Motivational Career Counselling and Coaching

What this book can offer you:

- ✓ A thorough understanding of CBT theory
- ✓ A range of cognitive behavioural approaches you can use with clients in employment or education and with jobseekers
- ✓ Self-help tools you can photocopy and use with clients
- ✓ Original methods for supporting clients in making career decisions by helping them to identify personal values
- ✓ Models for assessing the effectiveness of your newly acquired cognitive behavioural skills
- ✓ Techniques for improving your self-care as a practitioner and your life in general

Motivational Career Counselling and Coaching

Cognitive and Behavioural Approaches

Steve Sheward and Rhena Branch

Los Angeles | London | New Delhi
Singapore | Washington DC

Los Angeles | London | New Delhi
Singapore | Washington DC

SAGE Publications Ltd
1 Oliver's Yard
55 City Road
London EC1Y 1SP

SAGE Publications Inc.
2455 Teller Road
Thousand Oaks, California 91320

SAGE Publications India Pvt Ltd
B 1/I 1 Mohan Cooperative Industrial Area
Mathura Road
New Delhi 110 044

SAGE Publications Asia-Pacific Pte Ltd
3 Church Street
#10-04 Samsung Hub
Singapore 049483

Editor: Alice Oven
Editorial assistant: Kate Wharton
Production editor: Rachel Burrows
Marketing manager: Tamara Navaratnam
Cover design: Francis Kenney
Typeset by: C&M Digitals (P) Ltd, Chennai, India
Printed by: CPI Group (UK) Ltd, Croydon, CR0 4YY

MIX
Paper from
responsible sources
FSC
www.fsc.org   FSC® C013604

First published 2012

Library of Congress Control Number: 2011938232

British Library Cataloguing in Publication data

A catalogue record for this book is available from
the British Library

ISBN 978-1-4462-0181-7
ISBN 978-1-4462-0182-4 (pbk)

This book is dedicated to my parents and my wife Stella – Steve Sheward

Thanks to Steve for all his hard work – Rhena Branch

Contents

A number of worksheets for use with clients are available to download in
A4 format from www.sagepub.co.uk/sheward

About the Authors

Steve Sheward is qualified as both a Career Counsellor and Cognitive Behavioural Therapist and has used his experience of working in both professions to develop a unique combination of cognitive behavioural approaches with career counselling and coaching. Steve is accredited with the BABCP, AREBT and BACP. He has worked as a senior manager within the careers service for over ten years and was director of the Connexions Service in South London and also managed a range of national adult career counselling services including projects targeting support at unemployed clients. Steve currently works in London for the National Health Service as High Intensity CBT Therapist where he treats patients for a range of psychological problems including depression, anxiety, obsessive compulsive disorder and post-traumatic stress disorder. Steve has also delivered numerous training courses throughout England combining cognitive behavioural approaches with the use of career counselling and coaching to motivate clients. Steve also practises Karate and holds a 2nd dan black belt.

Rhena Branch is a CBT therapist accredited with the BABCP and UKCP and a member of the AREBT. She is also a qualified supervisor. Rhena has her own private practice in North London. In the past she has worked in a variety of settings including alcohol and drug rehabilitation centres, NHS settings and with the Priory Hospital. Rhena teaches and supervises on the Masters course at Goldsmiths University of London. Co-authored publications to date include: *CBT for Dummies, Self-esteem for Dummies, CBT workbook for Dummies, The Fundamentals of Rational Emotive Behaviour Therapy* and *The Cognitive Behaviour Counseling Primer*.

Introduction

Motivational Career Counselling and Coaching: Cognitive and Behavioural Approaches adapts scientifically proven cognitive behavioural therapy (CBT) theory and practice for use within career counselling and coaching for the first time as a detailed support programme for clients. The book is written specifically for practising career counsellors and coaches who wish to add to their professional skills and also for students or trainees undertaking related courses in preparation for entry into these occupations. Teachers in secondary, further and higher education may also find the book helpful as a resource in supporting learners, as well as anyone with a line management or mentoring role.

CBT is the fastest growing and most widely researched treatment in the UK used to help people deal with mental health challenges and has a 50 per cent success rate (UK National Health Service statistics quoted in Layard, 2010) in treating common psychological disorders such as anxiety and depression, considerably higher than other talking therapies. Approximately £173 million of public money has been invested in training 3,600 CBT therapists within the NHS over a three-year period following recommendations from Lord Layard's *The Depression Report,* published in 2006. One of the strongest arguments made in the report is that the government will see a return on its investment through helping people to overcome anxiety and depression, return to work and come off benefits. The use of CBT to help people overcome psychological problems is not confined to the health service. CBT was also used as a major part of the government funded Pathway to Work scheme delivered through Job Centreplus aimed at helping incapacity benefit claimants to deal more effectively with anxiety and depression and thereby facilitate their return to work.

During the same period, there has been an increasing emphasis on using career counselling and coaching to help individuals cope with redundancy, find employment and hold on to jobs in challenging times. Major public funded career counselling initiatives (including work with offenders in prisons) focus on helping clients obtain and sustain employment.

There is now an unprecedented need to provide career counselling and coaching practitioners and trainees with a new set of skills that will enable them to meet the increasing challenges of supporting clients in times of economic uncertainty. *Motivational Career Counselling and Coaching: Cognitive and Behavioural Approaches* is aimed at meeting this need.

When Albert Ellis and Aaron T. Beck developed CBT, their aim was to help clients overcome a range of psychological problems and this approach is still used by practitioners in the health service and private practice. In recent years, Martin E. P. Seligman (former president of the American Psychological Association) has used CBT to develop a form of positive psychology that helps individuals deal with the challenges of daily life without assuming a 'medical model' of CBT which assumes that clients have a 'mental health' problem that needs treating. This approach has influenced career counselling and coaching theories: one of the best known models is Gerard Egan's *The Skilled Helper* – widely taught on career counselling courses. We explain this influence more fully in Chapter 1.

Career counselling and coaching has a strong focus on collaborative problem solving and action planning with clients. Jennifer Kidd provides a succinct definition of this approach in *Understanding Career Counselling* (Kidd, 2006):

> *A one-to-one interaction between practitioner and client, usually ongoing, involving the application of psychological theory and a recognized set of communication skills. The primary focus is on helping the client make career-related decisions and deal with career-related issues.*

The cognitive and behavioural positive psychology approach helps clients to think and act more effectively in challenging situations in order to obtain their goals. *Motivational Career Counselling and Coaching: Cognitive and Behavioural Approaches* combines both of these approaches. By studying the theory and techniques set out within the book, practitioners and trainees will obtain a powerful model for helping clients achieve their career aims.

Motivational Career Counselling and Coaching: Cognitive and Behavioural Approaches is distinct from motivational interviewing (MI), developed principally by Miller and Rollnick (2002), in that our approach is used specifically within a vocational or educational context. It does, however, share certain features of MI in that it is collaborative and seeks to enhance the client's confidence and ability in coping with obstacles and succeeding in positive change through the combined use of cognitive behavioural approaches with career counselling and coaching.

Chapter 1 provides an introduction to the theory of cognitive and behavioural approaches within the context of career counselling and coaching. The reader is given an explanation of the way in which thoughts, emotions, behaviour and physiology interact and are influenced by the client's perception of challenging situations (e.g. job interviews). The role of unhelpful thoughts is explored and described as a self-imposed obstacle to achieving clients' goals. Two strategies for tackling unhelpful thinking are presented: the 5-areas model describing the environment, thoughts, moods, behaviour, physiology cycle and the ABCDE model. Instructions are provided for using these approaches with clients and a detailed table of helpful and unhelpful negative emotions is offered, describing the cognitive and behavioural characteristics related to different moods clients experience in challenging situations and typical thinking styles that trigger these emotions.

Having obtained an understanding of cognitive and behavioural theory in relation to career counselling and coaching, the reader is introduced to a range of motivational techniques in Chapter 2 aimed at helping clients to achieve success at interview. These include strategies for managing anxiety, focusing attention, maximising motivation, using positive imagery, relaxation and visualisation techniques. Advice is also provided on helping clients to overcome sleep problems before the interview (or any major event).

An important aim within career counselling and coaching is helping clients to make effective vocational or educational choices. A number of exercises are provided in Chapter 3 including building a compelling vision for the future, goal setting and maintaining motivation. A great deal of emphasis is placed on helping clients to make career decisions by identifying their personal values, and the reader is taught to use the Value Directions Questionnaire in one-to-one or group situations. The concept of 'flow' is introduced and its significance to career satisfaction explained. Psychological barriers to success are explored in addition to strategies for helping clients to go outside their comfort zone. Practical advice is also given on goal setting and action planning.

Chapter 4 provides a series of cognitive and behavioural strategies for helping clients to achieve success in the workplace. These include assertiveness, using the ABC model to manage stress and an adaptation of Steven Covey's Time Management Matrix. The chapter begins with an important section on helping the client to maintain mental focus and avoid distractions in pursuit of short- and long-term goals.

In Chapter 5 we deal with the vitally important subject of supporting unemployed clients in the knowledge that this is the main area of work for many practitioners and an increasingly challenging one within the dynamic fluctuations of the modern global economy. We begin the chapter with an outline of how unemployment can impact negatively on mental and physical health and research findings on how men and women can be affected differently in this respect. A new method for formulating clients' problems within the context of being unemployed is presented so that a detailed understanding can be obtained before selecting appropriate strategies to provide support. Behavioural activation is introduced as a method for motivating unemployed clients and a range of problem-solving strategies are presented with detailed instructions.

Chapter 6 is dedicated to using cognitive and behavioural approaches to career counselling and coaching in educational settings. The role of emotional intelligence (EI) within education is considered and how using cognitive behavioural approaches to underpin career counselling and coaching can be seen as an important addition to this new development by equipping learners with essential skills to gain self-insight and manage mood. We introduce new methods for identifying students' barriers to achievement and the effects these have on their thoughts, feelings and actions and offer methods for identifying solutions and new strategies for achieving success in education. The chapter concludes with advice on using metaphors to teach students helpful strategies including methods of increasing resilience and motivation while studying.

Having focused on imparting cognitive behavioural theories and techniques throughout the earlier part of the book, we offer advice to practitioners and trainees in Chapter 7 on evaluating their effectiveness in using these different approaches. The notion of evidence-based practice and reflective practice is introduced with specific reference to Kolb's learning cycle. A detailed checklist of criteria for evaluating the use of the techniques presented within this book is provided along with a marking scale to help measure ongoing improvement in practice. We consider some of the challenges faced by practitioners and trainees in using psychometric tests and offer an alternative model for measuring the client's progress against specific domains in their life. We also present a range of on-line resources that practitioners and trainees can draw on to supplement their use of the approaches set out within this book as part of their work with clients.

Chapter 8 deals with important ethical issues and challenges the reader to use cognitive behavioural theory as a tool for monitoring their perception of clients as individuals, as gender, ethnicity and cultural identity will inevitably influence our view of others. We provide advice on understanding the client within the context of their cultural identity and invite the reader to consider how their world view has been shaped by their own cultural identity. We present essential knowledge on maintaining client confidentiality and managing risk as these two areas of professional practice are gaining increasing importance as the nature of career counselling and coaching becomes more complex. The chapter concludes with a detailed exploration of the client–practitioner relationship and offers advice on agenda-setting and devising effective homework assignments.

Chapter 9 is devoted to helping the reader to use their newly acquired knowledge of cognitive behavioural approaches for self-help purposes in recognition of the increasing demands placed upon career counsellors and coaches. Common symptoms of work-related stress are described so that early warning signals can be noted and appropriate action taken. Detailed instructions are provided for using the tools set out within the book for self-help purposes and we provide a range of methods for achieving work–life balance and maintaining mental and physical wellbeing. The final section introduces the practice of mindfulness as an excellent method for reducing stress and increasing mental clarity. We end the book by offering a simple but effective mindfulness exercise aimed at helping practitioners to calm their mind and focus on the present moment. We hope that the reader is able to learn from and enjoy the material set out within this book and improve their ability to support clients as a result.

How to use this book

As with most instructional books, the reader may prefer to focus on specific chapters or sections depending on personal interest and professional or training needs. However, we suggest that you read Chapter 1 first as it provides theoretical underpinning knowledge for subsequent material in the book. We also strongly recommend that you read Chapter 2 before embarking on any of the other specialist sections as this chapter will equip you with many of the fundamental skills referred to throughout the book. Having gained a grounding in cognitive behavioural theory and practice, you can turn your attention to specific areas of their application within career counselling and coaching such as working within educational settings or the workplace and supporting unemployed clients. We recommend that you read Chapter 3 at some stage as this section provides important material aimed at helping clients to make effective career decisions and is a central plank within any career counselling or coaching approach.

Once you have experimented with some of the techniques described in this book as part of your professional practice or training, you may wish to study Chapter 7 and use the tools on offer as a method for refining your newly acquired skills. You can enhance your practice by drawing on the range of those assessment and self-help tools and go on to gain an awareness of the ethical issues explored in Chapter 8. Finally, we urge you to find time to read Chapter 9 at some stage as we consider self-care to be a vitally important issue for all trainees and practitioners and one that is often neglected. Having delivered training courses in cognitive behavioural approaches for career counsellors and coaches over the past five years, one of the most consistent messages we receive from participants is how beneficial they have found applying these theories and strategies to their own lives as well as those of their clients.

All of the tools and diagrams featured within this book are available to download in A4 format from www.sagepub.co.uk/sheward for use with clients as part of group exercises or one-to-one sessions.

1

Introduction to CBT Career Counselling Theory

This chapter is designed to help you to:

- gain an understanding of the theory and practice of cognitive behavioural therapy and how it can be used in conjunction with career counselling and coaching
- become proficient in using the 5-areas model with clients and understand the interaction between environment, thoughts, feelings, behaviour and physiology
- recognise unhelpful patterns of thinking
- learn how to use the ABC model with clients
- obtain a thorough understanding of helpful and unhelpful negative emotions and also use a quantitative versus qualitative model of negative emotions
- use the zigzag technique with clients to strengthen their helpful beliefs

---

What is cognitive behavioural therapy?

The fundamental aim of CBT is to examine how thinking and behaviour are related to understanding our emotions – how we feel. Put simply: our thoughts and behaviour affect how we and our clients feel. There are two famous quotes that are often used to illustrate these fundamental aspects of CBT:

'People are not disturbed by things but by the views which they take of them.' Epictetus *(c.55 – 135 AD)*

'Between stimulus and response lies the freedom to choose.' Viktor Frankl *(1905–1997)*

Epictetus was born into slavery but eventually obtained freedom and became one of the most influential stoic philosophers in history. One of the most important aspects of his teachings was that if we master our responses to the adversities of life, we will be better able to live a life filled with purpose, tranquillity and dignity (Irvine, 2009).

Viktor Frankl was a Jewish psychiatrist initially influenced by Freudian psychology and determinism which suggests that childhood influences shape personality and, to a large extent, the course of one's life. He was sent to Auschwitz while his parents, wife and brother died in other concentration camps. Frankl's experience of torture and degradation in Auschwitz enabled him to make a remarkable discovery that contradicted his early determinist outlook, and he later referred to this as 'the last of the human freedoms' (Frankl, 1984). Essentially, Frankl chose to respond to the horror of his surroundings with dignity and courage. Through this exercise of inner-freedom, Frankl did not allow his captors to degrade him.

Epictetus and Frankl offer dramatic examples of the way in which the exercise of the human mind can be used to tolerate extreme hardship, and you can probably think of many other historic figures such as Nelson Mandela who have chosen a positive response to adversity. CBT provides us with a framework that enables us and our clients to choose our own cognitive, behavioural and emotional responses to the challenges of life and is particularly relevant to career counselling and coaching in this respect.

What does CBT actually mean?

C = Cognitive: Basically all mental processes, including thoughts, memories, images, perceptions, dreams, attention.

B = Behaviour: Everything we do and how we respond to things. This includes what we say, how we act, what we avoid, how we solve problems. This can also include *not acting*, which is still a behaviour (e.g. stopping yourself from making your point of view heard).

T = Therapy: A systematic method for overcoming a problem or illness.

One of the key features of CBT is that it provides clients with a range of techniques to become self-sufficient in meeting present and future challenges. It does this by defining emotional and behavioural challenges (e.g. anxiety and poor performance at interview) and setting goals in terms of how the client would prefer to feel and behave (e.g. alert and focused). Therefore, CBT is a systematic, action-oriented and problem-solving approach to managing thoughts, emotions and behaviours more effectively.

Why CBT is becoming increasingly popular

CBT is a fast-growing and widely recognised treatment used to help people deal with psychological challenges. Due to its substantial evidence base demonstrating its effectiveness as a therapy, CBT is recommended by the National Institute for Health and Clinical Excellence (NICE) as a treatment within the British National Health Service (NHS) for a wide range of psychological disorders. The UK government has invested significantly in CBT as a treatment through the Increasing Access to Psychological Therapies (IAPT) programme (Department of Health, 2007). The kind of problems CBT can help with include:

- addiction
- anger problems
- anxiety
- body dysmorphic disorder
- chronic fatigue syndrome
- chronic pain
- depression
- eating disorders
- obsessive-compulsive disorder
- panic disorder
- personality disorders
- phobias
- post-traumatic stress disorder
- psychotic disorders
- relationship problems
- social phobia

It is highly unlikely that you will encounter the majority of these psychological problems when helping clients and, as we will go on to explain, you will be using CBT-based techniques in a career counselling and coaching specific context.

Important: *It is essential that you recognise your **professional boundaries** at all times. If your client indicates that they need help with any of the above problems, encourage them to see their General Practitioner.*

Is CBT used only to deal with psychological problems?

Albert Ellis and Aaron T. Beck are widely acknowledged to be the 'founding fathers' of CBT. When they established and refined their therapy the emphasis was on helping clients to overcome psychological problems, and this is still the approach that therapists use working in the NHS or private practice.

However, in recent years CBT has been developed as a means of *optimising* the way we think, feel and behave in our everyday lives when tackling challenges (such as job interviews), rather than just dealing with psychological problems. One of the most active individuals in developing this approach is Martin E. P. Seligman, former president of the American Psychological Association and Professor of Psychology at the University of Pennsylvania.

Seligman has used CBT to develop a form of positive psychology that helps people deal with the challenges of life more effectively and to achieve greater levels of satisfaction. He has published a great many books on the subject that are highly influential including *Learned Optimism* (2006), *Authentic Happiness* (2002) and *The Optimistic Child* (2007).

How does CBT work in conjunction with career counselling and coaching?

Career counselling theories have developed over the last century and have been influenced by other different counselling theories including psychodynamic and person-centred approaches. Cognitive behavioural approaches have rarely influenced career counselling theories apart from Krumboltz's model (Mitchell & Krumboltz, 1996) and social cognitive career theory. For a more detailed overview of this subject, consult Jennifer Kidd's excellent *Understanding Career Counselling* (2006). One of the best-known recent counselling models is Gerard Egan's *The Skilled Helper* (2002) and it is widely taught on career counselling courses.

In the latest edition of *The Skilled Helper*, Egan introduces an emphasis on positive psychology and the work of Martin E. P. Seligman (mentioned above) and Mihaly Csikszentmihalyi and integrates it within his model. Egan summarises the purpose of individuals working within helping professions (including career counselling and coaching) as:

> *Seeing problem management as life-enhancing learning and treating all encounters with clients as opportunity-development sessions that are part of the positive psychology approach.*

What Egan means by this is that practitioners can use each session as an opportunity to teach clients a range of problem-solving skills and thus increase their self-efficacy, and is congruent with the Chinese proverb 'Give a man a fish and you feed him for a day. Teach a man to fish and you feed him for a lifetime'. The career counselling and coaching approach has a strong focus on collaborative problem solving with clients and joint action planning. The CBT positive psychology approach encourages clients to think more effectively in challenging situations in order to improve the way they think, act and feel.

These combined approaches offer a powerful model for helping clients to succeed in their career and learning aims.

Our world view defined within the CBT 5-areas model

The 5-areas model shown in Figure 1.1 can be used to examine the complex interactions between thoughts, moods, behaviour, physiology and the world we live in (our environment). (A copy of the 5-areas worksheet for use with clients can be downloaded from www.sagepub.co.uk/sheward.)

We all live in some type of *environment*: for example, family, community, work. We are influenced by both our current environment (what is happening in our lives at this moment in time) and by our past environments (whether we experienced successes, losses or failures). Within the CBT model recognition is given to the fact that we are *influenced by* our environment and that it contributes to the way we think, feel and act. But CBT also maintains that we can make a difference to the way we feel by changing unhelpful ways of thinking and behaving – *even if we can't change our environment* (as in Viktor Frankl's example).

The other four aspects of the model are our *thoughts, moods, behaviour and physiology*. These four aspects interact with one another and the external environment as well. What we feel is closely connected to what we think, how we behave, and our physiology (physical responses such as increased heartbeat and sweating).

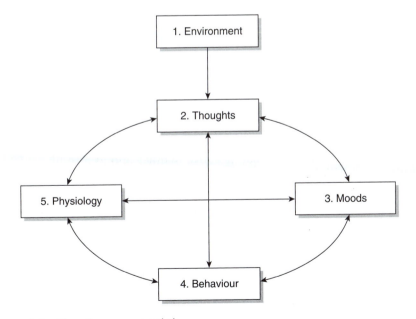

Figure 1.1   The 5-areas model

Changes in our behaviour influence how we think and feel emotionally (mood) and our physiology (bodily responses). Changes in our thinking can affect our behaviour and mood.

Understanding how these parts of our life interact with one another provides us with a means of analysing how we and our clients approach various challenges and whether or not our chosen strategies are effective.

Example

A client attending a job interview may have the thought, 'I'll say something stupid at the interview' (**thought**). This thought might make them feel anxious (**mood**) which may lead them to act in a nervous manner (**behaviour**) and they may feel their heart beating fast (**physiology**).

The thought–feeling link

If something happens to you in life, like most people you may believe that this event *makes* you feel a certain way. For example, you may have to give a presentation at work and conclude that the situation *makes* you anxious. CBT encourages you to examine how your thoughts and beliefs stand between you and the event and that they influence the way you feel and act in situations.

Therefore, as far as CBT theory is concerned, the prospect of having to give a presentation at work doesn't *make* you anxious. However, by thinking that you will look stupid if the presentation doesn't go well, *you make yourself anxious*.

Pattern of thinking

Often when people experience unhelpful negative emotions (such as anxiety) they are thinking in an irrational, negative manner and as a result act in self-defeating ways. This negative thinking can become a bad habit which keeps some people trapped in their unhelpful negative emotion (e.g. anxious all the time).

An individual's thinking can become *biased* because of a bias in the way they process information from their own thoughts and from the interactions with events around them (you could regard biased thinking as a distorted 'lens' through which some people view life). As a result, sometimes people make decisions based on self-defeating assumptions or they incorrectly interpret life situations or judge themselves harshly. They also jump to inaccurate conclusions or fail to cope with everyday challenges that life brings.

Interpretations

As mentioned previously, it is often not so much what happens to us in life that makes us happy or sad – it is frequently our *perception* of events that affects our feelings. For example, if a client attends a job interview and the interviewer does not smile very much, different *interpretations* would make the client feel different emotions. If they interpreted the interviewer's behaviour as proof that they did not like them, the client might feel anxious. But if the client's interpretation was that the interviewer had a formal interview style they would have a better chance of remaining calm in the situation. Other examples of these thinking errors include:

All-or-nothing (or black-or-white) thinking: extreme thinking that can lead to extreme and negative emotions and behaviours. A client may think that if they do not receive a promotion it will be the end of the world and suffer from anxiety prior to the interview and depression afterwards if they are unsuccessful. To counter this, the client could be encouraged to engage in *realistic* and *flexible* thinking and consider other benefits of going for the promotion (e.g. showing ambition) and developing contingency plans if unsuccessful at this point in their career.

Fortune-telling: making negative predictions of what will happen with future events. The client who considers going for the promotion may actually fear success because their negative prediction is that they would not be able to cope with the additional responsibility. The antidote to this style of thinking is to *be prepared to take calculated risks and develop a tolerance of uncertainty*. The latter is very important for career progression as a desire for certainty of outcome will inhibit advancement.

Mind-reading: similar to *interpretations* in terms of unhelpful, negative assumptions about what others are thinking and that their motives are less than charitable. The client may believe that their manager is annoyed with them because they are less communicative than usual, leading to feelings of stress which undermine performance. A more helpful approach would involve *generating alternative reasons* for this situation – that the manager may be preoccupied because *they* are finding work stressful at the moment.

Emotional reasoning: interpreting what is happening (or about to happen) based exclusively on how you feel emotionally. A client may feel naturally nervous when they are about to attend an interview or give a presentation but focusing excessively on this feeling may render them hyper vigilant, continually looking for evidence that things are going wrong to confirm their feeling of anxiety. This is a very subtle tendency which can lead to distorted interpretations of events as we instinctively rely on our emotions to guide us. In fact, the word 'emotion' derives from the Latin *emovere* or *movere* 'to move'. Emotions are very powerful internal messages that call upon us to take action and we have inherited them from our ancient ancestors for their survival utility through natural selection. However, we need to be guided by our emotions but not misled by them. In order to achieve a more balanced perspective, we and our clients need to *pay attention to what we are feeling and then balance our emotional responses with rational thinking*. Acknowledging, for example, that we are about to enter a challenging situation and the sensation of nervousness is a helpful and natural response providing us with additional energy and focus but not a sign of impending catastrophe.

Overgeneralising: the tendency to draw global conclusions from one or a few events, often referred to as the 'part/whole error'. A client may have experienced homophobic behaviour from a manager while working in a specific industry and concluded that the whole sector is populated by managers who will act in this way. Although it may be true that there is evidence of higher than average instances of homophobic behaviour in certain sectors (e.g. from industrial tribunal data), generalising these trends to the whole sector would be inaccurate and limit occupational choice if this acted as a psychological barrier for the client. If your client engages in this type of thinking you can help them to *suspend judgment and obtain a more balanced perspective* on their particular situation. This will typically involve testing their belief by looking for alternative evidence (e.g. organisations within the sector that are members of Stonewall, the lesbian, gay and bisexual charity).

Labelling: similar to overgeneralising, this tendency involves rating oneself, people and events in a negative limiting way also referred to as 'self- or other-downing'. A client with low self-esteem may label themselves as a 'failure' because they haven't achieved a promotion, the management team as 'bastards' for appointing another colleague and the world of work as an 'unfair place'. The problem with this distorted perspective (particularly with regard to the self) is that it does not accommodate the notion of *human fallibility* and the possibility of change and improvement. Just because the client failed once in their attempt to achieve a promotion does not mean that they are a complete failure. If prompted, they could provide evidence of previous successes (they managed to get a job with the company in the first place). Similarly, the client's managers have made a decision that hasn't been to their advantage in this instance but there may be examples of instances when they have acted more favourably.

Making demands: engaging in extreme or rigid thinking that does not allow an alternative outcome or point of view usually expressed through use of the words 'must', 'should', 'need', 'got to' and 'have to'. Albert Ellis (1913–2007) founded rational emotive behaviour therapy (REBT) in the late 1950s – one of the first CBT therapies (Neenan & Dryden, 2011). Ellis believed that a tendency to make demands is the greatest determinant of emotional problems and placed a huge emphasis on helping clients to challenge this unhelpful response. A client facing the prospect of a competitive interview may tell themselves that they absolutely *must* get the job for any number of reasons (money, status, self-esteem). The problem with approaching the interview in this frame of mind is that the client is more likely to feel increased anxiety, which will interfere with their performance, and a sense of devastation and hopelessness if they fail to achieve their desired outcome. This style of thinking is also common in clients who have perfectionist tendencies, which commonly lead to increased stress and missed deadlines. The counterbalance to making demands is to *hold flexible preferences* about oneself, other people and the world and is expressed in terms such as 'prefer', 'want' and 'wish'. This does not underestimate the strength of your client's motivation as they can hold a very strong flexible preference (e.g. to want the job very much or wish to maintain high standards at work). It does, however, accommodate an alternative to the desired outcome and facilitates contingency planning.

Mental filtering/disqualifying the positive: processing and internalising information that is consistent with a negative belief the individual may hold. A client who believes that others find them boring when engaged in interpersonal activities will have a tendency to seek negative evidence to confirm this belief while at the same time discounting any positive aspects that occur. They will be more inclined to take notice of instances when colleagues seem distracted or preoccupied but forget situations in which conversation flowed and was mutually beneficial. Mental filtering is also an insidious and cumulative process whereby increasing amounts of negative data are taken in and build up over time, strengthening unhelpful beliefs. This is particularly common among individuals who suffer from low self-esteem and usually becomes a self-perpetuating bad habit. The key to helping clients counter mental filtering is to encourage them to *gather alternative positive evidence* to disconfirm their negative beliefs. A simple but effective technique involves asking clients to keep a *positive data log* recording specific examples. Although this may seem like a rather obvious strategy, it is an important first step of reorienting clients who have got into the habit of automatically discounting any positive experiences due to their mental bias.

Low frustration tolerance: believing that the discomfort associated with pursuing a particular goal is intolerable rather than uncomfortable and worth enduring in order to achieve the desired outcome. Low frustration tolerance has many forms but its consistent theme is the inability to endure physical, emotional or psychological discomfort in the short term in order to achieve a positive goal in the long term. This style of thinking is probably the greatest barrier to achievement in life and restricts clients by keeping them trapped within a self-imposed comfort zone.

«

Exercise

What do you consider to be your greatest achievements? Think of the effort that was involved in accomplishing these successes. It is highly likely that you will have endured some discomfort or made certain sacrifices in order to achieve your aim.

Examples of low frustration tolerance include:

- putting off applying for promotions or more challenging roles due to fear of failure
- avoiding speaking up in meetings or giving presentations because of feelings of anxiety

(Continued)

(Continued)

- postponing further study essential for career advancement because it will require additional effort and disrupt leisure activities
- procrastinating on reports because of the boredom and rigor involved
- waiting until the last moment when the looming deadline forces action but creates stress
- comfort eating as an antidote to boredom
- putting off taking physical exercise because it seems to require too much effort (particularly after a hard day at work)

You can help your client achieve success in the workplace (and life in general) by encouraging them to develop a *high frustration tolerance* philosophy. This means actively seeking out experiences that involve some level of physical or mental discomfort on a regular basis to develop 'psychological muscle'. It might be helpful to use the metaphor of a 'resilience bank account'. Each time your client engages in a challenging activity that requires effort and discomfort, they make a deposit in the account. This could be a mundane but necessary task such as setting up a much needed filing system or a very challenging endeavour like doing a parachute jump for charity. Conversely, each time your client engages in avoidant or self-indulgent behaviour, such as procrastination or comfort eating, they make a withdrawal from the account. In his excellent book on the subject, *Developing Resilience: A Cognitive-Behavioural Approach* (2009), Michael Neenan refers to this approach as 'discomfort practice' and provides a wealth of techniques for developing resilience in the workplace. A key message worth emphasising to clients is that if they exercise high frustration tolerance during day-to-day moments that involve personal struggle (e.g. getting out of bed 10 minutes earlier or speaking up at meetings), they will be far better equipped to deal with greater challenges such as stressful presentations and crises at work.

Personalising: believing that what happens and the way people act relates directly to oneself. This often leads people to take an inappropriate amount of responsibility for situations that are beyond their control leading to feelings of guilt or hurt: a meeting with a colleague is more tense than usual and this is reflected in their language and gestures; the department fails to meet its targets for the month and the manager circulates a group e-mail expressing concerns about team performance. Individuals prone to personalising would naturally assume that they had done something to offend their colleague and that the department manager thought badly of them even if they had met their own personal performance target for the month. This tendency can be countered by *exploring different reasons* for events or people's behaviour while taking oneself out of the equation.

Hopefully you will now have a better understanding of common thinking errors that your client may make and how this can act as a barrier to achieving vocational goals. It will be helpful to refer to this list in relation to the 'Thoughts' component of the 5-areas model and the 'Beliefs' section of the ABC model in the following section when carrying out formulations with clients, as it will enable you to detect particular themes in their thinking errors. A formulation is an analysis of the client's cognitions, feelings, behaviours and physiological reactions in response to situations they encounter where there is some element of challenge.

Carrying out a 5-areas formulation

The amazing thing about the human mind is that we are able to deliberately change the way we think (and consequently act and feel) so that we can achieve big improvements in our lives. The 5-areas model can be used to help clients become more aware of the relationship between their thoughts, feelings, behaviours and physiological responses when they are faced with challenging situations while attempting to achieve their goals. As we shall see in subsequent chapters, the model is used both to help clients gain an awareness of psychological and behavioural flaws in their existing strategies and to develop more constructive approaches to achieving their goals.

In order to gain a better understanding of how to carry out a formulation with clients, it will be helpful for you to carry out your own 5-areas formulation of a recent challenging situation.

«

Exercise

Think of a recent situation that your found particularly challenging – this could be in the work place or a social situation.

Which unhelpful emotion did you feel (anxiety, depression, anger, shame, hurt, jealousy, envy, guilt) and what was going through your mind? What were your thoughts? How did they affect your behaviour? What effect was there on your body?

Use the 5-areas thoughts, emotions, behaviour, physiology form as part of this exercise. We will explore the use of this model with clients in subsequent chapters as a means of analysing the way in which these parts of their life interact and how they can take more control over their thought processes.

Now that you have gained an understanding of how to conduct a 5-areas formulation, we will introduce you to the ABC model and provide you with instructions on how to use it with clients.

The ABC model

The ABC model is similar to the 5-areas review process in that it provides a structure for determining any psychological or behavioural barriers that clients may be experiencing when seeking to achieve their vocational goals. Having determined what the specific barriers are, the model also provides a means of devising more effective strategies for enabling clients to achieve their goals. We will begin by providing you with a brief overview of the model and then explore each component and its precise use in detail.

'A' = activating event: Whether the situation is in the future, present or past, some specific aspect seizes our attention and triggers our thoughts. 'A' is sometimes referred to as 'adversity' in CBT literature because it represents some challenge that the client faces in their life.

'B' = belief: Essentially any cognitive process that gets triggered by the activating event including thoughts, visual images, personal meaning attributed the event and beliefs about the situation.

'C' = consequences: These are the emotional and behavioural consequences that flow from the thoughts triggered at 'B'. Other more subtle consequences include thoughts (a thought at 'B' can trigger a further unhelpful thought at 'C') and physical sensations (e.g. increased heart beat, rapid breathing).

This can also be rendered into the formula $A \times B = C$ as the more intense the trigger or activating event is at 'A', the greater the potential emotional, behavioural and physical consequences at 'C'. 'B' plays a crucial mediating role between the event and how the individual responds as their thoughts may either magnify and distort the nature of the challenge or interpret it in a constructive way. We will now consider each component of the model in detail.

Component 'A'

As mentioned, 'A's are specific aspects of situations that seize your client's attention and trigger a thinking process. Generally speaking, our attention as human beings is in a state of constant flux to enable us to function while being continually bombarded by different visual, aural and sensory stimuli. Consider the process of driving a car. The driver's cognitive reactions to the flow of traffic are relatively neutral, enabling a constant shifting of attention between different tasks such as changing gears and indicating. However, a change in the traffic lights to amber will focus the driver's attention on a specific element of the overall situation and trigger the (very rapid) thought that he or she needs to stop the car followed by the behavioural consequence of braking. There may also be an emotional consequence resulting in a slight feeling of concern. An important distinction that we need to make is between 'A's that are *actual events* and 'A's that are *inferred events*.

Example

Tony is an accountant in a law firm and has just received formal notification from the company's human resources department that he will be made redundant in three month's time. If we consider Tony's situation within the ABC model we would find that the announcement of redundancy is an actual event at 'A' and triggers thoughts about the risk of unemployment at 'B' which in turn gives rise to feelings of concern at 'C'.

Inferred events are far more subtle in that they represent the client's subjective interpretation of events, or a hunch about the situation, that goes beyond the available evidence and may or may not be correct. Consider Michelle's example:

Example

Michelle works for a company that has won a contract to deliver child care within a local community. This was quite a controversial decision as Michelle's company is a private sector provider and beat off competition from various charities in the area. Michelle is about to give a presentation to the local stakeholder group, which numbers 40 members. As she is about to begin her presentation, Michelle's attention is caught by a woman in the second row who seems to have a very disapproving look on her face. Michelle starts to think that this woman will ask awkward questions and begins to feel anxious. She notices that her mouth has gone very dry and her hand trembles slightly. As she begins her presentation Michelle becomes flustered and clicks on the wrong slide.

You can see from the above example that Michelle's 'A' was an inference as she *interpreted* the woman's expression as one of disapproval although there was no categorical evidence to support this hunch (the woman could have been concentrating very intently). You will have noticed that this inference at 'A' triggered a distressing thought at 'B' which resulted in a number of unhelpful emotional, behavioural and physical consequences at 'C'.

'A's can also be *internal* as well as *external* events. In the above example Michelle's activating event was external as she focused on the woman in the audience's facial expression. If that incident had not taken place, Michelle may still have noticed her mouth going dry and this (internal) physical sensation may have triggered the thought that she would not be able to speak during the presentation and result in feelings of anxiety. Bodily sensations are common internal 'A's, and we can also include different emotions as a trigger as outlined in the section on *emotional reasoning* above.

Critical 'A's can also relate to events in the past, present or future. Being notified that she had to give a presentation to the local stakeholder group may have triggered unhelpful thoughts of potential failure in Michelle's mind. She may also have thought about past presentations that had gone badly with the same effect.

Component 'B'

Although 'B' stands for 'belief' within the ABC model, we can include any cognitive process that gets triggered by the activating event including thoughts, visual images, personal meaning attributed to the event and beliefs about the situation as previously mentioned. These can be further categorised into three types of unhelpful thinking that your client may engage in:

Negative automatic thoughts (NATs): These unhelpful thoughts are probably the easiest to identify as they are near the surface of the client's conscious awareness and can be accessed through careful questioning. When drawing your client's attention to this type of thinking you may offer a comparison with gnats, annoying, irritating things that buzz around your head. Similarly, NATs fly into the client's mind spontaneously and quickly when they find themselves in stressful situations.

Underlying assumptions and rules: Your client may carry a set of unspoken rules or assumptions they have developed as guiding principles while pursuing their career. Examples include standards of behaviour and quality in the workplace. These may serve your client well until they encounter situations in which they have to compromise their personal rules and assumptions. If the latter are too inflexible, it is highly likely that your client will suffer from stress if the conditions are not met. For example, clients with perfectionist tendencies underpinned by the rule 'My work must always be of the highest standard' may find it difficult to cope with situations that require fast output which is 'good enough' due to tight deadlines. This type of thinking is closely related to core beliefs.

Core beliefs: Similar to rules and assumptions, your client may have developed core beliefs from childhood onward that are only triggered in stressful situations. For example, a client may have developed a core belief that they must be liked by everyone and engage in approval-seeking behaviour to obtain this outcome without being aware that they hold this belief. But circumstances may change and the individual may find it more challenging to obtain approval from the majority of people. A promotion and the need to make necessary but unpopular decisions may result in a cool response from certain colleagues and trigger the client's core belief. A useful metaphor for describing core beliefs is the image of traffic-calming 'sleeping policeman': small bumps in the road that discourage drivers from speeding. Sometimes drivers only become aware of them once they have driven over them and felt the bump.

Component 'C'

As mentioned previously, 'C' stands for emotional, behavioural and physiological consequences. We will start by exploring the concept of helpful and unhelpful negative emotions and the way they interact with one another and then introduce you to the emotions table, which also contains behavioural, physical and thinking consequences that are triggered by the client's thoughts and/or beliefs at 'B'.

Understanding helpful and unhelpful negative emotions

This subheading description may seem contradictory and you would be entitled to ask: 'How can *negative* emotions be helpful? Also, what about positive emotions?' The reason for this focus on negative emotions is that working with clients in career counselling and coaching almost always involves supporting them to overcome some challenge on the way to attaining their goals. Experiencing positive emotions seldom causes a problem for clients but if they find themselves in challenging circumstances (e.g. redundancy or long-term unemployment) it is highly likely that they will experience negative emotions that may become additional barriers to achieving their goals. As we will see in later chapters, it is far more preferable for your client to experience *concern* when about to attend a competitive job interview than *anxiety* which could have a detrimental effect on performance. Fortunately helping your client to *think* and *act* constructively when facing challenges will mean that they are more likely to experience helpful rather than unhelpful negative emotions.

You may find similar descriptions of emotions in CBT literature using the words 'healthy' and 'unhealthy' to make a distinction between the two types of negative emotions, particularly REBT (Dryden & Branch, 2008). We prefer to use the terms 'helpful' and 'unhelpful' to avoid the impression of pathologising the emotions in question and also to emphasise their pragmatic value (or otherwise) in helping clients achieve their goals. It is also worth mentioning that the terms used to describe emotions that follow are general and your clients may have different ways of describing their internal experiences: for example, *terrified* at the prospect of giving a presentation rather than 'anxious'. The important issue is for you to be able to recognise whether the client's description of being terrified is consistent with the characteristics of anxiety in order to help them think and act more constructively when facing their challenge so that they are more likely to experience concern (as opposed to anxiety). Experiencing concern takes into account the fact that the client may not feel comfortable in the situation (because the outcome is very important to them), but it will hopefully sharpen rather than inhibit their performance.

The interactive processes of emotions

As you can see from Figure 1.2, thoughts, moods and behaviours interact with one another in complex ways. Whenever you feel an emotion, a complex process

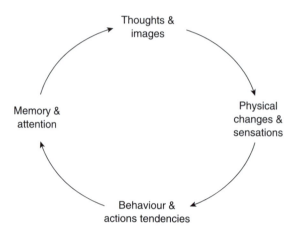

Figure 1.2   The interaction of emotional processes

is triggered. The process includes thoughts and images that enter your mind, memories you may recall, aspects of yourself or surrounding environment that you focus on, physical and mental sensations, your behaviour and things you *feel* like doing. For example, if you were about to give a presentation, focusing your attention on *potential* threats would increase the likelihood of anxious thoughts entering your mind as would recalling previous failed attempts at public speaking. Drinking coffee beforehand will increase your adrenaline and contribute to feelings of nervousness. Behaving in a fearful manner by hiding from the audience behind the projector will also add to your anxiety.

The advantage of understanding the interactive processes of emotions is that you will be able to help clients identify unhelpful negative emotions that they experience along with related thoughts and behaviours. As mentioned, clients frequently experience these unhelpful negative emotions when they encounter obstacles to achieving their goals. However, if they change the way they think and behave, clients will be more likely to experience helpful negative emotions that will strengthen their ability to overcome obstacles and achieve goals.

Distinguishing between helpful and unhelpful negative emotions can be difficult, particularly if this type of assessment is new to you. Table 1.1 contains a comprehensive list of helpful and unhelpful negative emotions and their characteristics. Everything you need to identify the emotions your clients experience is contained in the table. You will notice that some emotions are more commonly experienced by clients seeking support from career counselling and coaching than others (e.g. anxiety, anger). However, we thought it important to provide you with the full range of emotions for the sake of completeness and because we cannot underestimate the complexity of each practitioner's role in supporting clients.

Table 1.1 CBT emotions table: helpful and unhelpful negative emotions

Emotion	Type of belief	Theme	Thoughts	Behaviour
Anxiety	Unhelpful Rigid or extreme	Threat or danger	**Attention Focus:** *Monitors threat or danger excessively* • Overestimates how great the threat actually is • Underestimates ability to cope with the threat • Creates an even greater threat in one's mind • Thoughts about the threat get in the way of thoughts about taking constructive action • Perceives physical symptoms of anxiety as an increased threat (e.g. increased adrenalin)	• Withdraws physically from the threat (runs away) • Withdraws mentally from the threat (buries head in the sand) • Uses superstitious behaviour in an attempt to prevent threat happening • Numbs feelings of anxiety through alcohol or drugs • Seeks reassurance that the threat won't happen • Finds it difficult to tolerate the physical symptoms of anxiety (e.g. increased adrenalin)
Concern	Helpful Flexible and preferential	Threat or danger	**Attention Focus:** *Doesn't see threats where no threats exist* • Views the threat realistically • Realistically assesses ability to cope with the threat • Does not create an even greater threat in one's mind	• Faces up to threat • Deals with the threat constructively • Doesn't keep seeking reassurance • Tolerates the physical symptoms of concern (e.g. increased adrenalin)

(Continued)

Table 1.1 (Continued)

Emotion	Type of belief	Theme	Thoughts	Behaviour
			• Less likely to let thoughts about the threat get in the way of thoughts about taking constructive action • Perceives physical symptoms of concern (e.g. increased adrenalin) as uncomfortable but not an increased threat	
Depression	Unhelpful Rigid or extreme	Loss (with implications for future) Failure	**Attention Focus:** *Dwells on past loss or failure and personal flaws and failings* • Sees only negative aspects of the loss or failure • Thinks of other losses and failures that one has experienced • Ruminates on unsolvable problems • Believes oneself to be helpless • Thinks about negative world events • Thinks future is bleak and hopeless	• Withdraws from others and becomes less active • Withdraws into oneself • Creates a depressing home environment consistent with one's mood • Neglects self and home environment • Tries to lessen feelings of depression in self-destructive ways (e.g. alcohol, drugs, excessive eating)
Sadness	Helpful Flexible and preferential	Loss (with implications for future) Failure	**Attention Focus:** *Focuses on problems that one can change and personal strengths and skills* • Able to see both negative and positive aspects of the loss or failure	• Talks to significant others about feelings of loss or failure • Continues to take care of oneself and one's home environment

Emotion	Type of belief	Theme	Thoughts	Behaviour
			• Less likely to think of other losses and failures than when depressed • Is able to help self • Has balanced view of positive and negative world events • Is able to think about the future with hope	• Engages in positive activities that will help lift mood • Avoids self-destructive behaviour
Anger	Unhelpful Rigid or extreme	Frustration Personal rule is broken Self-esteem is threatened	**Attention Focus:** *Looks for malicious intent in the motives of others and evidence of offensive behaviour* • Has rigid and extreme attitudes (e.g. prejudices) • Assumes the other person has acted deliberately • Thinks of self as definitely right and other person as wrong • Unable to see the other person's point of view • Plots to exact revenge	• Attacks the other person physically • Attacks the other person verbally • Acts in a passive-aggressive manner • Takes out one's anger on another innocent person, animal or object • Withdraws aggressively (e.g. slams doors) or sulks • Recruits allies against the other person
Annoyance	Helpful Flexible and preferential	Frustration Personal rule is broken Self-esteem is threatened	**Attention Focus:** *Looks for evidence that the other person does not have malicious intent* • Has flexible and preferential attitudes	• Asserts oneself with the other person without resorting to physical or verbal violence • Asks, but not demands, that the other person changes their offensive behaviour

(Continued)

Table 1.1 (Continued)

Emotion	Type of belief	Theme	Thoughts	Behaviour
			• Considers that the other person may not have acted deliberately • Considers that both self and the other person may be right to some degree • Can see the other person's point of view • Doesn't think about getting revenge	• Doesn't seek revenge • Doesn't take out annoyance on others • Stays in the situation and tries to resolve issues with the other person • Doesn't sulk
Guilt	Unhelpful Rigid or extreme	Moral code or personal rule is broken by failing to do something or committing a 'sin' Hurts the feelings of a significant other	**Attention Focus:** Looks for evidence of retribution or others blaming one for the 'sin' • Thinks that one has definitely committed the 'sin' • Assumes more personal responsibility than the situation warrants • Has rigid and extreme attitudes • Ignores other people's responsibility for the situation • Ignores mitigating factors • Thinks that one deserves to be punished	• Tries to escape from guilty feelings in self-defeating ways • Begs for forgiveness • Promises (unrealistically) that the 'sin' will never be committed again • Punishes oneself physically or through deprivation • Attempts to deny responsibility for wrongdoing in an attempt to ease feelings of guilt

Emotion	Type of belief	Theme	Thoughts	Behaviour
Remorse	Helpful Flexible and preferential	Moral code or personal rule is broken by failing to do something or committing a 'sin' Hurts the feelings of a significant other	**Attention Focus:** *Doesn't look for retribution or others blaming oneself* • Considers behaviour in context and with understanding before making a final judgement about whether one has 'sinned' • Takes an appropriate level of personal responsibility for the 'sin' • Allocates an appropriate level of responsibility to others for the situation • Has flexible and preferential attitudes • Takes into account mitigating factors • Does not think one will receive punishment	• Faces up to the healthy pain that comes with knowing that one has sinned • Asks for forgiveness • Understands reasons for wrong doing and acts on that understanding • Atones for the 'sin' by taking a penalty • Makes appropriate amends • Doesn't make excuses for one's behaviour or act defensively
Shame	Unhelpful Rigid or extreme	Shameful personal information has been publically revealed by self or others	**Attention Focus:** *Sees disapproval from others where it does not exist* • Overestimates the 'shamefulness' of the information revealed	• Hides from others to avoid disapproval • May attack others who have 'shamed' self in an attempt to save face

(Continued)

Table 1.1 (Continued)

Emotion	Type of belief	Theme	Thoughts	Behaviour
		Others will look down upon or shun self	• Overestimates the likelihood that others will notice or be interested in the information • Overestimates the degree of disapproval from others • Overestimates how long disapproval will last	• May act in self-defeating ways in an attempt to protect threatened self-esteem • Ignores attempts by others to return situation to normal
Regret	Helpful Flexible and preferential	Shameful personal information has been publicly revealed by self or others Others will look down upon or shun self	**Attention Focus:** *Focuses on evidence that one is accepted by the social group in spite of 'shameful' evidence revealed* • Is compassionate and self-accepting about the information revealed • Is realistic about the likelihood that others will notice or be interested in the information • Is realistic about the degree of disapproval one will receive from others • Is realistic about the length of time any disapproval will last	• Continues to participate in social interaction and doesn't avoid others • Responds to attempts by others to return situation to normal • Acts in a self-accepting, unapologetic manner

Emotion	Type of belief	Theme	Thoughts	Behaviour
Hurt	Unhelpful Rigid or extreme	Other person treats self badly (self undeserving)	**Attention Focus:** *Looks for evidence of the other person not caring or being indifferent* • Overestimates the unfairness of the other person's behaviour • Thinks the other person doesn't care • Thinks of oneself as alone, uncared for or misunderstood • Tends to think of past 'hurts' • Thinks that the other has to make the first move to put things right	• Stops communicating with the other person/sulks • Punishes the other person through silence or criticism, without stating what one feels hurt about
Disappointment	Helpful Flexible and preferential	Other person treats self badly (self undeserving)	**Attention Focus:** *Focuses on evidence that the other person does care and is not indifferent* • Is realistic about the degree of unfairness of the other person's behaviour • Thinks the other person acted badly but doesn't think they don't care • Doesn't see oneself as alone or uncared for • Doesn't dwell on past hurts • Doesn't wait for the other person to make the first move	• Communicates about one's feelings to the other person • Tries to influence the other person to act in a fairer manner

(Continued)

Table 1.1 (Continued)

Emotion	Type of belief	Theme	Thoughts	Behaviour
Jealousy	Unhelpful Rigid or extreme	Threat to relationship with partner from another person	**Attention Focus:** *Looks for sexual/ romantic connotations in partner's conversations and behaviour with others* • Sees threats to the relationship when none really exists • Overestimates threats to the relationship • Thinks partner is always on the verge of leaving for another • Pictures visual images of partner being unfaithful • Thinks partner will leave for another person they admitted finding attractive	• Seeks constant reassurance that partner is faithful and loving • Constantly monitors partner's actions • Continually searches for evidence that one's partner is involved with someone else • Attempts to restrict the movements and activities of partner • Sets tests which partner has to pass • Retaliates for partner's imagined infidelity • Sulks
Concern for relationship	Helpful Flexible and preferential	Threat to relationship with partner from another person	**Attention Focus:** *Doesn't actively look for evidence of partner having an affair* • Doesn't see threats to the relationship when none exists • Views partner's conversations with others as normal • Doesn't create images of partner's infidelity • Accepts that partner will find others attractive but does not see this as a threat	• Allows partner to express love without seeking reassurance • Allows partner freedom without monitoring them • Allows partner to show a natural interest in other men or women without imagining infidelity

Emotion	Type of belief	Theme	Thoughts	Behaviour
Unhealthy Envy	Unhelpful Rigid or extreme	Another person possesses and enjoys something desirable that the self does not have	**Attention Focus:** *Focuses on how to get the desired possession without regard for any of the consequences* • Thinks about the desired possession in a negative way to try and reduce its desirability • Pretends to be happy with one's possessions even when this is untrue • Thinks about how to acquire the desired possession regardless of its usefulness • Thinks about how to deprive the other person of the desired possession	• Criticises the person who has the desired possession • Criticises the desired possession • Tries to take away the desired possession from the other person • Spoils or destroys the desired possession so that the other person does not have it
Healthy Envy	Helpful Flexible and preferential	Another person possesses and enjoys something desirable that the self does not have	**Attention Focus:** *Focuses on how to get the desired possession after considering the consequences for self and others* • Honestly admits that one desires the possession • Doesn't pretend to be happy with one's possession when one is not • Thinks about how to obtain the desired possession for positive reasons • Can allow the person to have and enjoy the desired possession without criticising the person or the possession	• Tries to obtain the desired possession if it is truly what one wants

The emotions table explained

Here we explain the contents of each section contained within the emotions table.

Emotion and type of belief

The emotions table is arranged in pairs of emotions that are either helpful or unhelpful to clients (and people in general) in achieving their goals. For example, it would be unhelpful for a client to experience *anxiety* at an interview as the emotion interferes with mental and physical performance. *Concern*, on the other hand, will enable the client to tolerate the uncertainty of the situation while remaining alert and focused. If the client feels very strongly about the outcome (getting the job) it might be unrealistic for them to feel confident and relaxed if they have come to you for support with their anxiety. If they insisted that this was how they wanted to feel, you could compromise by getting them to aim at moving from anxiety to concern before making the transition to confidence. Note also that unhelpful beliefs are rigid and extreme whereas helpful beliefs are flexible and preferential.

Themes

Themes describe certain aspects of the *situation* that the clients find themselves in (or anticipate) and are the same for both helpful and unhelpful negative emotions. For example, the theme for anxiety is threat or danger (e.g. the risk of performing poorly at interview) and is exactly the same for concern, but the thoughts and behaviours that the client is likely to experience are different depending on the emotion.

Thoughts

If the client experiences an unhelpful negative emotion, they are more likely to focus on negative and/or catastrophic aspects of the situation and overestimate the likelihood of bad things happening. This can become a vicious cycle as even the slightest evidence of 'bad things happening' (e.g. a stern-looking interviewer) will confirm and strengthen the client's negative belief. The attention focus consistent with helpful negative emotions, however, is more positive in outlook and constructive.

Behaviour

Helpful negative emotions are accompanied by constructive behaviours that enable clients to overcome the challenges they face on the way to achieving their goals. Unhelpful negative emotions are usually linked to self-defeating behaviours that get in the way of achieving goals. This is an important point as one of the key strategies used to move from an unhelpful emotional state is to *act* and *think* in a way that is consistent with helpful emotions. It is also worth emphasising that the urge to behave in a certain way is indicative of the emotion that your client may be experiencing even if they do not act on this feeling. For example, if your client were about to give a presentation and felt the urge to run away, this would indicate that they were experiencing anxiety rather than concern even if they managed to resist the urge.

Quantitative versus qualitative models of negative emotions

Having reviewed the contents of the emotions table, you may decide that using qualitative distinctions to help clients discern what they are feeling when facing certain challenges is too complicated a process. At the very least, the table will provide you with a better understanding of client's emotional reactions and enable you to devise more effective helping strategies. An alternative method that you can employ when addressing clients' emotional reactions is a quantitative model. Consider this in the case of anxiety:

No Anxiety .... Intense Anxiety

0   1   2   3   4   5   6   7   8   9   10

With this approach, your initial endeavour is to ascertain the intensity of the client's feeling in relation to their challenge by using *likert scales*. The most helpful question to ask is:

'On a scale of 0 to 10 where 0 is no anxiety at all and 10 is the most intense anxiety you could experience, how would you rate your feelings about (attending the interview/giving the presentation)?'

Having identified a baseline for the client's specific feeling, you are now both in a position to formulate an emotional goal as part of your overall strategy. This needs to be realistic as the client may wish to aim at 0. This issue can be dealt with by using the following response:

'Given that you feel very strongly about (wanting to get the job/successfully achieve the presentation), how realistic is it for you to aim at feeling no anxiety at all?'

Assuming the client had rated their current level of anxiety at 8 and agreed that a realistic emotional goal would be to reduce this to 2, your next step is to consider what cognitive and behavioural strategies the client will need to develop in order to bring about this reduction:

'Let's consider ways in which you could think and act that would bring your anxiety level down from 8 to 2.'

You can then revisit the emotions table and review the thoughts and behaviours associated with concern to help you formulate your strategy. This process will work for any emotion that the client identifies.

Having provided you with a theoretical overview of the ABC model, we will now present you with an extended version including detailed instructions for its use with clients.

The ABCDE Model

The ABCDE model can be used to:

- understand how clients create additional barriers to achieving their goals through unhelpful thinking
- help clients to understand the problems they create for themselves and break down specific challenges by using the ABCDE framework

The different components of the model are:

'A' =**activating event** sometimes referred to as *adversity* because it often represents a challenge. An activating event means an actual *external* event that has occurred in the past or is happening in the present or a future event that the client antici- pates. The activating event can also be *internal* (in the mind) such as an image, dream or memory. 'A' referred to as an activating event because in this model it is a *trigger* for the client's thoughts and beliefs.

'B' =**beliefs** that clients automatically have when they are triggered by the *activating event*. Beliefs include clients' thoughts, rules, demands they make (on them- selves, the world and other people) and the meanings they attach to events (both external and internal).

'C' = the consequences of beliefs that clients hold about an *activating event* includ- ing emotions, behaviours and physical sensations that are caused by experiencing different emotions.

'D' = **disputing**, which involves challenging the unhelpful thought or *belief* that largely contributes to the negative emotional and physical *consequences* at 'C'.

'E' = **new and effective thinking** that will help the client deal with their challenge more constructively and lead to improved emotional and physical consequences at 'C'.

You can use the ABC part of the model to analyse problems your clients may be experiencing as a result of their unhelpful thinking through careful ques- tioning. There are three ways in which you can do this depending on your preference and your client's abilities:

- Use the ABC model as a mental framework for analysing the client's problems.
- Write down the problem with your client using the ABCDE worksheet (availa- ble to download from www.sagepub.co.uk/sheward).
- Teach your client to analyse their own problems by completing the ABCDE form.

We can use our earlier example to carry out an ABC analysis:

A: Client imagines failing a job interview (an inference about a future event).

B: They believe, 'I've got to make sure that I don't perform badly at the interview or it will mean that I'm a failure.'

C: The client experiences anxiety (emotion), a churning stomach (physical reaction) and drinks alcohol in an attempt to calm themselves (unhelpful behaviour).

You can use this example as a guide to completing the ABCDE form with your clients or teach them to complete it if, in your judgment, they have the ability and inclination. You can see that following the example will help make sure you record:

- the facts of the *event* and specific trigger under 'A'
- your client's *thoughts* about the event under 'B'
- how your client *feels* and *acts* under 'C'

Developing a clear ABC of your client's problem can help them to see how their (often negative) thoughts at 'B' lead to their emotional and behavioural responses at 'C'.

The next section provides a detailed description of how to complete the ABCDE form with your client.

Completing the ABCDE form

The following guidelines will enable you to complete the ABCDE form with your clients or help them to become proficient in completing the form themselves so that they can use it as a self-help tool for dealing with challenges in achieving their goals.

Step 1: Ask the client to describe what they want to achieve under the 'What is your goal?' section

Encourage them to make their goal as specific as possible (e.g. doing well at the interview). You could link this to the client's action plan.

Step 2: In the Consequences (C) section, point 1, encourage your client to identify the emotion they are feeling about a particular situation

You don't have to start at 'C' but it makes sense if the client has presented a barrier to achieving their goal in terms of how they *feel* about the situation. An example of an unhelpful emotion could include *anxiety* about attending a job interview.

The emotions table in the previous section will help you (and your client) to understand and identify emotions.

Step 3: In the Consequences (C) section, point 2, encourage the client to describe how they acted (or felt like acting)

This could include an unhelpful behaviour related to the emotion identified at point 1 like *withdrawing physically from the threat* (e.g. wanting to avoid attending the interview).

The 'Behaviour' section of the emotions table will help you and your client to describe how they act or feel like acting when confronted with a barrier to achieving their goal.

Step 4: In the Activating Event (A) section, get the client to describe what triggered their feelings

As mentioned in the previous section, the 'activating event' (sometimes described as 'adversity') is the *trigger* for unhelpful thoughts and feelings and is usually specific and personally significant. Activating events (or triggers) can include situations that:

- happen in the present (attending the interview)
- happened in the past (did badly at the interview)
- will happen in the future (due to attend the interview)

More subtle examples of activating events (or triggers) can include *physical sensations* (increased heart rate or breathing) and even thoughts or emotions.

In order to make your assessment as accurate as possible, encourage the client to be specific about the most challenging aspect of the situation. There are two simple ways in which you can do this. Ask:

'What is the most challenging (or disturbing) thing about the situation?'

or:

'If there's one thing you could change to make you feel OK about the situation, what would it be?'

If the client finds it difficult to be specific about the situation, you could ask them to list the various aspects they find challenging or disturbing and then rank them accordingly. This method will enable you to pinpoint the main concern.

Step 5: In the Belief (B) section, get the client to describe any unhelpful thoughts and beliefs about the situation

This could include unhelpful thoughts like:

'I have to get the job or it'll prove that I'm a failure.'

'I always do badly at interviews so I'm bound to mess this up.'

'The other applicants will be better qualified than me.'

It's worth noting that many people think in *images* as well as words. Your clients may *see* themselves doing badly at the interview in their mind. You can capture *catastrophic images* in this section.

Step 6: In the Dispute (D) section, encourage the client to consider mistakes they are making with their thoughts and beliefs about the situation

The following questions will help you to identify your client's thinking errors:

'Are you thinking about the worst thing that could happen?' (catastrophising)

'Are you thinking in extreme, all-or-nothing terms?' (black and white thinking)

'Are you using terms like "I *always* fail" or "I *never* do well"?' (over-generalising)

'Are you predicting the future or waiting to see what happens?' (fortune-telling)

'Are you jumping to conclusions about what other people will think about you?' (mind-reading)

'Are you focusing only on the negative without considering any positive aspects?' (mental filtering)

'Are you putting yourself down excessively, for example, as a failure?' (labelling)

'Are you paying too much attention to your negative gut feelings instead of considering the facts of the situation?' (emotional reasoning instead of rational reasoning)

'Are you telling yourself that the situation is unbearable – for example, nervousness before an interview – when it is in fact tolerable and worth putting up with for the sake of your goal?' (low frustration tolerance)

Step 7: In the Effective Thinking (E) section, encourage your client to come up with specific thoughts

Examples of effective thinking are:

- a helpful alternative for each thought, attitude or belief entered in column B at point 1
- how they would prefer to feel at point 2
- how they would prefer to act at point 3

This stage is very important as one of the key principles of CBT is to encourage clients to *think* and *act* against their negative beliefs with the aim of getting them to *feel* better about their challenging situation.

The following questions will help your client to identify more positive alternatives:

'What is a more helpful way of looking at the situation?'

'What evidence do you have for your unhelpful belief about the situation?'

'If your best friend were thinking this way about the situation, how would you encourage them to come up with a more positive approach?'

'Even if things didn't go the way you want them to, what could you gain from the situation?'

Step 8: Help the client develop a plan to move forward

This final stage draws everything together. Take all of the agreed actions in Section E, 'Action plan'.

Guided discovery and Socratic questioning

Plato said of the ancient Greek philosopher Socrates (c. 469–399 BC) that he was a man who thought for himself and taught others to think for themselves (Magee, 1987). Socrates bequeathed his method of Socratic questioning centuries ago and its practice has been used in philosophy ever since. It is also used extensively within CBT to facilitate guided discovery: using questioning to enable clients to see flaws in their thinking or strategies aimed at achieving their goals and helping them to realise potential solutions. There are two ways you can use this approach where:

- neither of you have the 'answer' to the client's problem and are exploring possibilities collaboratively through the method of question and answer
- you can see a possible solution ahead of the client but lead them to this conclusion through questioning rather than simply telling them.

In the case of the second approach, it is important that you do not simply manipulate the client to arrive at the answer you desire. You need to maintain a genuine interest in stimulating their problem-solving ability while keeping an open mind that you may not have the correct solution or that the client can arrive at a better one. Here is an example of helping a client to prepare for a job interview using Socratic questioning:

Counsellor:	You've mentioned that you're very nervous about attending the interview. What's the worst thing that could happen as far as you are concerned?
Client:	That I'd dry up – that I wouldn't be able to answer the question.
Counsellor:	And if that happened, what would that mean to you?
Client:	It would mean that I'd look stupid, a complete idiot.
Counsellor:	So is that your biggest fear, looking an 'idiot' in front of the interview panel?

Client:	Yes it is.
Counsellor:	How much time do you spend thinking about this?
Client:	Most of the time.
Counsellor:	And how is thinking that you'd look an 'idiot' affecting you ability to prepare for the interview?
Client:	It's getting in the way, I can't concentrate on preparing.
Counsellor:	And if you think this way on the day of the interview, what's likely to happen?
Client:	There's an even greater chance of me drying up.
Counsellor:	So what could you do to help yourself?
Client:	Change the way I'm thinking about it I suppose.
Counsellor:	How?
Client:	I could be less hard on myself and think that if I went blank it would be due to nerves rather than stupidity.

In the above exchange the learning outcome would have had far less potency if the practitioner had simply told the client to stop thinking they would look an idiot if they failed to answer the question. Bearing this point in mind, if you find yourself about to make a didactic teaching point, try to turn your statement into a question. This will be more effective in terms of keeping the client mentally engaged in the process in addition to strengthening their sense of self-efficacy with regard to problem solving. This approach is particularly helpful if you find yourself working with overly passive clients whose lack of participation compels the practitioner to do most of the work but with little gain for the client. To help remind you of this principle, remember the saying, 'Let the client's brain take the strain'. Although there are great merits in using guided discovery and Socratic questioning, this approach needs to be used sensitively to avoid making the client feel that they are being interrogated. Also, if it becomes apparent that the client is unable to move forward as a result of Socratic questioning, it will be necessary to make a didactic input before reverting to guided discovery.

Using the zigzag technique to strengthen clients' helpful beliefs

Using the ABCDE approach is a useful way of helping clients to challenge unhelpful beliefs they may have about overcoming any particular barriers they face on the way to achieving their goals. However, even if you elicit a more effective outlook at 'E', clients may accept it at face value but still have hidden reservations about putting this constructive thinking style into action. This is often because they have gained *intellectual* insight into their problem but not *emotional* insight.

Intellectual versus emotional insight
Albert Ellis (1963) distinguished between both types of insight that clients obtain when they realise that their cognitive and behavioural approaches to achieving their goals are flawed. He described intellectual insight in terms of a

superficial acknowledgement from clients that their beliefs about a situation are irrational, inconsistent with reality, illogical and self-defeating and that adopting an alternative perspective (e.g. rational, consistent with reality, logical and self-helping) would be constructive in achieving their goals. This can be described as an 'ah ha' moment: a sudden epiphany that can of itself provide clients with a great deal of satisfaction because they may have gained an insight into consistent thinking errors they have made for the first time. Clients may be seduced into thinking that gaining this insight alone is sufficient to bring about change and will enable them to overcome any psychological barriers that they have previously faced when trying to achieve their goals. It might be, for example, that they have detected unhelpful patterns of thinking and acting when faced with specific stressful situations (e.g. interviews, presentations) that are consistent with childhood experiences (being very embarrassed at having to talk in front of the class at school). This type of insight, however, is insufficient for enabling your client to think, feel and act more constructively when overcoming their specific challenge: to do this requires emotional insight.

The process of moving from intellectual to emotional insight can be described in terms of transferring the new constructive outlook from the head to the heart. This requires a commitment on behalf of the client to think and act consistently with their new effective attitude when under pressure and attempting to achieve their challenging goal and to dispute their old, negative thinking style as it occurs. Without sufficient resolve on the client's part, their intellectual insight will merely help them to understand why they fail to achieve their goal before, during and after they attempt it. This also means acknowledging that some discomfort in goal attainment is inevitable (e.g. feeling concern rather than anxiety) but is not an indication that maintaining a more constructive thinking and behavioural strategy is not working.

You can help your client to strengthen their effective new thinking strategy by teaching them to use the zigzag technique. This involves encouraging the client to play devil's advocate by both attacking and defending their new thinking strategy. The more adept your client becomes in challenging attacks on their constructive outlook, the more conviction and emotional insight they will gain. When encouraging your client to take part in this exercise, it is helpful to suggest that they mount progressively aggressive attacks on their constructive belief until they have fully exhausted any doubts in their own mind about the efficacy of their new belief. This process can be likened to a judo practitioner fighting in sequence a series of increasingly proficient opponents in order to gain strength and confidence. The following example shows Corrine's completed zigzag form to illustrate this process.

Example

Corrine has been feeling very ambivalent about applying for a promotion within her organisation. Having carried out an ABCDE assessment, it became apparent that she maintains unhelpful beliefs that: (a) failure will be humiliating in front of her colleagues; (b) even if she were successful, she would not be able to cope with the additional responsibilities. Having disputed these negative beliefs, Corrine has formulated (see Figure 1.3) an effective new outlook that she now wishes to strengthen.

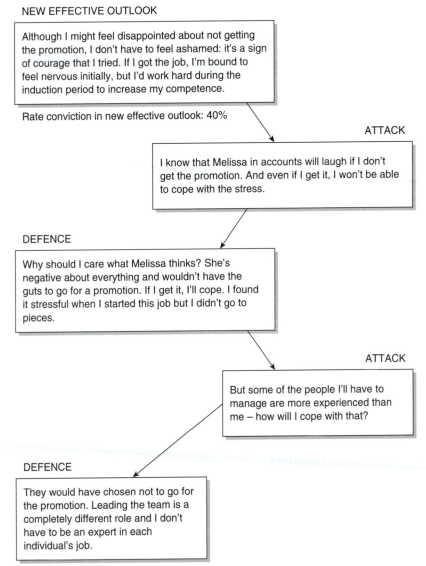

NEW EFFECTIVE OUTLOOK

Although I might feel disappointed about not getting the promotion, I don't have to feel ashamed: it's a sign of courage that I tried. If I got the job, I'm bound to feel nervous initially, but I'd work hard during the induction period to increase my competence.

Rate conviction in new effective outlook: 40%

ATTACK

I know that Melissa in accounts will laugh if I don't get the promotion. And even if I get it, I won't be able to cope with the stress.

DEFENCE

Why should I care what Melissa thinks? She's negative about everything and wouldn't have the guts to go for a promotion. If I get it, I'll cope. I found it stressful when I started this job but I didn't go to pieces.

ATTACK

But some of the people I'll have to manage are more experienced than me – how will I cope with that?

DEFENCE

They would have chosen not to go for the promotion. Leading the team is a completely different role and I don't have to be an expert in each individual's job.

Rate conviction in new effective outlook: 80%

Figure 1.3 Corrine's zigzag form

The zigzag form

You can use the blank zigzag worksheet (available to download from www. sagepub.co.uk/sheward) to carry out this process with clients or coach them in using it as a self-help technique. The following steps apply in both instances.

Step 1: Summarise the new effective outlook in the top left hand box (or any other helpful belief/s that the client wishes to strengthen). Rate the strength of conviction on a scale of 0 to 100 per cent.

Step 2: In the next box, summarise any reservations or doubts about the new effective outlook. When performing this step, it is essential to attack the helpful belief as vigorously as possible to ensure that it is robust and will not dissolve in a 'live' situation.

Step 3: In the next box down, do battle with the attack by seizing on weakness in the argument. Counter each point with constructive rebuttals. It is important to remain focused on defending the effective new outlook or helpful belief and not become sidetracked by other points raised in the argument.

Step 4: Repeat steps 2 and 3 as often as is necessary until all attacks on the effective new outlook or helpful belief have been exhausted. This process may require using several zigzag forms until all doubts are dealt with adequately and a sense of firm conviction is obtained. Also, it is very important to stop on a defence of the effective new outlook or helpful belief rather than an attack to engender a feeling of positive conclusion.

Step 5: When all doubts and attacks have been answered, re-rate conviction in the effective new outlook or helpful belief on a scale of 0 to 100 per cent. If conviction has not increased, or has only increased moderately, examine the client's zigzag form and check that they have followed the instructions correctly.

As with many of the tools outlined in this book, clients can begin using the zigzag technique as a paper and pencil exercise but then internalise the process as a cognitive method for disputing unhelpful thoughts and beliefs for subsequent challenging situations.

Reflect and discuss

1   What do you consider to be the most important aspects of CBT theory and application in relation to your professional practice? How will you integrate these within your current working methods?
2   How can you apply the 5-areas model to a particular client case that you are currently working on? How can you apply it to a personal or professional situation?
3   Which are the most common unhelpful patterns of thinking that you come across in your work with clients?

4 How can you apply the ABC model to one client case and one personal or professional situation?
5 Which helpful and unhelpful negative emotions to you encounter most frequently in your work with clients?
6 How can you integrate the zigzag technique into your current professional practice?

2

Enabling Clients to Succeed at Interview

This chapter is designed to help you to:

- develop a formulation of your client's challenges in relation to their forthcoming interview using both the 5-areas and ABC models
- teach clients to use the 'as if' technique to manage anxiety and prepare for interview more effectively
- teach clients a relaxation and breathing technique to feel calm before and during the interview
- use the 'worry tree' to encourage clients to adopt a problem-solving approach to concerns they experience prior to interview
- coach clients in taking control of their attention at will
- become proficient in the use of a pre-interview visualisation technique with clients
- provide clients with useful advice on practising effective sleep hygiene prior to interview

Now that you have gained an understanding of CBT theory set out in Chapter 1, we will help you to apply this knowledge to one of the most common (and important) situations career counsellors and coaches experience when working with clients: enabling them to succeed at interview. In this chapter we will introduce you to a range of motivational and confidence-building techniques including two visualisation exercises. But first of all you need to determine what your client's state of mind is as they contemplate achieving their goal and to do this you can use the 5-areas review or ABC model introduced in Chapter 1.

Developing a formulation of your client's challenges

As part of your work, you will have probably supported your client in terms of practical preparation. This would typically involve elements that are within your client's *external* range of control such as:

- researching the company
- rehearsing potential interview questions
- practising interview technique in role play
- deciding on self-presentation style

You can explain that the next level of preparation you will be working on together are elements within your client's *internal* range of control.

As we have already seen, gaining a shared understanding of the way your client thinks and feels about achieving their goals will provide you both with valuable information on potential thinking errors and will enable your client to develop an optimum psychological strategy. In our experience clients can often put a great deal of pressure on themselves by seeing it as of absolute importance that they succeed in a particular interview. Using the approaches outlined within this chapter will help clients to deal with this and other common psychological issues that confront them when attending interviews. Let's start by using a 5-areas review with a client who is due to attend an interview for a graduate-entry retail management job.

In Chapter 1 we used the 5-areas form to carry out a thoughts–feelings review with a client. An alternative way of introducing this approach is to develop a formulation with the client on a flip chart (or a blank piece of paper if space does not permit). This is a more subtle method and has the advantage of engaging you both in working collaboratively on a shared endeavour. Instead of getting the client to fill in a series of boxes, you can elicit their thoughts and feelings in relation to their goal through *Socratic dialogue* so that the formulation develops naturally as you both gain new insights. This is demonstrated in the following example.

Example

Steve: OK Shakira, we've been working on your interview technique through role-play at the last session. Are you feeling more confident about your body language and self-presentation?

Shakira: Yes, watching the recordings has really helped.

Steve: That's great. Now the interview's next week and we've done all we can to help you prepare in practical terms. Today I'd like us to work together on your mental preparation, how does that sound to you?

Shakira: Sounds good.
Steve: So when you think about the interview, is there anything that concerns you in particular?
Shakira: Definitely. I've got this real fear that they'll ask me a question I haven't prepared for.
Steve: That happened at the last interview didn't it? So let me jot it down on the flip chart.

Situation
Interviewer asks question I haven't prepared for

Steve: So if that did happen, what sort of thoughts are you likely to have?
Shakira: Well, from past experience I know I'll just think, 'Oh God, I can't answer that – I've trashed the interview!'
Steve: OK, let's put that up there.

Situation
Interviewer asks question I haven't prepared for

Thoughts
'God, I can't answer that'
'I've trashed the interview'

Steve: So if you started to have those kinds of thoughts at that point, how do you think you'd start to feel?
Shakira: I'd feel that I was making a complete idiot of myself.
Steve: That's another negative thought you might have. What I mean is how do you think you'd feel emotionally? [*Clients often fail to differentiate between thoughts and feelings they experience so you may have to clarify this.*]
Shakira: Really panicky, like I'd want to disappear. [*This suggests that Shakira is experiencing the behavioural characteristics of anxiety rather than concern – see Table 1.1 on CBT emotions.*]
Steve: So pretty anxious then?
Shakira: That's right.

Situation
Interviewer asks question I haven't prepared for

Thoughts
'God, I can't answer that'
'I've trashed the interview'

Feelings
Panicky
Anxious

Steve: And if you started to feel panicky and anxious, how would that affect your performance during the interview?

Shakira: I'm pretty sure I'd start saying things like, 'um' and 'err' because my mind's going blank and I'm panicking inside. If I'm not careful, I'll start waving my hands around nervously – I did that last time this happened.

Steve: OK, so you'd lose focus and become less articulate.

Situation
Interviewer asks question I haven't prepared for

Thoughts
'God, I can't answer that'
'I've trashed the interview'

Feelings
Panicky
Anxious

Behaviour
Loss of focus
Less articulate
Erratic gestures

Steve: And what sort of physical symptoms might you notice at this point?

Shakira: I'm sure I'd start blushing, that always happens, and I'd probably start sweating. And the worst thing is my mouth might go dry and I'd find it even more difficult to speak.

Steve: Sounds pretty unhelpful – let's put those down.

Situation
Interviewer asks question I haven't prepared for

Thoughts
'God, I can't answer that'
'I've trashed the interview'

Physiology
Blushing/ Sweating
Dry mouth

Feelings
Panicky
Anxious

Behaviour
Loss of focus
Less articulate
Erratic gestures

Steve: Can you see any sort of pattern emerging here?

Shakira: Definitely. I can see that if I start thinking that way, it's bound to lead to feelings of panic that'll have a knock-on effect on my performance and physical responses.

Steve: So we can actually link these different aspects.

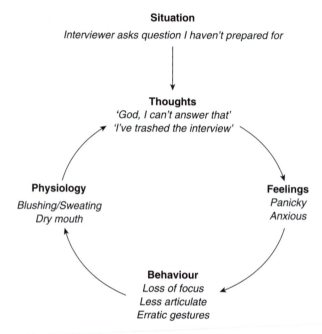

Situation
Interviewer asks question I haven't prepared for

Thoughts
'God, I can't answer that'
'I've trashed the interview'

Physiology
Blushing/Sweating
Dry mouth

Feelings
Panicky
Anxious

Behaviour
Loss of focus
Less articulate
Erratic gestures

Figure 2.1   Shakira's emotional processes, stage 1

Steve: What do you make of that?

Shakira: Well, it's a bit of a vicious cycle isn't it? Once I notice that I'm blushing and my mouth's dry, I'll panic even more and really screw the interview up.

Steve: Exactly. So how can you reverse this vicious cycle given that there's a real chance you might be asked a question you haven't prepared for?

Shakira: I guess I need to change the way I'm thinking about it now and also prepare how I'd respond if it happened in the interview.

Steve: Great! Any ideas?

Shakira: I suppose I can tell myself that if an unexpected question comes up, I don't have to panic. I can give it my best shot because the whole interview doesn't depend on one question.

Steve: That's right. And if you thought that way, how do you think you'd feel and act in the interview?

Shakira: I'd probably feel calmer and give myself time to answer the question rather than babbling on to conceal my ignorance.

I reckon my breathing and heartbeat would be more even too.

Steve: Shall we make some changes on the flip chart and see how that looks now?

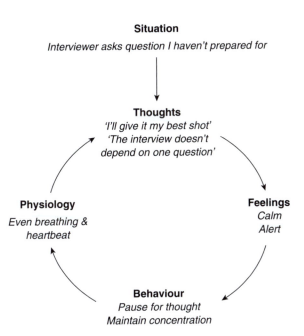

Situation
Interviewer asks question I haven't prepared for

Thoughts
'I'll give it my best shot'
'The interview doesn't depend on one question'

Feelings
Calm
Alert

Physiology
Even breathing & heartbeat

Behaviour
Pause for thought
Maintain concentration

Figure 2.2   Shakira's emotional processes, stage 2

Steve: The key learning point I want to emphasise here is that the way you think, before and during the interview, will have an effect on the way you feel and act. And as we can see from this, if you think constructively, you're more likely to feel better and perform well on the day. The model we've just used is called a 5-area review. Do you think it might be useful for you in other situations?

Shakira: Yes, definitely. Part of the selection process involves facilitating a discussion with other candidates competing for the job and I've been getting myself in a bit of a state about that.

Steve: I'll give you a copy of the 5-areas review model. I'd like you to use it in the same way that we've been working today before our next session. Analyse the sort of unhelpful thoughts that you're having about the situation and consider their effects on your feelings and behaviour. Once you've done that, come up with a more helpful mental strategy that'll make you feel better and help you to perform well when you're facilitating the group.

I would then record this as a homework assignment in the client's action plan, having obtained her commitment to carrying it out.

You will have probably realised that the ABC model can be used to develop formulations of challenges clients face in the same way as the 5-areas review model. Both methods have their advantages. The 5-areas review is excellent for illustrating the interrelation between thoughts, feelings, behaviours and physiology whereas the ABC model stresses the causality that ensues from interpretations of events and their emotional and behavioural consequences. In Chapter 1 we explored using the ABC model by helping clients to complete the ABCDE form. In the following example the model is used to develop a formulation with the client on a flip chart using a Socratic style (see Chapter 1). In this instance, Rhena is helping a client to prepare for a social event (a buffet lunch) that will be part of the selection process for potential trainee solicitors at a very traditional law firm.

Example

Rhena: OK Tom, I know this means a lot to you because if the firm takes you on, they'll pay for you to do your articles and give you a permanent position after training.

Tom: That's right, but my one dread is this bloody lunchtime buffet. I'm sure I'll mess that bit of it up.

Rhena: Why are you so sure?

Tom: Well if I'm honest it probably boils down to the fact that I come from a working-class background and I know that most employees and the other applicants were educated at public schools.

Rhena: We could help you prepare by doing a role-play, how about that?

Tom: I don't think that would help really. I've read up on etiquette and I know what to do. It's more a question of how I feel about the situation.

Rhena: Sounds as though our time would be better spent helping you to prepare for it mentally. Perhaps we could explore the way you think about the situation in detail and see what effect that's having. Do you want to give that a try?

Tom: Might as well.

Rhena: OK. So we're both agreed that the situation you will find challenging is attending the buffet lunch: let's write that on the flip chart.

Situation:
Attending buffet lunch at law firm

Rhena: So what's the worst thing about the situation as far as you're concerned?

Tom: I'm not sure.

Rhena: Let me put it to you like this. If I had a magic wand and could change one thing about the situation that would make you feel better, what would it be? [*I'm attempting to use the 'magic question' to determine Tom's critical 'A'. If this fails I could resort to the listing method outlined in Chapter 1*]

Tom: Now that you put it like that, I guess it's the possibility that I might drop my food or spill my drink.

Rhena: Let's jot that down.

Situation:
Attending buffet lunch at law firm
'A' = The possibility of dropping my food or spilling my drink

Rhena: So if that did happen, what would you think?

Tom: That I look like a clumsy working-class idiot. [*Note that Tom is engaging in labelling or self-downing by using this description of himself. He is also engaging in mind reading by making inferences that others will regard him in this way – see Chapter 1*]

Rhena: Let's make a note of that. [*Notice that I am not disagreeing with the client's interpretation of events at this point.*]

Situation:
Attending buffet lunch at law firm
'A' = The possibility of dropping my food or spilling my drink
'B' = I'll look like a clumsy working-class idiot

Rhena: And if you think like that, how are you going to feel?

Tom: Really embarrassed – I'd want to make my excuses and leave right there and then. [*We can see from this that Tom is describing the behavioural consequences of shame: wanting to hide from others to avoid disapproval.*]

Rhena: And how is thinking and feeling like that going to affect your performance socially?

Tom: Well I guess I'd become so self-conscious that I'd pay less attention to what the other people were saying. I'd probably become more clumsy.

Rhena: So the consequences of what you're thinking might look something like this?

Situation:
Attending buffet lunch at law firm
'A' = The possibility of dropping my food or spilling my drink
'B' = I'll look like a clumsy working-class idiot
'C' = Embarrassment, increased clumsiness and reduced concentration

Tom: I'd say that's spot-on.

Rhena: The question I have for you is this: does it logically follow that committing one social gaffe will mean that you're a complete idiot? [*I am using a logical argument to dispute Tom's self-downing belief: making one mistake does not make him a complete idiot.*]

Tom: I see where you're going with this. No, probably not.

Rhena: And the other important question to ask yourself is, will thinking this way help you perform well on the day when your goal is to get the job? [*I use an additional pragmatic argument to further weaken Tom's unhelpful belief – posing the question 'How useful is it to think this way?'*]

Tom: Put like that, no.

Rhena: I hope you can see from the ABC model we've just used that the way you're thinking about the event is lowering your confidence now and could cause your mood and behaviour to deteriorate on the day. If you accept that, how could you solve this problem?

Tom: I guess I could think differently about the situation. I've never really considered what an impact my thoughts have on my feelings and actions.

Rhena: So what would be a more constructive view that you could take?

Tom: I could tell myself that even if I made a mistake, it doesn't mean that I've failed the selection process. Even posh people drop their food!

Rhena: And even if you did make a mistake, how do you think you'd feel if you told yourself that?

Tom: I think I'd feel OK. I could accept myself and stay on top of the situation.

Rhena: Let's make some changes.

Situation:

Attending buffet lunch at law firm

'A' = The possibility of dropping my food or spilling my drink

'B' = Even if I make a mistake, it doesn't mean I'm an idiot. Even posh people drop their food!

'C' = Self-accepting; calm but alert; focused

Rhena: You mentioned that this is the first time you've realised how your negative thinking can affect your mood and behaviour. Has this model helped give you that insight?

Tom: I think it helps to break the whole process down and examine it objectively.

Rhena: Would it be helpful if I taught you this model so that you could use it to spot any other thinking errors you might be making and rectify them?

Tom: Yes, I think that would be useful.

Having won Tom's confidence in this approach, I would then go on to teach him the ABC model and set him a homework task of carrying out similar formulations.

Using both the 5-areas review and the ABC model will enable you to identify negative thoughts that clients have prior to attending the interview or detrimental cognitions that may occur to them during the interview. In Chapter 1 we considered the type of unhelpful beliefs clients may hold about themselves, others or the situations they experience. It would be helpful to review this section in addition to the list of unhelpful thinking styles when carrying out formulations with clients.

It is vitally important that clients put into practice the constructive thoughts and behaviours that you have developed together as part of your formulation. However, some clients may be sceptical and respond by saying that although they accept the positive aspects of the new thoughts and behaviours, they simply don't feel right. For example, Tom may have agreed that practising a self-accepting belief and acting confidently at the law firm's buffet lunch may seem like a good idea in principle but it would feel unnatural as it isn't consistent with the way he normally thinks and acts. This is exactly the point as practising new constructive beliefs and behaviours feels a little strange *initially* but they begin to feel more natural when put into action. In order to help your client overcome this initial hurdle you can teach them the 'as if' approach described below.

The 'as if' exercise

This exercise involves encouraging your client to practise their new helpful attitudes and behaviours *in spite of* scepticism and feelings of anxiety in the knowledge that confidence will grow the longer they persist. This technique requires a leap of faith and is sometimes described as 'fake it until you make it'.

The starting point for acting 'as if' is to build on the various positive attitudes and behaviours that you and your client have identified as part of your formulation. It may be helpful to review Table 1.1, with particular regard to the thoughts and behaviours associated with helpful negative emotions as prompts. You can help your client by asking them what sort of attitudes and behaviour would help them succeed in their challenging situation or how would someone who possessed these resources think and act. In Tom's case this would require posing the following questions and then modelling and internalising the helpful attitudes and behaviours that have been revealed:

Example

Tom, if you believed that you were socially equal to other applicants, how would you behave at the law firm buffet? By:

- making eye contact and smiling when appropriate
- giving yourself time to think about questions you're asked and responding confidently
- adopting a relaxed but upright posture and breathing calmly but evenly
- focusing your attention on the other person and the conversation rather than being over concerned about the possibility of making mistakes
- giving yourself permission to make mistakes without feelings of shame
- telling yourself that if you have been invited to take part in the selection process it means that you're highly regarded already

The main thing to emphasise to clients when acting 'as if' is that the way they *act* will affect they way they *think* and *feel*. This is because it is possible to 'trick' your brain into believing that you are confident because you are behaving this way even if you do not feel it to start with. As you have seen from the various 5-areas reviews and ABC formulations we have presented, thoughts, feelings and behaviours are linked, although when helping your clients to bring about positive change does not necessarily require you to work in that sequence. In this instance you are helping your client to initiate a positive behavioural change that will have beneficial emotional, cognitive and physiological consequences. This is because when your client's brain is presented with evidence that they are acting confidently, it is highly likely that they will begin to feel more confident.

Try this experiment

If your client is willing to experiment with this technique, ask them to try acting 'as if' in different situations by practising attitudes and behaviours that they desire but that do not always come naturally. You could suggest the following example to get them started.

Next time your client is involved in a conversation (work or social) and does not feel particularly confident, encourage them to experiment with adopting a more confident tone of voice – even if this feels unnatural to start with. They may notice that when they hear themselves sounding confident, they will feel an increased sense of confidence.

Helping clients to manage anxiety

Most clients experience interviews as stressful situations prior to and during the event. There is often a lot at stake in terms of wanting to get the job in an increasingly competitive market but also potential threats to the client's self-esteem. All of these factors can lead to increased anxiety, which will have a negative impact on the client's thoughts, actions and physiology as we have seen when carrying out formulations using the 5-area review and ABC models.

An important role that careers counsellors and coaches can play at this juncture is in *normalising* the experience of anxiety for their clients and helping them to regard their symptoms as *healthy concern* for an important outcome. In order to provide this support it is helpful to have a basic understanding of how anxiety works.

Many people experience anxiety as a deeply unsettling experience because it usually involves intense physical and mental sensations that are perceived as a *danger signal*. These include some or all of the following:

- churning stomach and need to use the toilet
- pounding heart and rapid breathing
- muscular tension and tingling sensations
- sweating and feeling hot
- dry mouth
- trembling and feeling unsteady
- difficulty focusing and light-headedness

Understandably, these unpleasant symptoms are often misinterpreted as a signal that something very bad is about to happen (see *emotional reasoning*, in Chapter 1) and this distracts attention away from the main task (e.g. doing well at the interview). If the experience of anxiety is particularly intense, the individual concerned might believe that their churning stomach will cause vomiting or the light-headedness they feel will precipitate a fainting spell. But why are we and our clients often subject to such an intense emotional experience when faced with nothing more threatening than a formal interview?

Evolutionary psychologists maintain that all of the negative emotions we encountered in Chapter 1 had a very important survival function for our ancient ancestors and were passed on to us through successive generations. With regard to fear, our ancestors who responded most readily to threat were more likely to survive and pass on their 'high anxiety' genes to their offspring. When we or our clients feel the onset of anxiety, we experience a primitive emotion that signals danger even if this response may not be appropriate to modern day situations (such as interviews) that are challenging but not life threatening. As Daniel Goleman pointed out in *Emotional Intelligence* (1996):

> For better or for worse, our appraisal of every personal encounter and our responses to it are shaped not just by our rational judgements or our personal history, but also our distant ancestral past.

There are a number of ways in which we can help clients to deal with anxiety before and during interview, and these are described below.

Accepting anxiety

Encourage your client to accept the fact that *nervousness is normal* during an interview and that the sensations listed above are common symptoms of anxiety – not an indication that they are losing control. You could also encourage clients to reframe their view of the physical aspects of anxiety and regard these sensations as an internal gathering of resources that will help sharpen their performance (e.g. secretion of adrenaline leading to increased mental alertness).

Acknowledge anxiety then focus outwards

It is important for clients to acknowledge any feelings of nervousness if they occur – they can even say 'hello' to their nerves. Trying to suppress or deny these sensations is likely to have the paradoxical effect of intensifying them. You could use the 'pink elephant' metaphor to explain this concept: 'I'd like you to try as much as possible *not* to think of a pink elephant for the next minute.' (Try this yourself – chances are you will not be able to). In much the same way, if clients try to deny their nervousness, they will inadvertently focus greater attention on the sensations.

Having 'gone inside' and acknowledged any feelings of nervousness, advise the client to concentrate their attention on the external environment. We explain this process fully later on in this chapter.

Relax and focus on breathing

Teaching a wide range of relaxation techniques is beyond the scope of this book. However, instructing clients in the use of a simple breathing technique will help them to counteract any excessive symptoms of anxiety. It is always advisable to seek your client's consent before offering to show them this technique as they may consider it to be a form of meditation and object on religious grounds (some faiths discourage the practice of formal meditation). It is also helpful to emphasise that this is a relaxation technique rather than meditation.

Start by explaining to your client that many people find it helps them to become calmer if they breathe in a certain way that involves relaxing the stomach and inhaling deeply: this is often referred to as abdominal or *diaphragmatic breathing*. Many people breathe this way naturally, but most engage in shallower chest breathing. When we breathe slowly and deeply while involving the diaphragm, it can have a soothing effect on our parasympathetic nervous system.

Invite your client to sit comfortably, preferably with their back straight, and ask them to place one hand on their stomach. Encourage them to exhale slowly while contracting their abdominal muscles. Encourage them to feel their hand move up and down as they inhale and exhale focusing on slow, natural breathing all the way down to the stomach.

Encourage them also to focus their attention on the sensation of the breath entering through their nostrils as they inhale and exhale.

Once they have become used to breathing this way, suggest that they recite a relaxing word slowly in their mind each time they exhale, for instance, 'c-a-l-m'.

Your client can use this breathing technique in a number of ways. If they feel agitated several days before the interview, they may find it helpful to spend at least five minutes twice each day (or whenever they feel stressed) practising in a quiet place. In addition to calming the parasympathetic nervous system (a physical benefit), deep rhythmic breathing has the effect of quieting the mind (a psychological benefit) as its focus shifts to each breath rather than troubling thoughts.

The worry tree

Although you may have worked hard with your client to identify any specific negative thoughts about the forthcoming interview and re-framed them, it is still likely that they may engage in random worrying either before the interview or on the day. Most people have a tendency to *ruminate* about concerns if there is nothing immediately to occupy their mind, and this can often lead to negative thinking and result in feelings of anxiety. Mihaly Csikszentmihalyi (pronounced 'cheeks-sent-me-high') is author of *Flow* (1991), the ground-breaking work on optimal psychological conditions. He described this state as *entropy* – the tendency of the human mind to drift towards rumination about worry and other negative thoughts.

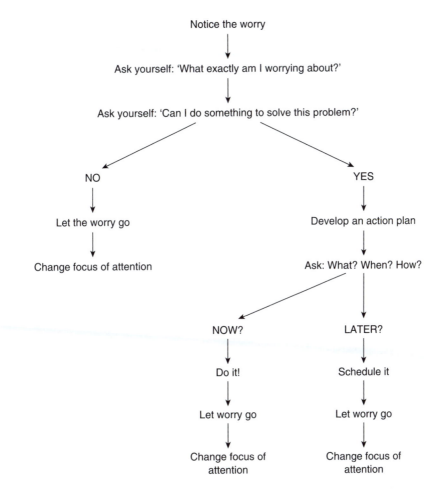

Figure 2.3   The worry tree (adapted from Butler & Hope, 2007)

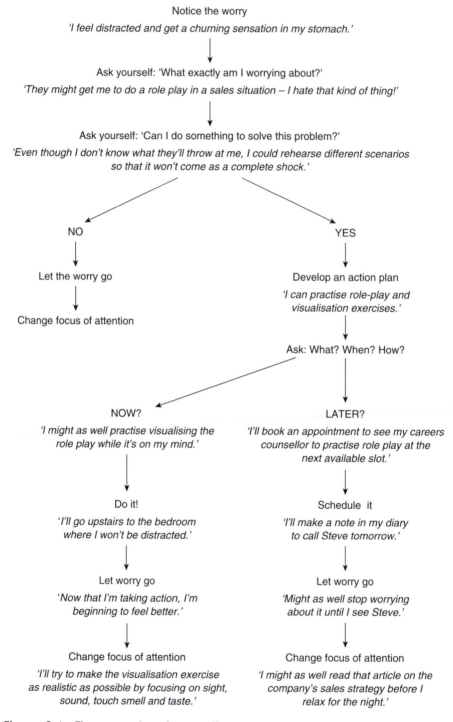

Figure 2.4 The worry tree in practice

But when we are left alone, with no demands on attention, the basic disorder of the mind reveals itself. With nothing to do, it begins to follow random patterns, usually stopping to consider something painful or disturbing. Unless a person knows how to give order to his or her thoughts, attention will be attracted to whatever is most problematic at the moment: it will focus on some real or imaginary pain, on recent grudges or long-term frustrations. Entropy is the normal state of consciousness – a condition that is neither useful nor enjoyable. (1991: 119)

Worry, like other 'negative' emotions we have encountered, has a useful function: it is call to action. It is that nagging concern which prompts us to prepare adequately for an interview or exam when we would rather do something less demanding and more pleasurable like socialising or watching television. But it becomes a dysfunctional activity when worries begin to spiral out of control and lose their specific focus on what needs to be done. At its most extreme, this tendency can result in *generalised anxiety disorder* (GAD) in which worries feed off themselves and self-multiply. *The worry tree* is a useful tool for helping clients tackle each concern as it arises, differentiating between problems that can be dealt with constructively and random worries that are outside of the client's control. Figure 2.3 provides a general template for dealing with worries in this way.

The key thing to emphasise when using this model with clients is that if they find themselves worrying about the forthcoming interview, they need to use this emotion as a catalyst for problem-solving action. You could also suggest that once the client has practised using the worry tree as a paper and pen exercise, they will be able to internalise the model and add it to their repertoire of tools for succeeding at interview.

Let's look at a practical application of the worry tree to a client's concerns prior to attending a job interview (see Figure 2.4).

Hopefully it will be clear from the example in Figure 2.4 that the worry tree will also identify if the object of the client's worries is beyond their control and does not merit further thought. The essential point here is that if the client has exhausted every practical solution to dealing with their concern, there is absolutely no point in expending valuable energy worrying about it further. 'Letting the worry go' may seem like a difficult thing to expect of clients in practice, but the techniques and attitudes set out in the following section will supplement this approach.

Helping clients to take control of their attention

As we have already seen in previous examples of interview scenarios, the client's focus of attention will often be *internal* as well as *external*. Physical symptoms of anxiety may cause significant distraction and inhibit performance. Clients may also attempt to rehearse what they are about to say, monitor their performance as they deliver each answer and carry out a rapid 'post-mortem' on what they have just said. It is also common for them to become self-conscious about their appearance. This behaviour is perfectly understandable as they may have a panel of interviewers scrutinising their every move, but is unhelpful when clarity of thought is required.

One of the key principles for helping clients to effectively manage their anxiety at interview (or any other situations requiring social interaction) is to coach them in refocusing attention away from themselves. In CBT this is often referred to as training in *task concentration*. You have seen from the 5-areas model that the client's anxious feelings can lead to anxious thoughts and behaviours which, once triggered, initiate a vicious cycle leading to deterioration in performance. Fortunately getting the client to direct approximately 80 per cent of their attention on the *task* and *environment* will improve performance at interview.

As you can see from Figure 2.5, the individual's focus of attention is divided between the task in hand (the interview in this instance), the surrounding environment and the perception of the self. Your aim should be to encourage the client to divide their attention between these three areas but reduce the focus on *self* as much as possible while at the same time expanding focus on *task* and, to a lesser extent, *environment*. Remember, you're not asking your client to deny their feelings of nervousness – that would be counterproductive. Instead, encourage them to 'go inside' and acknowledge normal feelings of slight apprehension but then concentrate on developing an external focus of attention.

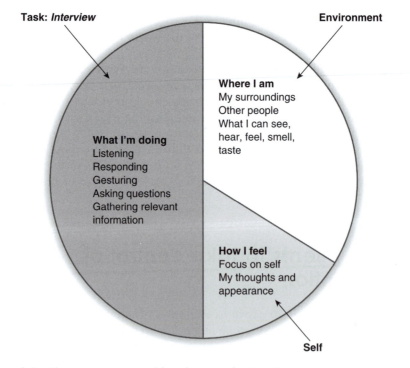

Figure 2.5   Three areas requiring focus of attention

A good starting point in helping the client to take charge of their attention is to use *guided discovery* as a method for enabling them to consider the way in which they already practice filtering out distractions on a daily basis. Potential examples could include:

- Focusing intently on a conversation with a friend in a noisy environment such as a pub or restaurant. In this instance the client will have filtered out background noise because they are eager to hear what their friend is saying.
- Becoming engrossed in a television programme ignoring the sound of conversation from other people in the room or noises from the street.
- Engaging in physical exercise while distracting oneself from feelings of fatigue and discomfort by listening to music or watching television.
- Completing chores, study or work assignments with looming deadlines ignoring unpleasant symptoms of minor ailments such as colds or headaches.

The key learning point to get across to clients is that they can control the focus of their attention when sufficiently motivated to do so. The reason for this is that there is usually an obvious *reward* for doing so: an engrossing conversation, an entertaining programme, an urgent deadline met. The next step is to coach clients in practising task concentration *at will*. In order to do this you need to negotiate an appropriate homework assignment.

Step 1: Get the client to nominate a future event that will enable them to practise task concentration but that will not be too challenging to start with. For example, your client might be planning to meet a couple of colleagues for coffee the next day.

Step 2: Instruct your client to focus exclusively on themselves during the initial stage of the meeting with colleagues. Ask them to notice their thoughts, feelings and their perception of themselves (e.g. how they think they appear to colleagues).

Step 3: Ask your client to turn their attention to the external environment after a couple of minutes. What can they see, hear and smell? What are the physical sensations associated with the environment (the feeling of their body weight on the seat, their hand resting on the table)?

Step 4: Get the client to deliberately focus their attention on the task they are engaged in. Ask them to immerse themselves in the conversation paying particular attention to the other person's tone of voice, facial expressions and gestures as well as the content of the conversation.

Step 5: Evaluate this experience with the client identifying any difficulties they experienced in focusing their attention at will and considering tactics for over coming these obstacles. Importantly, ask them how they felt when they switched attention away from themselves and on to the environment and task. Reinforce any positive insights the client has gained and encourage them to reflect on how this skill will help them at interview.

Step 6: Negotiate a more challenging assignment for your client to practise task concentration. This could be a situation in which your client does not feel completely comfortable (a meeting at work) or where there may be a greater number of distractions (reading a detailed report on public transport).

Hopefully your client will begin to realise that they can exercise a considerable amount of control over their attention and in doing so ignore negative thoughts and feelings that may occur leading up to or during the interview. This skill is well worth developing and can be used in many situations other than formal interviews. It can also be used in conjunction with the techniques described in Chapter 3 in the section on 'Maintaining Motivation'.

Using visualisation techniques with clients

Formal interviews are future events and clients' inferences about what may or may not happen can lead to negative thoughts and subsequent feelings of anxiety. A major reason why clients make themselves anxious about future events is because they are unfamiliar. Even if your client prepares thoroughly for the interview they will not be able to predict the outcome with any certainty. Coaching your client in visualisation techniques will help them to reduce some of the uncertainty associated with the event by helping them to mentally rehearse attending the interview. This will enable your client to psychologically 'ease into' the situation on the day of the interview by reducing their sense of unfamiliarity and going in 'cold'.

Imagery is used widely within CBT and a great many professionals working in high-pressure situations use visualisation techniques to optimise performance (athletes, politicians, senior managers). The reason these techniques are so effective is that the human brain does not necessarily make a distinction between something that is imagined and something that is actually taking place. If your client is sceptical about this explanation or you need a vivid illustration of this concept, try the following exercise with them.

Exercise

Ask your client if they are interested in experiencing a practical example of how visualisation techniques work. Obtain permission that they will (ideally) practise this brief exercise with their eyes shut. You can adapt the following script to suit your own personal style:

I'd like you to close your eyes and sit in a comfortable but upright position. Imagine that in front of you there is a small table about waist height. In the centre of the table there is a light brown wooden chopping board and on top of this there is a large yellow lemon and a small silver knife.

Concentrate on the appearance of the lemon and notice how bright its yellow skin is and how its shiny surface reflects the light slightly.

Now pick the lemon up and feel its smooth, waxy skin with your fingertips. You might also notice the slight indentations and how it is firm but pliable when you squeeze it.

Place the lemon on the board and take the small silver knife in your hand. Now cut the lemon in half and listen for the hiss of juice escaping and the chopping sound when the blade makes contact with the wooden board.

Raise the lemon until it is just beneath your nose. Now slowly inhale the sharp, tangy smell and linger on the freshness of its fragrance.

Finally, bite into the flesh of the lemon and taste the sharp bitterness as its juices flow over your tongue and into your mouth. Notice the moist, pulpy texture of the lemon in your mouth.

Ask your client to open their eyes and question them about the exercise. If they have followed your instructions, they should have noticed an increased amount of saliva in their mouth. Draw attention to this point as it illustrates vividly how an imagined event can trigger the same physiological reaction as an actual event.

You may have noticed that this particular visualisation exercise also drew on the additional four senses of sound, smell, taste and touch in order to make the experience more vivid. This forms an important part of the next exercise, which is aimed at enabling your client to rehearse attending the forthcoming interview 'in their mind'.

Mentally rehearsing the interview: exercise 1

Step 1: Practical preparation

By now you should have ensured that your client has done enough practical preparation for the interview attending to essential issues such as:

- researching the company
- anticipating potential questions based on an evaluation of the person and job specification
- scoping out answers and preparing for impromptu role plays
- planning the route and allowing sufficient time
- deciding what to wear based on an assessment of the organisation's dress code

(Continued)

(Continued)

This basic preparation alone will make the client feel more confident as it will reduce any uncertainty that they will not be able to answer the questions. Carrying out a role play utilising appropriate techniques outlined in the chapter will also be a positive aid.

Step 2: Building a visual image of the interview

If at all possible, encourage your client to visit the venue where the interview will be held. Not only will this help them plan their journey and anticipate any potential problems that an internet search might not reveal, it will also enable them to build a visual image of the venue that will aid mental preparation. If it is not possible for your client to visit the venue, you can encourage them to build a visual image by visiting the company website or examining company brochures.

It will also be extremely helpful for your client to create a picture of what the interviewer looks like (or interviewers if it is a panel), although this may not always be possible. Again, company websites and brochures are a helpful resource. If all else fails, encourage your client to build up a picture of the interview by using their imagination based on whatever knowledge they have about the venue and individuals involved. In this way they can still 'teach their mind' that the interview is not a completely unfamiliar and therefore nerve-wracking situation.

Step 3: Find a quiet place to rehearse

Advise your client to find a quiet place where they will be alone and free from distractions. Suggest that they sit in a comfortable but upright position, preferably with their eyes shut to enhance concentration. They may wish to practice the relaxation breathing technique described earlier in this chapter in order to feel a sense of calm and clear their mind before commencing the visualisation exercise.

Step 4: Immerse yourself in the situation

The important thing to emphasise to your client is that they can add intensity to their visual image by making the mental rehearsal as vivid as possible so that they feel as though they are actually experiencing the situation as it unfolds. To assist them in this task you need to help them work with their five senses as part of their 'virtual experience':

- **Sight**: Instruct your client to associate themselves fully in the situation. This means seeing what is happening in each moment through their eyes and not observing themselves in a detached manner. This is an important part of the process as it ensures that they feel as though they are actually experiencing the situation. Ask them to pay particular attention to what they see. As they approach the venue, what colours do they notice? Are they muted or bright? Is it a sunny day or overcast? Are the images hazy or clear?

- **Sound**: As your client enters the building, get them to focus on the sounds that become apparent, perhaps the voice of the receptionist and the sounds of the work environment: doors opening and closing, people talking. Ask your client to distinguish which direction the sounds come from.
- **Smell**: Perhaps there is a smell of fresh coffee brewing or the pleasant fragrance of furniture polish.
- **Taste**: In order to make the experience more vivid, your client could imagine drinking a cup of tea or glass of water as they wait for the interview to take place, focusing on the calming effect of the taste and temperature when sipping the liquid.
- **Touch**: Encourage your client to imagine the physical sensations of pushing open the door and entering the room, shaking hands confidently with the interviewer (or interviewers) and taking a seat calmly. Get them to focus on the reassuring feeling of being physically grounded: the weight of their body seated in the chair and the solid feeling of placing their feet firmly on the ground.

Step 5: Act calm, feel calm

By now your client should feel fully immersed in the imaginary interview as if it were actually taking place. At this point it is important for your client to imagine how they would prefer to feel mentally and emotionally as well as physically. Returning the focus to the client's breathing will help to engender a feeling of calm if the rhythm is slow and regular and attention paid to how soothing it is to feel each slow breath enter and leave the body.

Step 6: Don't get nervous about feeling nervous

If your client begins to feel nervous at any stage during the visualisation exercise, encourage them to accept this sensation without trying to force it away or catastrophise about its sudden presence. Reassure them that these feelings are normal, and indicate an increase in adrenaline which will sharpen their performance. They may perceive this nervousness as uncomfortable but it should not be mistaken as a danger signal. Encourage your client to acknowledge their 'butterflies' and gently return their focus to mentally rehearsing the interview.

Step 7: Practice, practice, practice

Encourage your client to practise this visualisation exercise as much as possible. The more times they attend the interview in their mind, the more confident they will feel on the day as the experience will no longer seem unfamiliar.

The above exercise emphasises accepting and tolerating moderate feelings of nervousness that are a natural consequence of attending the interview. The next visualisation exercise is subtly different in that it enables clients to:

- identify any self-defeating thoughts that may arise prior to or during the interview in a pre-emptive manner
- draw on their own resources by identifying mental strategies for dealing with negative thoughts and the stress of attending interviews

The technique is adapted from a branch of CBT called rational emotive behaviour therapy (REBT), which places an emphasis on changing irrational beliefs as a method for helping clients deal with psychological challenges.

Mentally rehearsing the interview: exercise 2

- **Step 1:** Ask the client to find a quiet place, close their eyes and imagine themselves taking part in the interview process drawing on their five senses to make the experience as vivid and realistic as possible.
- **Step 2:** Ask the client to imagine that the actual interview has started and get them to be aware of any physical sensations that become markedly noticeable. Get them to pay particular attention to sensations of tension, increased heartbeat and breathing, or hot flushes.
- **Step 3:** Get the client to attend to the thoughts they are having during the interview that are not relevant to process. Ask them to note carefully any self-defeating thoughts arising from feelings of anxiety.
- **Step 4:** Encourage the client to imagine themselves coping successfully with their anxious feelings. Having registered the physical symptoms of anxiety, they should refocus their attention on the interview itself and away from bodily sensations such as increased heartbeat and breathing. Ask them also to focus on calm, regular breathing and imagining their muscles relaxing as the interview progresses.
- **Step 5:** Get the client to do battle with any negative thoughts that have arisen. Ask them to imagine holding a positive attitude and countering each negative thought with positive, encouraging responses. The latter could take the form of short, powerful messages like, 'I'm doing fine! Keep focused and don't worry about the butterflies!'
- **Step 6:** Get your client to follow through by imagining themselves coping successfully with the interview from beginning to end. Encourage the client to see themselves doing the best they can and being satisfied with their overall performance.
- **Step 7:** Having completed the visualisation exercise, ask the client to note carefully any helpful statements or images they developed that enabled them to cope with nervous feelings and negative thoughts.

This last step is vitally important as it will enable the client to develop an idiosyncratic strategy for coping with stress before and during the interview as well as creating a positive mental attitude. Try to emphasise this when instructing the client prior to carrying out the exercise and afterward during the debriefing. As with the first visualisation exercise, repeated practice will reward itself.

If you have encouraged your client to carry out the exercises summarised in this chapter, they should be better able to control any anxiety and have developed a positive outlook prior to the interview. The final section in this chapter provides essential advice for your client on getting a good night's sleep before the interview (and generally).

Getting a good night's sleep

Although the situation described in this section is the night before the interview, all of the advice and techniques that follow can be adopted by your client as effective habits for ensuring a good night's sleep.

It is perfectly understandable for your client to be more mentally aroused than usual the night before an interview and at the same time concerned that they will sleep soundly in order to feel well-rested and mentally alert the following day. Problems may occur if they tell themselves that they *must* get a good night's sleep, and if this is not possible they will feel awful and fail the interview.

Figure 2.6 is an example of how demanding a good night's sleep can have the opposite effect.

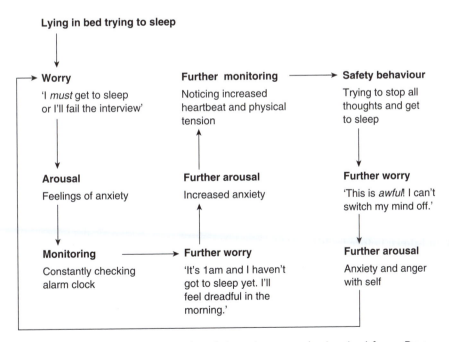

Figure 2.6   Jane's vicious cycle of sleeplessness (adapted from Ree and Harvey,2006, 'Night-time cycle of insomnia', in the *Oxford Guide to Behavioural Experiments in Cognitive Therapy*. p. 289)

The more Jane tries to get to sleep and forces herself to stop thinking, the worse her problem becomes. This is because her thoughts are triggering anxiety which in turn leads to increased adrenaline and physiological arousal. However, simply telling herself to stop thinking has the paradoxical effect of increasing thoughts. As we have seen in Chapter 1, Jane would be best advised to adopt *flexible preferences* about falling asleep rather than *rigid demands*. Jane would be better off telling herself that even if she was not able to sleep, she would still manage the interview. After all, it will only last an hour and a cup of coffee and adrenaline will ensure that she is sufficiently alert. Although this strategy may seem counter-intuitive, it will reduce the pressure that Jane is putting on herself with *all-or-nothing thinking* and will short-circuit the vicious cycle.

The other error Jane is making concerns the constant monitoring of her alarm clock. This simply draws attention to how late it is and prompts her to calculate how many hours' sleep she has left which leads to further feelings of anxiety. Many people get into the habit of glancing at the clock periodically when they experience difficulty sleeping without even being aware of the tendency and its unhelpful consequences. In this instance it is advisable to put the clock out of sight or turn it around so that the luminous dials are not visible.

Similarly, paying excessive attention to physical symptoms such as heartbeat and breathing will lead to increased arousal. Acknowledging these symptoms but focusing on calm, rhythmic breathing using the technique described earlier in this chapter will yield better results. This can also be combined with techniques outlined in the first visualisation exercise. The client can create an image of the most relaxing scenario they can think of using their five senses as we have previously instructed. For example, the memory of lying on a beach and dozing, listening to the sound of the sea lapping against the shore, feeling the soothing rays of the sun and smelling the pleasant fragrance of suntan lotion. Combined with calm, rhythmic breathing this visualisation will reduce arousal and provide a distraction from anxiety provoking thoughts.

There are a number of other helpful things you can advise your client to do or avoid in order to increase their chances of getting a good night's sleep before the interview:

Wind-down before bedtime: Although it is sometimes tempting to use the evening before an interview to prepare thoroughly, reading background information or mentally rehearsing interview questions may lead to a heightened state of alert or even anxiety. Advise your client to curtail these tasks at least two hours before bedtime and engage in more relaxing activities. Eating late, engaging in strenuous physical exercise or watching enervating television programmes (e.g. thrillers, horror films) are all calculated to increase physical and mental arousal before bedtime. A more helpful course of action could include taking a warm bath, listening to a relaxing radio programme or music, sipping a warm milky drink and reading an undemanding book.

Avoid alcohol or caffeine: Many people drink alcohol to help themselves relax if they are tense and mistakenly think that it will help them to sleep more soundly. The problem with this approach is that alcohol disinhibits and the individual may throw caution to the wind, drink excessively and find themselves with a hangover on the morning of the interview. Also, although people sometimes find it easy to fall asleep after drinking, their subsequent sleep pattern is disrupted because alcohol is a diuretic and prompts frequent trips to the bathroom. Caffeinated drinks including tea, coffee, cola and hot chocolate should be avoided from late afternoon onwards. This is because caffeine stays in the bloodstream for hours after consumption and increases alertness. It is also worth bearing in mind that some headache tablets contain high levels of caffeine.

Don't lie in bed tossing and turning: As we have seen in Jane's cycle of sleeplessness, lying in bed *trying* to get to sleep has the opposite effect to the one desired. If sleep becomes elusive it is far better to get out of bed, keep warm and do something boring like reading a dull book or newspaper article. Eventually tiredness will come and is usually preceded by the sensation of eyelids feeling increasingly heavy which is a signal to return to bed.

Create on optimum environment for sleep: Basic details include ensuring that the bedroom is neither too warm nor too cold and that any external light is excluded. If noise is a problem and can't be dealt with immediately (e.g. inconsiderate neighbours impervious to complaints), foam ear plugs can provide a temporary solution. At a more subtle level, it is advisable to remove any reminders of work (e.g. laptops, company literature) or clutter that creates a sense of disorder. Ideally the bedroom should be a relaxing environment that is associated only with sleep or sex. Watching television in bed is not generally conducive to a good night's sleep.

Reflect and discuss

1 What are the advantages and disadvantages of using either the 5-areas model or the ABC model to help clients deal with challenges they are encountering when preparing for interviews?
2 How can you adapt the visualisation exercise outlined within this chapter in your own professional practice?
3 Which techniques described in this chapter would be effective for use in group work with clients? How could you use the group dynamic to teach these skills more effectively?

3

Supporting Clients in Decision Making

This chapter is designed to help you to:

- understand Gerard Egan's three processes of information gathering, analysis and making a choice in relation to client's decision-making processes
- use cost and benefit analyses to help clients make more informed career decisions especially when they experience ambivalence about specific options
- become proficient in the use of Tol Bedford's FIRST model and setting SMART goals for clients
- encourage clients to maintain motivation
- understand the theory of flow in relation to career satisfaction
- help clients identify their personal values as part of their career decision-making process

Gerard Egan's *The Skilled Helper* (2002) has had a huge influence on career counselling and his model is taught widely on post-graduate and other courses. With regard to decision making, Egan stresses three important processes:

Information gathering: In the context of career counselling, this will require clients to gather all of the necessary information available to make an informed decision about which course to study or occupation to enter. This applies at any stage in the client's life from deciding study options in secondary education to making radical decisions around changing careers in mid- and later life. Although you do not need to have a detailed knowledge of every occupation and educational course, it will help your client enormously if you can advise them where to obtain relevant and up-to-date information (e.g. careers literature, professional institutions' websites).

Analysis: Once the client has obtained sufficient information, you can support them in processing this data by exploring the implications of various career or study options. This may involve a certain amount of *challenging* and *reality testing* if clients have unrealistic expectations and will require a great deal of subtlety on your part. You may find, for example, that your client wishes to enter a profession or course of study that requires higher entry level qualifications than their predicted grades for forthcoming exams will yield (e.g. medicine). If you meet with resistance in acknowledging the reality of the situation, a potentially helpful strategy is to introduce the notion of developing *contingency plans* as a compromise (this is generally helpful in any decision-making process). The client who insists on applying to study medicine with lower than required predicted grades may be encouraged to consider other medical occupations with less stringent entry requirements as a back-up plan. This will, of course, depend on the client's motivation behind their primary choice: opting for a career in medicine may be driven by notions of status rather than a desire to care for others and will need to be explored carefully before on appropriate contingency plan can be developed.

Making a choice: If you have helped your client to process the available data effectively, they should be left with a range of potential options for final decision making and subsequent action. This is not always straightforward as clients may become confused or ambivalent about the options available to them. As we have seen in previous examples, when clients become emotionally agitated about a particular issue, their ability to think rationally may be impaired, and this applies equally to decision making. Egan suggests prompting clients to consider the potential advantages and disadvantages associated with each option. You can improve upon this approach by helping clients to construct a more detailed *cost and benefit analysis* (CBA). Below is an example of Gregg's cost and benefit analysis.

Example

Gregg is 45 and currently employed as a marketing manager within a large retail company. He has grown increasingly disillusioned with his role and is considering retraining to become a secondary school language teacher as he is bi-lingual in Spanish. Gregg is married with two young children and has a mortgage. His wife works full time and is an assistant branch manager within a local building society. As Gregg already possesses a combined degree in Spanish and French, he is able to apply for a one-year, full-time post-graduate certificate in education specialising in his subject area. If he were to pursue this option, Gregg's plan would be to apply for secondary school teaching posts within travelling distance from home. He currently spends one and a half hours each way commuting to and from work and finds this tiring and frustrating. Both the one-year course of study and subsequent career change will mean a significant drop in income for Gregg and his family.

After Gregg had completed the cost and benefit analysis shown in Table 3.1, he was able to obtain a better overview of the various advantages and potential disadvantages associated with taking this career decision both for himself and his family in the short and long term. Gregg noted that most of the short-term costs were *material* whereas both the short- and long-term benefits offered a

Table 3.1   Gregg's cost and benefit analysis

Costs and benefits of: Retraining to be a secondary school teacher	
Costs (disadvantages)	**Benefits (advantages)**
Short-term	**Short-term**
For self:	*For self:*
Reduction in income Loss of company car Loss of professional 'status' Risk of disillusionment with new career	Studying an intellectually stimulating subject Pursuing a career linked to personal values Less time spent commuting
For others:	*For others:*
Less disposable income for family Risk of financial insecurity if teaching job does not materialise	Long school holidays provide increased opportunities for child care Spending more time with the children
Long-term	**Long-term**
For self:	*For self:*
Teaching profession subject to changes due to government policies	Less time spent commuting Teaching profession offers more security than current employer Final salary pension scheme Better career prospects Pursuing a career linked to personal values
For others:	*For others:*
	Better able to teach the children languages Long school holidays provide increased opportunities for child care

potential increase in quality of life for himself and his family. Critically, the CBA helped facilitate discussion between Gregg and his wife around whether they could realistically sustain a short to medium-term reduction in family income to finance Gregg's career change and whether this investment would benefit the whole family. After carrying out a series of careful calculations, Gregg and his wife realised they could manage on her salary until he obtained employment as a teacher and that the overall benefits to the family outweighed the risks and sacrifices required to make this career change. (A blank CBA worksheet can be downloaded from www.sagepub.co.uk/sheward.)

In addition to Egan's focus on *information gathering*, *analysis* and *making a choice*, you may find it helpful to impose some sort of order onto the decision-making process with your client. Tol Bedford's FIRST model provides a useful structure that can be used in conjunction with the other techniques described in this chapter.

The FIRST model

As we have mentioned, helping clients to make effective decisions can be challenging in a number of ways. You may have to deal with a range of complex needs in a short amount of time if you only have a limited number of sessions with the client (or just one session). It is a common experience for practitioners (particularly trainees) and their clients to get confused during sessions focusing on decision making and run out of time before dealing adequately with the issues in hand. The FIRST model will give you a framework within which to use your career counselling and coaching skills to support the client, and because you have reference points within the model you can navigate the session without getting lost. The model is also sufficiently flexible to enable you to change the order of the main components to suit your client's needs.

The FIRST model was developed as the result of research published in 1982 by the then chief occupational psychologist of the Department of Employment in England, Tol Bedford. He video-recorded a number of careers advisers' interviews and questioned the interviewees before and after the interviews, and concluded that there were five dimensions on which an interviewee might be expected to move or change during such an interview – Focus, Information, Realism, Scope and Tactics. He put them in that order to create the mnemonic 'FIRST' out of the initial letters.

Focus

Establish rapport
Most people appreciate it when others pay attention to them and *visibly tuning in* is an expression of empathy that lets the client know that you are with them

and prepared to listen carefully to their concerns. You can focus on key non-verbal skills that will enable you to establish rapport by using 'SOLER':

S: Face the client *Squarely*: this posture indicates involvement.

O: Adopt an *Open posture:* an open posture can be a sign that you are open to the client and what he or she has to say.

L: Remember that it is possible at times to *Lean* toward the other: a slight inclination towards the other person can be interpreted as 'I'm with you, I'm interested in you'.

E: Maintain good *Eye contact:* maintaining good eye contact with a client is another way of saying 'I'm with you; I'm interested; I hear what you have to say'.

R: Try to be relatively *Relaxed* or natural in these behaviours: a respectful, empathic mind set might lose its impact if your client does not see these internal attitudes reflected in your external behaviours.

Contract with the client

At the start of the interview you will want to negotiate a contract or *working charter* (Egan, 2002) with the client so that you both agree on what can be achieved within the time available. You may both wish to renegotiate this during the session if other priorities emerge.

Prioritise client objectives

You both need to narrow down the client's objectives to a manageable shortlist. It is very difficult to make a decision if your client has too many things to choose from so try to establish what their most important options are (e.g. which occupations are they committed to working towards?).

Specific rather than general goals drive behaviour, so broad goals need to be translated into more specific goals and tailored to the needs and abilities of each client.

Information

Prior to setting your client the task of information gathering, you need to determine how much they know about the options they have prioritised (e.g. occupations, vocational or academic courses). However, as Egan points out, there is no such thing as completely objective decision making as all information received by the decision maker (client) takes on a subjective hue. As well as ensuring that your client has accurate information on which to base their decisions, you can help them to discriminate instances in which they are filtering information in a subjective way and distorting its meaning. For instance, a female jobseeker may falsely infer from occupational material that careers in the construction industry are exclusively the domain of male employees.

Realism

The options your client ends up with should be realistic opportunities that they can take advantage of, not just fantasies, and some sensitivity is called for by the practitioner in facilitating this process. The notion of 'realism' can be somewhat problematic as nobody has the right to tell your client that they are being 'unrealistic' because they are aiming high or want to do something that is difficult. Encourage your client to aim high if they have realistically appraised their chances of achieving a particular option and encourage them to develop a suitable contingency plan (see below). Encouraging realistic decision making is a delicate balance between making sure your client achieves what they are capable of and sometimes enabling them to accept certain limitations and the sense of disappointment that may bring.

Scope

If you have helped your client to consider the costs and benefits of various options and potential strategies for achieving their objectives, you will both have the raw material for developing suitable contingency plans.

It is generally helpful to formulate contingency plans but they are particularly indicated when clients have highly competitive ambitions and objectives. Having back-up plans helps clients develop a more flexible outlook rather than rigid all-or-nothing thinking that almost inevitably increases stress. Having a contingency plan in mind while taking part in a high-pressure selection process for a competitive job will help your client reduce some of the mental pressure. They will be able to reassure themselves that they have other 'irons in the fire' if their desired outcome does not materialise in this instance.

Tactics

Egan observes that planning for action should not be confused with action itself and that without action a programme for change is nothing but a wish list. Additionally, clients who have goals but have not developed a range of tactics in order to achieve them will find it difficult to make the next step. This is where you need to work collaboratively with your client to formulate goals that they will remain committed to and stand a solid chance of achieving. To give your client the best chance of reaching their goals, always endeavour to make them 'SMART':

S-pecific

M-easurable

A-ttainable

R-ealistic

T-ime bound

Specific

Your client's goals need to be very clearly defined. Stating that they wish to change careers in order to achieve a better work–life balance gives a broad but rather vague indication of what they want to achieve. You may need to use your *Socratic questioning* skills (see Chapter 1) to help the client pin down exactly what it is they want to aim for. Examples of Gregg's specific goals are:

- To apply for a post-graduate certificate in education that offers a specialism in teaching languages at secondary school level.
- To apply for language teaching posts in secondary schools within one hour's travelling distance of home.
- To develop a medium-term domestic finance strategy that will allow for a reduction in income while studying.

Keeping goals as specific as possible will help you and your client to identify the steps they need to take in order to achieve their aims. It will also provide the psychological benefit of breaking down a seemingly overwhelming task into manageable steps that the client can believably see themselves taking (and will help with any subsequent visualisation exercise that you might construct).

Measurable

Developing specific goals makes it far easier for you and the client to measure progress towards achievement and will increase motivation. Clearly, Gregg will be able to measure whether or not he has achieved the first two goals by obtaining a place on a post-graduate course and subsequently receiving a suitable job offer. The third goal is more subtle, and one of the measures he devised is:

- To have agreed an interest-only fixed-term mortgage of less than 4.5 per cent covering the next two years.

Attainable

Your client's goals need to be attainable based on their current or potential skills and abilities. In Gregg's case, he possessed fluency in two languages and a degree-level qualification but needed to acquire additional teaching skills in order to change careers. It is also important for your client to consider whether planned goals are consistent with their personal values as any kind of inner-conflict may render them harder to achieve. We will explore the issue of helping clients to make decisions based on their personal values in some detail later in this chapter.

Realistic

Setting goals that are challenging but achievable can motivate clients to take constructive action. However, overambitious goals run the risk of overwhelming the client and demotivating them over time. Gregg's goals were realistic because they took into detailed account his skills, abilities and practical circumstances (e.g. financial viability and family support). All of the points made above concerning realism and decision making are equally valid in relation to goal setting.

Time bound

It can be challenging to set a timeframe around certain goals as they may not lend themselves to a definite deadline. For example, helping a client to find a new job after being made redundant may take more or less time than anticipated due to a number of variable circumstances. The aim of setting a timeframe around goals is to keep the client motivated as an absence of deadlines can easily lead to procrastination. A rough guideline is to allocate short-term goals to tasks that can be completed within the next few days or a week. Medium-term goals can include tasks that take from a week up to six months depending on the timeframe agreed, and long-term goals can take anything

Table 3.2 Gregg's timeframe for achieving his goal

Long-term goal	Timeframe
To get a job as a secondary school modern languages teacher	1 year

Short-term goals	Timeframe
Purchase *Times Educational Supplement* to research current teaching profession	Tomorrow
Visit Teaching Development Agency (TDA) website to research salary scales and opportunities	Monday
Research teacher training courses offering modern language specialism within travelling distance from home	Wednesday
Research secondary schools teaching French and Spanish within 1-hour travelling distance	Friday

Medium-term goals	Timeframe
Meet building society manager to review options for temporary interest-only mortgage	Within 2 weeks
Devise shortlist of teaching colleges that meet criteria	Within 4 weeks
Make final selection of teaching courses and apply	Within 6 weeks
Research local teaching opportunities and apply to appropriate vacancies	Within 8 months

between six to twelve months to achieve. The guiding principle of negotiating a timeframe with a client is to give them sufficient time to achieve their short-, medium- and long-term goals but not so much slack that they do not feel any sense of urgency to progress them.

Table 3.2 sets out Gregg's timeframe for his long-term goal, broken down into individual tasks listed under short- and medium-term goals.

Maintaining motivation

Once you have enabled your client to make effective decisions and devised SMART goals, encouraging them to take sustained action towards achieving their objectives is essential. It is quite common for clients to be swept away on an initial tide of enthusiasm only to find that this dwindles when they meet with challenges or the inevitable boredom associated with completing some necessary tasks. It is helpful if both you and your client consider potential obstacles to achieving their goals and devise appropriate contingency plans for dealing with these. An important hurdle that clients may encounter on the way to achieving their ultimate goal is declining motivation and even the temptation to give up altogether. You can pre-empt this potential barrier to success by discussing it openly and coaching your client in a few effective methods for maintaining motivation:

Know the point: It will help your client to remain focused on achieving their goal if they are able to remind themselves of the reason for committing to it in the first place. This may involve reviewing cost and benefit analyses or other decision-making processes that triggered the initial motivation for change. A vivid mental image of what success will look and feel like can act as a spur when energy begins to flag.

Keep goals in sight: Having outlined the goals in as much detail as possible, encourage your client to reduce these into smaller subsidiary tasks. For example, one of Gregg's medium-term goals was to meet with the building society manager to review options for interest-only mortgages. This could be broken down further into:

- Book appointment with building society (tomorrow morning)
- Obtain permission from line manager to take annual leave for meeting (Tuesday afternoon)
- Review building society terms and conditions and calculate term of interest-only mortgage required (Saturday before meeting)

Record progress: Breaking tasks down into as many steps as possible reduces the chances of the overall goal becoming psychologically overwhelming. Acknowledging and celebrating the completion of each small step will provide positive reinforcement for effort made and fuel ongoing motivation. Also periodically reviewing progress made will provide a sense of achievement.

Remain positive: Encourage your client to give themselves as much encouragement and praise for their efforts as possible (in addition to any support you are able to provide them). Get them to anticipate occasional setbacks as a natural consequence of striving for achievement. It may be necessary for your client to refine their original strategy at various stages along the way, and they can enlist your help in doing so. Discourage negative thinking during these moments and remind them to use an objective, problem-solving approach to get back on track.

Supporting clients who bring *some* ideas to work on prior to making career decisions is often a relatively straightforward process. A far more challenging situation that career counsellors and coaches are sometimes faced with is dealing with clients who have no ideas whatsoever and who come to you seeking inspiration. One of the key principles of career counselling and coaching is that professional support should be *non-directive* and facilitative in enabling the client's decision-making process. Adhering to this principle is sometimes challenging when clients expect to be told which career path to pursue.

The most common strategy that practitioners deploy in response to this dilemma is the use of psychometric tests and occupational interest guides. Although this is a perfectly valid approach, many clients find the thought of 'tests' off-putting as they may hold negative associations for them. Similarly, clients may find the prospect of using various computer software packages alienating as they have come to you for a human interaction to find that valuable first spark of inspiration. Two creative methods that you can use with these clients include the use of visualisation techniques and the exploration of personal values. We will now consider both of these approaches in detail.

Helping clients build a compelling vision of the future

Sometimes it is necessary for us to dream of how our future lives may be before we take the next step on our career path. In this exercise you are seeking to stimulate your client's imagination with the aim of them obtaining a sense of direction and some ideas to work on, and also as a method for maintaining motivation by creating and working towards a compelling vision. If your client can build a strong image of themselves pursuing a desired career and enjoying an associated lifestyle in the future, it is likely that they will have more confidence and faith in their ability to take the required steps to achieving this ambition.

Most children imagine various scenarios of future adulthood including fantasies about what role they will play. Some very fortunate individuals have a sense of a calling at a young age and realise childhood ambitions later in life, often in spite of discouragement. A more common experience is that we lose the ability to imagine future possibilities in life as we grow older as the tendency to self-censor and think 'rationally' becomes ingrained. In spite of this tendency, most of us still engage in daydreams from time to time.

We have inherited our ability to visualise future scenarios from our ancient ancestors who created the first temples, artwork and agricultural implements. All human creativity stems from this unique ability to create a vision in the imagination and make this into a reality. We sometimes underestimate the power of this creative process, and the following exercise seeks to rekindle and strengthen your client's ability to 'daydream' with a constructive purpose so that they can build a strong, positive vision of their future career.

Exercise

Step 1

Start by outlining the purpose of the exercise to your client: to stimulate their creative thinking processes and to provide ongoing motivation. As with all of the exercises described in this book, you are not guaranteeing an instant solution but offering the client an opportunity to experiment with a range of approaches. If they are willing to try this exercise, agree the best method for carrying it out depending on their preferences. This could either involve you guiding them through the exercise or instructing them on how to complete it in their own time.

Step 2

Ask the client to sit somewhere quiet where they are unlikely to be disturbed and make themselves comfortable. Explain that completing the exercise with closed eyes will help enable the client to focus more effectively, but check that they are happy to do this. They may also wish to use the relaxation exercise described in Chapter 2 in order to settle into a calm state of mind. Either way, focusing on breathing will enable them to ease into the exercise. Next, ask the client to gradually let all thoughts go for the time being. They should not try to force their thoughts to disappear but simply let them drift away like passing clouds. It may be helpful for them to imagine wiping a board clean or turning over a crisp white piece of paper – whatever image the client finds helpful to clear their mind.

Step 3

Encourage your client to imagine how they would like their life to be. Tell them not to limit their thoughts with any practical issues at this point, just enjoy the fantasy. Ask them to pay particular attention to the type of work and home environment they are constructing in their mind, the clothes they are wearing, the people around them and what they are doing. Are they in an office or outdoors? Are there any particular implements that they are using such as a computer or specific equipment and machinery? What does an ideal day at work look like?

Step 4

Next encourage your client to gradually add more detail to their vision:

- How do they feel emotionally: calm? Excited?
- What do their work colleagues look like?
- What time do they get up in the morning and what daily routine follows?
- What can they smell, touch and taste as part of the vision?

Get them to add as many different details as they are able to make their visual image of the future complete.

Step 5

After indulging in this fantasy for a few minutes or longer, ask the client to bring their attention back to the present and open their eyes. Get them to reflect on any insights they have gained, in particular, clues for potential occupations that would enable them to realise their vision. Are there any ideas for research or discussion with you?

This exercise can be repeated frequently if your client found it a positive experience. They may wish to set aside time to practise as described above. They can also revisit and build upon their vision any time they are able to such as travelling on public transport, going for a walk or completing household chores. Hopefully the purpose of the client's vision will change from providing the inspiration for deciding on a particular career to providing motivation to achieve the various goals required to make a reality of the dream. Having a vivid, compelling picture of what the future could be like will provide your client's brain with a sense of direction at both a conscious and unconscious level and draw upon the various internal resources required to succeed. You can help your client make this vision even more compelling by helping them to identify their personal values.

Personal values and career satisfaction

Your client may never have taken the opportunity to explore their personal values or it may be some time since they considered them. If you help your client to identify their personal values and find an occupation that enables them to express these values, they will stand a very high chance of achieving job satisfaction and happiness in life. Some individuals are drawn to certain careers that reflect their values without knowing it: they are often said to have a calling or vocation. Examples of this include careers in nursing, medicine or teaching. People who enter these occupations usually have strong values in relation to caring for others and the power of education to empower individuals. The converse is also true and many people work in jobs that make them profoundly unhappy because their role is in conflict with their personal values.

Example

A client of mine (Steve Sheward) was a senior manager within a human resources (HR) department. She was quite successful in her role but had begun to feel an increasing sense of discontent that hung over her like a dark cloud. She had entered HR because she wanted to work with people, but found that she often had to compromise her sense of compassion because of organisational objectives (for example, helping to sack people or make them redundant). Having reappraised her values, my client realised that she wanted a job that would enable her to express the caring side of her personality and retrained as a relationship counsellor.

It is easy to see from the above example why pursuing a career that is in conflict with your personal values can create an uncomfortable state of dissonance. But why does carrying out work that is consistent with our personal values give us a sense of satisfaction and fulfilment? One explanation is the theory of flow.

The theory of flow in relation to job satisfaction

The psychologist Mihaly Csikszentmihalyi invented the concept of 'flow', a state of complete absorption in what you are doing, resulting in a deep sense of satisfaction and achievement. This concept is often encountered in sports psychology in which athletes describe being in 'the zone'. But activities that lead to the experience of flow do not have to be physical – examples also include playing chess or reading a thought-provoking book. More important is that the activities provide appropriate conditions for experiencing flow including:

- a challenging task that requires a certain level of skill
- the need to concentrate on the task in hand
- clear goals
- immediate feedback when performing the task

Not all of these conditions have to be met but their presence leads to an experience that is perceived as a sense of:

- deep, almost effortless absorption
- being in control
- the 'self' vanishing
- time stopping

In the novel *Saturday* written by Ian McEwan (2005), the protagonist Henry Perowne, a neurosurgeon, experiences this profound state of being completely immersed in the present moment while operating on a patient:

> *For the past two hours he's been in a dream of absorption that has dissolved all sense of time, and all awareness of the other parts of his life. Even his awareness of his own existence has vanished. He's been delivered into a pure present, free from the weight of the past or any anxieties about the future. In retrospect, though never at the time, it feels like profound happiness. ... This benevolent dissociation seems to require difficulty, prolonged demands on concentration and skills, pressure, problems to be solved, even danger. (p. 258)*

Pause for a moment

Try to recall a time when you experienced a similar state of total absorption that could be described as 'flow'. How could you create the conditions to experience this intense sense of living in the present moment at will?

Csikszentmihalyi carried out an interesting experiment measuring individuals' experience of flow during work and leisure time using an experience sampling method (ESM) (Csikszentmihalyi & LeFevre, 1987, 1989). Participants in the study were provided with pagers and signalled at random times during the day and evening. They were instructed to write down what they were doing at that moment, including their thoughts, feelings and level of engagement with the activity. The sample size was substantial, comprising thousands of participants from different socio-economic backgrounds. The results of the experiment were counter-intuitive as the data confirmed that participants experienced greater levels of flow at work rather than in leisure time. Professor Seligman (2002) has observed that this is probably due to the fact that one of the most popular leisure activities in America is watching television and 'The mood state Americans are in, on average, when watching television is mildly depressed'. This notion could equally be applied to Britain and other western European countries. Seligman goes on to suggest that engaging persistently in easily achieved hedonistic pleasures leads to a decline in psychological wellbeing whereas participating in challenging but absorbing flow activities helps build 'psychological capital'. To illustrate this he uses an analogy from economics whereby:

> Engagement in pleasure = withdrawal of psychological capital
>
> Engagement in flow activities = investment of psychological capital

Seligman further illustrates this concept by telling the story of an exotic Amazonian lizard kept by one of his teachers. Apparently the lizard refused all attempts to feed it to the extent that it began starving to death before the teacher's eyes. One day the teacher made a final, unsuccessful attempt to feed the lizard a ham sandwich and threw his newspaper on top of the snack in a gesture of defeat. Almost at once the lizard raised itself from its torpor, leapt on the newspaper ripping it to shreds and then devoured the sandwich voraciously. Seligman makes the point that the lizard needed to engage in hunting and stalking activities, impulses it had inherited through natural selection, before it could eat. He extends this notion to human beings: if we take shortcuts to gratification without exercising our far more complex array of skills and virtues, we run the risk of starving to death spiritually in the midst of great material wealth. Seligman goes on to present a compelling argument that work offers an ideal opportunity for us to practise our innately human skills and achieve greater satisfaction in life. This is, of course, not a completely original idea and has been reflected in Aristotle's notion of 'the good life' and the Protestant work ethic and seems slightly anachronistic when set against the modern attitude of individualism and a desire to escape the tyranny of enforced employment. But our need to work is explored by the modern-day philosopher, Alain de Botton (2009) in *The Pleasures and Sorrows of Work* and the teacher of Harvard University's most popular course, Tal Ben-Shahar. In his book on achieving satisfaction in life, *Happier* (2008), Ben-Shahar asserts that 'Even if we do not need to work for our survival, we are enslaved by our nature: we are constituted to want to be happy, and to be happy we need to work.' Seligman's main contribution to this idea is that work enables us to express our human virtues and thus experience flow. And our best chance of achieving this condition is to pursue employment that is consistent with what he refers to as our *signature strengths* or personal values.

Seligman's signature strengths

Seligman makes a distinction between talents, which are innate, and character strengths such as compassion and optimism, which can be learned and nurtured over time. He offers 24 strengths under the heading of six virtues:

Wisdom and knowledge

1 Curiosity/interest in the world
2 Love of learning
3 Judgment/critical thinking/open-mindedness
4 Ingenuity/originality/practical intelligence

5 Social intelligence/personal intelligence/emotional intelligence
6 Perspective

Courage

7 Valour and bravery
8 Perseverance/industry/diligence
9 Integrity/genuineness/honesty

Humanity and love

10 Kindness and generosity
11 Loving and allowing oneself to be loved

Justice

12 Citizenship/duty/teamwork/loyalty
13 Fairness and equity
14 Leadership

Temperance

15 Self-control
16 Prudence/discretion/caution
17 Humility and modesty

Transcendence

18 Appreciation of beauty and excellence
19 Gratitude
20 Hope/optimism/future-mindfulness
21 Spirituality/sense of purpose/faith/religiousness
22 Forgiveness and mercy
23 Playfulness and humour
24 Zest/passion/enthusiasm

Chapter 8 provides details of on-line resources that can be used to measure signature strengths and other aspects of personality and character.

Helping your client to identify their personal values

As we have mentioned, if you can help your client to identify their personal values (or signature strengths according to Seligman) and find work that enables them to express these on a daily basis, they will stand a better chance of achieving job satisfaction. Another way of helping clients to live according to their values in the workplace is to support them in re-engineering their job as far as possible to achieve greater harmony and job satisfaction. You can encourage your client to discuss this issue with their manager at personal development review meetings.

The *value focus questionnaire* in this section will help your client to examine specific aspects of employment that could enable them to live in greater harmony with their personal values. We use the term 'values' in this section to refer to the individual's principles and standards – what they hold to be important in life. It is worth emphasising that values are different to goals and commitments in this context: they can be thought of collectively as a 'compass' that guides the individual through life according to personal principles. Values are broader and more 'all-embracing', though they may be frequently reflected in your client's goals and personal commitments.

In this section we provide advice in helping your client to identify their personal values as a means of making more effective career choices whether seeking entry to the labour market for the first time or considering a complete change of direction mid-career. There are a great many psychometric tests and occupational interest guides available and the most widely used are listed in Chapter 7. Our suggestion is that these tools can be deployed more effectively if used in conjunction with an audit of the client's personal values.

If your client experiences difficulty in articulating any personal values, it may be helpful for them to recall an earlier stage in their life, perhaps early adulthood or even childhood, in order to rediscover certain ideals or guiding principles that were more self-evident at the time.

Ask your client to complete the following exercise.

Exercise

Reconnecting with your personal values

When you were younger, what were your interests? What basic principles did you hold? Did you have any personal mottos? What causes or issues were you passionate about?

Don't worry if you only come up with one or two answers to these questions. It may take some time for you to think clearly about what is important in your life.

You could also try talking to a close friend, partner, family member or someone else whose opinion you respect. Ask them what they think your personal values would be based on their knowledge of you. However, don't place their opinion above your own. The feedback and opinions of a trusted individual in your life can certainly help to point you in the direction of your personal values, but be sure to trust your own judgment as well as theirs.

Here is an example of how Michael was able to identify a number of personal values in response to the above questions.

Example

Michael has taken a sabbatical from his job in the pharmaceutical industry and has been using this time as an opportunity to consider different career options.

What were my earlier interests?
'I've always been interested in animal welfare. I love nature and used to be a keen bird watcher. I'm still very concerned about the effects of climate change on wildlife and follow developments in the media closely.'

What were my principles and personal mottos?
'I've always trusted the basic decency of human beings and believe that if you are honest and open with people they will usually respond in the same way. I still believe in the idea that we only have one planet and that we should take a collective responsibility for looking after it.'

When I was younger, what issues or causes was I passionate about?
When I was at university, I became an active member within a human rights campaign group. I also spent a vacation in Africa with Voluntary Services Overseas (VSO) participating in an agricultural programme.

After completing this exercise, Michael was able to recall a number of strong personal values that he had lost touch with. As a result, he was able to reflect on these neglected values and how much better he used to feel when he lived a life that was more in accordance with them. Michael began to consider ways in which he could re-connect with his personal values and pursue a career that would enable him to do so more freely.

Acknowledging shifting or conflicting priorities

It is reasonable to expect that your client's priorities may have shifted over time. Major life events such as having a child, starting a new relationship or experiencing bereavement will undoubtedly require a re-ordering of priorities. However, a change in life circumstances and priorities does not necessarily mean that your client's basic values have changed, and it can be a comfort to keep them in sight during more turbulent times.

Similarly, your client's priorities may conflict or contradict one another on occasions (e.g. balancing work and home-life commitments). Under these circumstances it may be necessary to prioritise work until certain debts have been paid before a more balanced, value-directed lifestyle can be attained.

Table 3.3　Value focus questionnaire

Area Examples of values include:	Valued focus
WORK	
SCOPE: having a variety of things to do	Variety is very important to me – I get bored by routine
LOCATION: place of work is important to you	I want to work close to where I live. I feel more connected with my local community
TRANQUILITY: you prefer to have few pressures or demands	Having a sense of calm is very important – I do not want to tolerate feelings of stress
COMPETITION: you enjoy competing against other people or groups	Competing with others brings out the best in me and provides me with strong motivation
AUTONOMY: you like to be able to work with minimum supervision	Ideally I'd like to be my own boss – I prefer making my own decisions
FLEXIBILITY: you prefer to choose your own times for doing things	I want to be able to arrange my life around personal priorities other than work
COMPANIONSHIP: you would like to socialise with the people in work	The social aspect of work is very important and I want to be with like minded people
DYNAMIC ENVIRONMENT: you enjoy working rapidly	I like a fast-paced, exciting work environment
HIGH STATUS: you enjoy being in a position that leads others to respect you	My job defines who I am and I enjoy the status associated with my role
INFLUENCE: you enjoy responsibility for making key decisions	I want my actions to have a major impact
CREATIVITY: thinking of new ideas and ways of doing things	I want to be able to express myself through my work
RISKS: you like to take risks	An element of risk excites me
VIBRANCY: it is important for you to have excitement at work	I prefer a dynamic work environment that's very energetic
REMUNERATION: earning a large amount of money is important to you	I'm highly motivated by material success
CARING: work that involves helping others individually or in groups	The most rewarding aspect of the job is helping others

Area Examples of values include:	Valued focus
HIGH PROFILE: you like working for organisations that are well known	I desire status as part of my work
CAREER PROGRESSION: you like to work where there is a good chance of promotion	I prefer to plan my career on the basis of clear routes for progression
CHALLENGE: you enjoy being stretched and given new problems to work on	I work best when my talents are stretched
PREDICTABILITY: you like a work routine which is fairly predictable	I prefer the security of knowing what I'm doing within a predictable structure
HIGH PRESSURE: you like working to deadlines	I need tight deadlines to motivate me
TEAMWORK: you like to achieve tasks with others	I enjoy collaborating with others to get things done
PHYSICALLY ACTIVE: you enjoy doing something that is physically demanding	I like to be physically active rather than sitting at a desk
SOLITARY WORKING: you like to work on your own	I don't miss the company of others and prefer to be on my own
AESTHETIC: you enjoy work involving drawing, designing, making music, making models etc.	I am artistic and require work that enables me to be creative
COMMUNICATION: you enjoy being able to express ideas well in writing or in speech	Connecting with others through written or verbal language is very important to me
APPRECIATION: you strongly desire recognition for your work	Having my efforts recognised is a strong motivator
SECURITY: it is important to know your work is always there for you	Job security provides me with a sense of stability
SOCIABLE: you enjoy having a lot of contact with people	I thrive in the company of other people
PRECISION: you like working at things which involve great care and concentration	I enjoy exactitude and precision in my work
SOCIALLY CONSCIOUS: you like to think that your work is producing something worthwhile for society	I need to make a contribution to society through my work

(Continued)

Table 3.3 (Continued)

Area Examples of values include:	Valued focus
MANAGERIAL: you enjoy being responsible for work done by others	I have a talent for leadership and organisation
INFLUENCING: you enjoy persuading people to buy something or change their minds about something	I enjoy using my powers of persuasion with others
KNOWLEDGE: it is important for you to learn new things	I need intellectual stimulation and ongoing learning
EXPERTISE: you like being known as someone with special knowledge or skills	I like the status that expertise bestows on me

EDUCATION and TRAINING

Questions to ask yourself with regard to education and training values include:	I am a firm believer in lifelong learning and am committed to studying for additional qualifications whilst working full-time
• What do you want to study or train in?	I am prepared to pay the full course fee and regard it as an investment in my career
• How long are you prepared to study or train?	
• Full-time, part-time or on-the-job?	
• Are you prepared to pay something towards your study or training?	

RELATIONSHIPS

Questions to ask yourself with regard to relationship values include:	I want to be a supportive partner and invest time in the relationship whilst balancing work commitments
• What sort of partner do you want to be?	My family is very important and I would place a high priority on helping them in times of need
• If you are single, what sort of relationship would you like?	
• What is important to you in how you act as a brother/sister/ son/daughter/father/mother?	

Area Examples of values include:	Valued focus
FRIENDSHIPS Questions to ask yourself with regard to friendship values include: • What is important to you in the friendships you have? • How would you like your friends to think of you? • What new friendships would you like and with what sort of people?	It is important for me to have a small number of close friends whom I can confide in and who know me very well Trust is essential. I hope my friends feel that they can turn to me for support when needed
RECREATION Questions to ask yourself with regard to recreation values include: • What hobbies, sports or other interests are important to you? • What new hobbies, sports and interests would you like to pursue?	I try to strike a balance between physical and mental recreation activities and enjoy being completely absorbed in either pursuit
SPIRITUALITY Questions to ask yourself with regard to spiritual values include: • Have I any spiritual values that are religious or non-religious? • How important are these values as guiding principles in my life?	I have a strong feeling of spirituality and a definite sense of right and wrong that guides my actions in life
HEALTH and WELLBEING Questions to ask yourself with regard to health and wellbeing values include: • What things are important to me to increase my health and wellbeing?	I believe in nurturing my mind and body and try to find time for both physical exercise and mental relaxation

The value focus questionnaire

Your client may find it helpful to complete the value focus questionnaire (Table 3.3) to generate ideas for you both to discuss in session. You will see that there are different cues under each heading to help your client consider their personal values. We have provided examples of answers to each question as a guide. (A blank copy of the value focus questionnaire for use with clients can be downloaded from www.sagepub.co.uk/sheward.)

The approaches outlined within this chapter have placed an emphasis on helping clients to make important decisions with regard to career change. They can also be used to help clients explore the option of staying within their current job by finding ways of dealing with problematic aspects of it rather than making dramatic changes to their lifestyle. For example, when using the cost and benefit analysis, try to ensure that the client is not engaging in *mental filtering* and completely discarding any positive aspects of their current job. As mentioned previously, helping clients to identify their key values can be a first step to re-engineering their current job so that it becomes more congruent with personal principles (and more conducive to experiencing *flow*). Having gone through this process with the client, you will then be able to help them design a SMART action plan for bringing about positive changes in their current role.

Reflect and discuss

1 What are the main characteristics of Gerard Egan's processes of information gathering, analysis and making a choice?
2 How can you integrate your current range of professional skills within Tol Bedford's FIRST model when working with clients?
3 How many experiences of flow have you experienced in your life? What were the conditions then and how could you experience more flow now?
4 What are your personal values and how much are they reflected in your current professional practice?

4

Cognitive and Behavioural Approaches to Career Counselling in the Workplace

This chapter is designed to help you to:

- enable clients to maintain motivation and focus within the workplace
- coach clients in a range of interpersonal techniques including reducing anxiety in social situations and assertiveness
- help clients identify symptoms of work-related stress and use a range of strategies to counter these
- teach clients effective time-management skills

Maintaining motivation

One of the many challenges clients are faced with in the workplace is how to maintain an optimum level of motivation and this task is often regarded as the responsibility of managers within the organisation. But if your client is unable to generate their own enthusiasm and energy, they may severely limit their chances of success in the workplace and, at worse, fall into a spiral of demotivation.

We have already presented methods for helping clients to develop effective goals and action plans in Chapter 3. Clients often find the 'blue-sky thinking' associated with this phase exciting and feel enthusiastic after you have helped them develop a compelling vision for the future. One of your responsibilities is to teach clients methods for following through this initial psychological momentum when they are confronted with the hard work involved in achieving their aims.

One of the most important skills that clients need to cultivate in order to maintain motivation is focus. We would like to introduce the Japanese concepts of *kime* and *mushin* at this point to serve as helpful metaphors that you can use with clients when working on developing their motivation.

Kime and *mushin*

In pre-industrial Japan the Samurai were elite warriors within the feudal society's nobility and highly skilled in the art of swordsmanship. They also practiced Zen Buddhism in order to train their minds to attain supreme levels of calm and focus when confronted with extremely dangerous situations. The Zen master Takuan Soho described this approach as follows:

> Whether by the man who strikes or the sword that strikes, whether by position or rhythm, if your mind is diverted in any way, your actions will falter and this can mean that you will be cut down (1986: 20).

When two Samurai warriors of equal physical skill met in a duel, the one with the best ability to control his mind was most likely to prevail. This psychological skill involved the practice of *mushin* (literally 'no-mindedness'), a state of supreme concentration in which the mind does not allow itself to be distracted by superfluous thoughts or external stimuli. This state of mind provides the conditions for *kime* (from the verb *kimeru*, 'to conclude'): total focus of one's mental and physical energy on the object of attention.

As you will see from Steve Covey's time management matrix later in this chapter, it is very easy for clients to get drawn into quadrant IV activities (not urgent and not important) and lose their focus. Potential distractions are becoming increasingly common in the modern workplace with the advent of multimedia and multitasking. A recent survey by the University of California calculated that on average office workers are subject to 34 gb of information each day – twice as much as they were 30 years ago. Sources of distraction include:

- phone calls
- emails
- texts

- multitasking
- interruptions from colleagues

The above are examples of external distractions; clients are also subject to more insidious *internal* distractions. We have already encountered Mihaly Csikszentmihalyi's notion of *entropy* in Chapter 2, that the mind has a tendency to drift towards worry and other negative thoughts if unoccupied. Our minds are also frequently inclined to drift away from the task in hand towards more pleasurable experiences without our being aware of it. Consider Sarah's example:

Example

Situation

Sarah has to write a report each month on her team's performance and ensure that it is circulated at least a week before the departmental meeting. It's not a task she relishes and Sarah often leaves it to the day before her circulation deadline. She has written one page of the report and is already feeling bored. It suddenly occurs to Sarah that if she searches for performance data on competitor organisations via Google, it will improve the report.

Distraction

Sarah keys in a sentence that she hopes will provide her with information on competitor organisations. A list of search options duly presents itself, but one of the links surprises Sarah as it concerns her favourite television series. Almost without thinking and compelled by a sense of curiosity, Sarah clicks on the link and is delighted to discover the television series' official website. It hosts behind-the-scenes glimpses, profiles of the different characters and a number of free games.

Outcome

Sarah becomes engrossed in the various articles on the website – one item seems to flow into another. Eventually a colleague reminds Sarah that it's nearly lunch time and she realises that she has spent nearly an hour and a half reading about her favourite television series. Sarah begins to panic as she realises that the deadline for circulation is looming and skips lunch to make up time. Her blood sugar drops, leaving her feeling light-headed, so she drinks coffee to keep going. The nearer the deadline looms, the more anxiety Sarah feels, and this causes her concentration to deteriorate further. Eventually Sarah manages to produce (in her view) a rather mediocre report. She feels tired and irritable and so misses her weekly gym session. Returning home that evening Sarah feels guilty and slightly gloomy because she normally feels energised after training at the gym. She also feels slightly apprehensive about the forthcoming departmental meeting.

Hopefully you can see from this example that Sarah lost her focus on a necessary task due to boredom and an almost unconscious desire for distraction – with very unhelpful consequences.

Pause for a moment

Try to think of occasions when you have experienced a similar drift in attention from the task in hand. What were the consequences? Where they negative (highly likely)?

One of the most important skills that clients need to cultivate in order to achieve their goals in the workplace is the ability to focus attention at will. This is an essential skill but one that is infrequently taught. You can help your client with this challenge by encouraging them to practise the following techniques:

1   **Take charge of your mind:** Encourage clients to consider the fact that their mind 'has a mind of its own' and will wander off if they don't pay attention to it. The first step to achieving this level of discipline is to become aware of the mind's inclination to wander. Get your client to use Table 4.1 to monitor this tendency for one day noting each situation, the distraction and the outcome.
2   **Clear your mind:** As you will see in Steven Covey's time management matrix later in this chapter, each day presents us with a range of conflicting priorities that continually distract us from the task in hand. The simple solution is for your clients to empty their minds of nagging responsibilities by writing a daily task list according to priority so that they no longer have to worry about them.
3   **Create an optimum working environment:** If your client's desk or workstation is cluttered, it will be difficult to maintain focus as their attention will be distracted by reminders of other unfinished tasks. In addition to de-cluttering the working area, it is helpful to anticipate what's needed to complete the task and have it to hand. For example, this will prevent your client wandering off to borrow a dictionary and become involved in a conversation. If possible, suggest that your client closes down all other media that are likely to cause interruptions until the task is complete (e.g. mobile, email, desk phone).

Table 4.1   Focus management log

Situation	Distraction	Outcome
What task was engaged in?	At which point did I become distracted? How did this happen?	What happened as a result of becoming distracted?

4 **Concentrate on the task in hand:** This is the antidote to fragmented concentration brought about by multitasking and requires practice. Coach your client in the Buddhist technique of *one-pointedness*. The whole working day provides an exercise in concentration, making each action the complete focus of attention. This requires *intent* from your client. They need to commit themselves (as far as possible) to the completion of the task they have started. This may require breaking larger tasks into manageable (e.g. hour-long) units.

5 **Don't let your mind get carried away:** If your client has carried out step 1, they should be able to notice the pull of the mind away from the task in hand and arrest this impulse. It may help your client to think of intruding thoughts and impulses as *buses* or *trains*. They can simply watch them go by without being carried away by them.

6 **Nourish the mind:** Depending on individual dietary requirements, light snacks that combine proteins and carbohydrates are optimum. Eating fruit is an excellent way to keep hydrated and draw energy from natural sugars. Caffeinated drinks need to be consumed in moderation as excessive amounts lead to spikes in concentration followed by a drop in mental energy. Getting into the habit of sipping water throughout the day is a far better way of maintaining concentration.

7 **Pace yourself:** It's important to take regular breaks to maintain peak levels of concentration, but this should not be confused with the temptation to engage in displacement activities (e.g. surfing the Internet). The best way of achieving this is to work relentlessly on one task for a set period of time – perhaps an hour – and take a very short break. It is essential to get up and move around if seated for long periods to relieve muscular tension and sore eyes. A brisk walk at lunchtime is an excellent way of increasing oxygen to the brain.

8 **Stretch yourself:** Help your client to reframe their mental approach to working on demanding or boring tasks. Instead of regarding sustained effort as a chore (mental torture for some), encourage your client to see it as an opportunity to develop *mental stamina*. Career success requires the cultivation of this very quality in the same way that an athlete needs to acquire supreme physical stamina.

9 **Reward yourself:** It may increase your client's motivation to provide themselves with regular but small rewards for the completion of tasks. This could be as modest as promising themselves a sip of water for writing a paragraph or a walk to the water cooler after an hour spent completing a section of the report. This will have the psychological effect of *reinforcing* productive behaviour as the client's brain begins to associate focus and sustained effort with reward.

Managing relationships in the workplace

Managing professional relationships with colleagues and clients is an essential skill that can make the difference between success and failure in a career. Daniel Goleman (1996) famously asserted that *emotional intelligence* (EI) is a better predictor of success than IQ. Although this claim has been contested by many academics, the concept of EI has had a major impact on the corporate world and most organisations place increasing emphasis on interpersonal, as well as technical, skills when recruiting. In this section we will introduce you to a number of methods that will enable your client to behave assertively in the workplace while also developing rapport with colleagues. But first we will start with a more subtle area that concerns helping clients to manage their psychological reactions in work-based social interactions and their effect on mood and behaviour. Consider the following example:

Example

Frank has just started work as a sales account manager at Saber Communications and is due to attend a 5-day residential training course as part of his induction. He won't know anyone else on the course but he is aware of the fact that it will be a competitive environment and everyone will be keen to impress. Frank is concerned that he will not be able to shine sufficiently and worries about the impression he will create and how this will affect his future with the company.

It's natural for your client to feel some concern when faced with an unfamiliar social situation in the workplace, particularly when the outcome might affect their career. However, it's important for your client to be aware of any potentially unhelpful thoughts or behaviours that could inhibit their chances of managing the situation successfully.

David Clark and Adrian Wells (1995) developed a model of social phobia that is widely used in CBT to help people deal with social anxiety. Although your client may not suffer from this condition, using aspects of the model will help you to pinpoint any areas for improvement in their interpersonal skills and coach them in developing more effective social interactions. For this reason, it is worth becoming familiar with some of the characteristics of social anxiety.

Characteristics of social anxiety

Many people suffer from episodes of social anxiety in the workplace and this tendency varies between mild self-consciousness that can be overcome by acquiring additional social skills to paralysing social phobia that requires clinical therapy. One of the main characteristics of social anxiety is fear that the individual will be judged negatively by others mainly due to a failure in performance of some sort. This commonly includes activities in which the individual is the subject of attention from others such as speaking to people (individually or in groups), writing or eating in public. When people suffer from social anxiety they often believe that they will behave in a way that is unacceptable to others and that this in turn will lead to rejection (compare this with the cognitive and behavioural consequences of *shame* in the emotions table in Chapter 1).

As we have seen in Chapter 1, unhelpful thoughts and beliefs often have negative physiological consequences. Hartmann (1983: 435–56) offered a model of social anxiety in which individuals focus on physical symptoms in addition to their fears about performance and negative judgment. This increased (internal) self-consciousness distracts the individual's attention from what is going on in the social situation (external) and makes social interaction even more difficult. These individuals are also more prone to making negative *inferences* about the situation and mistakenly assume that others do not like them or find them boring.

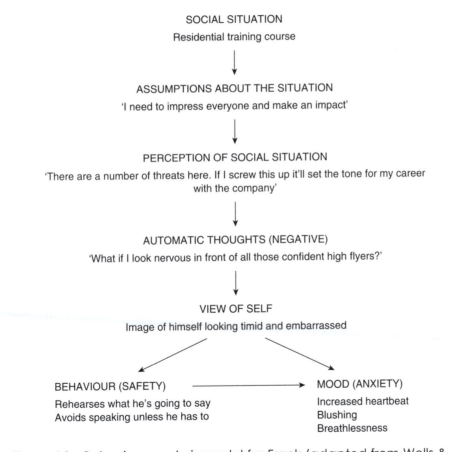

SOCIAL SITUATION
Residential training course

ASSUMPTIONS ABOUT THE SITUATION
'I need to impress everyone and make an impact'

PERCEPTION OF SOCIAL SITUATION
'There are a number of threats here. If I screw this up it'll set the tone for my career with the company'

AUTOMATIC THOUGHTS (NEGATIVE)
'What if I look nervous in front of all those confident high flyers?'

VIEW OF SELF
Image of himself looking timid and embarrassed

BEHAVIOUR (SAFETY)
Rehearses what he's going to say
Avoids speaking unless he has to

MOOD (ANXIETY)
Increased heartbeat
Blushing
Breathlessness

Figure 4.1   Behaviour analysis model for Frank (adapted from Wells & Clark, 1995)

In order to avoid the prospect of making mistakes and drawing disapproval, some people adopt *safety behaviours* such as avoiding eye contract or rehearsing what they are going to say to ensure that it is sufficiently interesting. Ironically these very behaviours have the opposite effect to that intended. The individual may appear unfriendly and experience rejection by others as a result. In this instance, their fears become a self-fulfilling prophecy and the outcome sets them up for increased anxiety when faced with future social interactions.

You can use the adaptation in Figure 4.1 of Clark and Wells's model to help your client analyse their patterns of behaviour when engaging in social interactions within the workplace. These will typically include meetings, appraisals, conferences, training courses and away days, not to mention purely social events such as the office Christmas party. We can see from the model how Frank approached the residential training course.

As you can see from the example in Figure 4.1, if you are coaching a client to improve the way they interact socially in the workplace, it helps if you have a recent or vivid example of a situation that they believe could have benefited from improvement. The key thing to determine is whether the example represents a standard pattern of behaviour. If this is the case, you can use this idiosyncratic formulation as a map for you and your client to develop more effective ways of interacting socially.

Explore what your client's assumptions are about situations involving social interaction: It is very common for situations at work involving social interaction to trigger off negative beliefs that your client holds about themselves which may normally lie dormant. As we have seen in Chapter 1, your client may have learned these unhelpful beliefs in childhood. For example, Frank revealed that he was always the last person to be picked for team events on school sports days and this has led him to form the belief that he is not popular. Frank only becomes aware of this belief when he enters social situations, particularly those in which he does not know the other people. Another common tendency is for clients to engage in *all-or-nothing thinking*: 'I must appear informed, intelligent and witty' or 'I have to make a positive impact'. It is important to draw your client's attention to any thinking errors they are making and challenge them, referring to the list set out in Chapter 1.

Perception of the social situation and negative automatic thoughts: Help your client to get the social situation in perspective if they perceive any potential threats. Encourage them to resist the urge to put even more pressure on themselves. Just how *awful* would it be if they did not appear informed, witty and abundantly charismatic? Remind your client that most social interactions in the workplace are pretty average and can actually backfire if they try too hard.

View of self: It's normal for your client to feel slightly nervous in social situations where they do not know the other people (e.g. conferences, training courses) or where the other individual(s) may hold power (e.g. appraisals). The big mistake is for your client to believe that just because they *feel* slightly nervous, they will *appear* nervous to others and develop an unhelpful mental image of themselves the way they think others see them. This tendency often leads clients to look for signs that the other person(s) has noticed their social awkwardness. This is rarely the case but a negative self-image will incline the client towards making unhelpful *inferences*. You may have realised by now that the process we have described is similar to *emotional reasoning* described in Chapter 1 and needs to be countered in the same way.

Mood (anxiety): A major problem that clients experience in social situations is a heightened awareness of the cognitive and physiological consequences of concern or anxiety. As we have seen previously, fixating on sensations such as increased heartbeat and a racing mind will create a vicious cycle of interpreting these symptoms as a sign of danger leading to increased anxiety followed by heightened physiological arousal. It is important for your client to realise that these (internal) symptoms are temporary and will fade away if ignored. The most effective strategy is for them to focus their attention on the other person and the environment (external).

Behaviour (safety): A common behaviour that people engage in when feeling anxious in social situations is to mentally rehearse what they are going to say. This is usually due to the fact that they hold unhelpful beliefs about *having* to appear intelligent and witty. They also monitor themselves as they are delivering the sentence. Both of these tendencies have unhelpful consequences. First, the conversation may have moved on and there is a risk of losing the thread due to lack of attention. Second, self-monitoring during delivery of a sentence leads to self-consciousness and interrupts the flow of thought. Having made a contribution to the conversation, the individual may conduct a 'post-mortem' of what they have just said, checking for any mistakes in delivery. As you can see, engaging in these safety behaviours can actually precipitate the outcome the individual is seeking to avoid. If you notice this tendency in your client, the best strategy you can advise is for them to engage in *focused attention* and *active listening*. If they really concentrate on the content of what the other person is saying and pay close attention to their body language and non-verbal cues, chances are that your client will become less self-conscious and more able to keep up with the flow of conversation. This, in turn, will lead to a reduction in anxiety and enable them to be more spontaneous in their contribution to the conversation.

Key learning point

Encourage your client to dispense with safety behaviours and go outside their comfort zone when engaging in social interactions at work. Coach them in increasing their contribution each time and work with them to conduct an objective analysis of the outcome. Gathering evidence that their negative predictions did not come true will disconfirm any negative beliefs your client may hold about their ability to interact socially at work and lead to increased confidence.

Having improved your client's ability to manage social interaction at work, you may need to coach them in the appropriate use of assertiveness.

Helping clients assert themselves in the workplace

Thinking and acting assertively in the workplace is a skill your client can learn – it is not an inherent quality they are born with. However, many people are slow to assert themselves when the need arises because they have developed unhelpful beliefs about this form of behaviour (e.g. that they *shouldn't* act in a confrontational manner). Unfortunately failure to behave assertively when necessary can lead to lack of self-confidence because the individual concerned will continually reinforce the belief that they are incapable of dealing with conflicts of opinion. This can result in *passive* behaviour and prevent career progression (e.g. going for promotions). Alternatively, lack of assertiveness can lead to growing resentment which often reaches boiling point and explodes in

---

☐ Do you usually let other people get their own way in the workplace when you have a different point of view?

☐ Do you often hesitate before expressing your opinions or saying what you want because there's a chance others might disagree with you?

☐ Even when you think you have a good idea or a good point to make, do you tend to hold back and go along with what other people are saying?

☐ If someone actually offends you, do you let the matter go unchallenged rather than bringing it to their attention?

☐ Do you find it difficult to raise the issue of promotion, pay rises or other benefits with your manager because you fear rejection or don't think you deserve these things?

☐ Are you reluctant to ask for support or instructions in carrying out tasks because you believe that you should be able to manage and others will think less of you?

☐ Do you make an effort to avoid disagreement with work colleagues because you worry about the possibility of getting into an argument?

☐ Are you concerned that if you disagree with others, they may stop liking you?

☐ Do you make every effort to avoid confrontations because you don't think that you would be able to cope with the situation?

☐ Do you sometimes allow resentment to build up and engage in outbursts towards others?

☐ Do you try to win the argument most of the time as failure to do so would be a sign of weakness?

☐ Do you openly criticise others and apportion blame?

☐ Do you find yourself using a harsh, loud tone of voice and displaying aggressive body language and eye contact?

Figure 4.2   Assertiveness checklist

aggressive behaviour. People often mistake the latter for assertiveness but overlook the negative consequences of acting this way such as alienating colleagues and increasing blood pressure. If your client asks for support with assertiveness training, it is worth getting them to complete the assertiveness checklist given in Figure 4.2 to obtain a better understanding of their needs.

If your client has ticked two or more of the items in the checklist, they probably require support in developing assertiveness skills in the workplace as their tendency to avoid what they regard as 'conflict' or default to aggressive behaviour will put them at a disadvantage and restrict career progression. Your starting point in helping your client to develop these skills is to ask for a *recent* and *vivid* example of an occasion when they wanted to assert themselves but found it difficult to do so and carry out an *ABC formulation* as described in Chapter 1. The following are typical beliefs at 'B' that individuals hold when they fail to assert themselves in situations in which it is perfectly reasonable to do so or act aggressively:

'I dislike confrontation and conflict. If I assert myself, I won't be able to tolerate the feelings of emotional and physical discomfort.'

'Confrontation could result in raised tempers and everyone involved will come away feeling badly.'

'Building positive relationships in the workplace takes a great deal of time and effort: a row risks causing a breakdown in communication.'

'Standing up for myself may end up in a fight – I don't want to make waves.'

'Arguments always end in a win-lose outcome, a nil-sum game.'

or:

'I *must* win the argument at all costs.'

'Other people *should* show me respect.'

'I won't let anyone get the better of me.'

'How dare they treat me this way.'

Having carried out an ABC formulation, you will have determined:

typical antecedents at 'A' (e.g. interdepartmental meetings)

unhelpful beliefs about the situation at 'B' (similar to those described above)

emotional and behavioural consequences at 'C' (usually anxiety, unhealthy anger or passivity)

The next stage involves *disputing* your client's unhelpful beliefs using the methods described in Chapter 1 and coaching them in more effective ways of thinking and acting.

Key learning point

Teach your client that although they can't control how others will react in a confrontational situation, they can exert a considerable amount of control over their own thoughts and behaviour which will influence the way they feel (confident as opposed to anxious or unhealthily angry).

You could explain to your client that they may not enjoy asserting themselves (particularly if they are not used to it), but they will probably feel better in the long-run if they deal with situations rather than avoid them. It is often helpful to make use of *metaphors* when coaching clients in cognitive and behavioural techniques (see Chapter 6 for more on this subject). Compare avoiding assertiveness behaviour as similar to having toothache and putting off going to the dentist. Preferring to avoid getting the tooth treated is understandable but putting up with short-term discomfort will lead to long-term relief (this is a further example of moving from *low frustration tolerance* to *high frustration tolerance*).

Clients are most likely to find themselves in two types of situations when the need to assert themselves arises:

Planned assertion: In this situation your client will have had time to consider what they want to say to the other person. They may have arranged a meeting and told them what they want to discuss. The main advantage with this situation is that your client can plan (and even script) what they intend to say in an assertive but non-aggressive manner. The potential disadvantage to be aware of is that they may start to worry about the outcome or make themselves angry in advance and end up thinking and acting in an unhelpful manner when they meet with the other person. Help your client to avoid this trap by telling themselves that they will act reasonably and that it will be *unfortunate but not awful* if the situation does not go as planned. All of the following guidelines apply irrespective of whether your client is asserting themselves with managers, subordinates or colleagues.

Unplanned assertion: In this instance, your client may find themselves in an adversarial situation without having the opportunity to prepare in advance. Typical examples include differences of opinions at team meetings, inconsiderate behaviour from a colleague, criticisms of your client's work or conduct. The advantage of this situation for your client is that they won't have much time to worry about the prospect of asserting themselves or building up resentment towards the other person, but they may have very little time to prepare. Emphasise that your client needs to behave in a calm manner *even if they do not feel this way*. Refer the 'acting as if' technique outlined in Chapter 2: if they *act* in a calm manner, chances are that they will *think* and *feel* calmer.

The following section provides both *cognitive* and *behavioural* guidelines for assertion. It may be helpful to practise these techniques with your client using role play.

Guidelines for healthy assertion

Make eye contact

Maintaining good eye contact conveys the impression that your client is confident and has conviction in the points they are making. Encourage them to hold their head up and meet the other person's gaze. It is worth emphasising that your client's gaze should be calm and even. If they are emotionally aroused, there is a danger that your client could stare or 'eyeball' the other person and appear aggressive.

Be clear in your mind about what you want to say

Encourage your client to summarise as clearly as possible the exact points they want to make to the other person. This method will enable your client to keep the exchange focused even if the other person attempts to sidetrack them. If they have the opportunity, it will be helpful to write a few notes to clarify thinking.

Speak slowly and stick to the points you want to make

Your client should endeavour to speak at a calm, even pace so that the other person is able to hear what they are trying to convey. It is particularly important to check any impulse to rush through each point due to feelings of nervousness and the desire to 'get it over and done with' or feelings of anger that can result in a barrage of comments. If your client speaks slowly and calmly, it is likely that they will begin to feel calmer (see above). Speaking in this way also gives the other person the impression that your client is confident. It is also important for them to stick to their key points and counter any attempts by the other person to lead them off at other tangents. If this happens, your client's best tactic is to calmly return to the point they are making until it is adequately addressed irrespective of attempts at digression. This is often referred to as the 'stuck record' technique.

Avoid aggressive behaviour or language

Although replacing anxiety with aggression may *feel* more empowering, this form of behaviour is more likely to draw an aggressive response and lead to a breakdown in communication. Even if your client feels angry, it is better for them to act in a firm, rather than aggressive manner. As it increases, anger obliterates the ability to think clearly and undermines the impact of any points made: it conveys an impression of loss of control. If your client is able to remain calm but firm in their communication, the other person is more likely to listen to their point of view and treat them with respect.

Take responsibility for the way you think, feel and act in the situation

Advise your client to take particular care with their choice of language and any intended criticisms. For example, this means communicating to the other person that when they (or the company) acted in a certain way, your client felt (hurt or angry) about it *because of their point of view*. This approach suggests that they have taken responsibility for their thoughts and feelings about the situation (because they are personal to your client), but there is a chance that they may have misunderstood the intentions behind the actions in question. This offers the other person an opportunity to clarify why they (or the company) acted in a certain way. The opposite approach is to use *global statements*, for example, 'You're always criticising me in team meetings'. This is a particularly unhelpful form of communication as it is not specific. Your client needs to be as precise as possible in describing the issue of contention.

The following are examples of helpful specific statements and unhelpful global statements.

Helpful and specific statements

'When you gave me feedback at my performance review last week, I didn't feel as though all the hard work I've put in over the past couple of months had been taken into account.'

'At last week's team meeting, when you said my financial projections for next year's budget were sloppy, I thought that it undermined my authority in front of colleagues and could have been discussed in private.'

'When we approach deadlines and you shout at me, it makes me feel nervous and that interferes with my ability to get the work done on time.'

'When the division introduced its new policy on late opening for customers without any staff consultation, I got the distinct impression that my opinion wasn't important.'

Unhelpful global statements

'You really don't care about all of the hard work I've put in for the department!'

'You constantly belittle me in front of everyone!'

'I feel completely ground down by the way you treat me!'

'This company rides rough-shod over staff opinions and just wants to drive its own agenda through!'

Make your point and give the other person a chance to respond

As with other activities that require regulation of emotional arousal, controlled breathing is a simple but effective technique for controlling anger or anxiety. Encourage your client to pause and take a deep breath after they have made their point. This will have a calming physiological effect, increase oxygen to the brain aiding clarity of thought in addition to allowing the other person to consider what has been said and formulate their response. As mentioned previously, it is important for your client to ensure that each point is resolved (as far as possible) before moving on to the next one. The temptation to bombard the other person with each point in quick succession should be avoided as both parties are likely to lose track of the main issues.

Practice regular assertiveness to increase confidence

Coach your client in practising the above assertiveness skills in situations that are challenging (and that they currently avoid due to anxiety or fear of losing their temper) but not overwhelming. As your client's confidence grows and they gather evidence that nothing *terrible* will happen when they assert themselves, they will be encouraged to take on more challenging situations. Remind your client that just like any other skill, assertiveness becomes easier with practice although they may still feel nervous or annoyed. It is worth stressing that tolerating this slight discomfort is a small price to pay for increased autonomy and self-esteem. Although your client may not always achieve their desired outcome, acting assertively will help them to feel more in control of their work situation and this belief alone will reduce stress and lead to increased confidence.

Managing stress in the workplace

The UK Health and Safety Executive (HSE) states that stress is the major cause of working days lost through occupational injury or ill health. HSE research indicates that during the period 2007–2008 an estimated 13.5 million working days were lost due to stress-related absence. Approximately one in five people state that they find work very or extremely stressful and over half a million people report suffering from work-related stress to the extent that they believe it has made them ill. Symptoms of stress are similar to the physiological consequences of anxiety and include:

- Heartbeat increases rapidly to pump blood around the body and provide oxygen and nutrients.
- Breathing intensifies, increasing oxygen supply to the blood-stream providing more energy.
- The adrenal glands secrete adrenaline and noradrenalin to provide additional energy and increase heartbeat and also Cortisol to reduce inflammation and enable joints to function after injury.
- Blood vessels leading to major muscle groups and the heart dilate, priming the body for action.
- Noradrenalin causes specific blood vessels to contract and decreases blood supply to the digestive system and peripheral circulation.

All of the above symptoms are consistent with the 'fight or flight' response described in Chapter 2: appropriate for threats to life and limb but inappropriate to most situations in the modern workplace. Also, although the physiological consequences of stress are useful in providing energy during an emergency, they can have a negative effect on health in the long term if continuously experienced.

The HSE define stress as:

> *the adverse* reaction *people have to excessive pressure or other types of demand placed upon them. (HSE, 2008: 1, our emphasis)*

We have emphasised the word 'reaction' to underline the subjective nature of stress. People vary enormously in the way they react to perceived challenges at work, and as we have seen, the way they *think* about the situation will affect the way they *feel* and *act* (e.g. stressed and anxious or excited and enthusiastic).

Example

Jacqui and Kalpana are chartered accountants and work for the same company. The finance director, Jack, has asked them both to give a presentation at the next senior management team (SMT) meeting on the strengths and weaknesses of the company's auditing procedures. Kalpana is delighted to be given this opportunity and feels highly motivated. She thinks 'This is excellent – it's the break I've been waiting for. I'll be able to show Jack how much hard work I've put into researching potential improvements and that's bound to win me points at my next formal appraisal.' Jacqui, however, is petrified about having to give a presentation in front of the SMT and thinks 'What if I get nervous and blush in front of everyone? They'll realise that I'm not very confident and that'll undermine my authority in the department.'

The key thing to note about the situation in the above example is that Jacqui and Kalpana have the same role within the company and were given the same task to perform. The critical difference between them was their different perceptions of the task and the resulting emotional consequences.

The ABC model is an extremely effective tool for countering stress in the workplace, and you can use it to help clients reappraise what they consider to be stressful situations and turn them into challenges and opportunities for growth.

Consider how you could use the model to support Jacqui in the above situation.

Example

Activating event/adversity: Jacqui has been asked to give a presentation at the next SMT meeting.

Beliefs/thoughts: 'If I blush it will be terrible and everyone will think that I'm unconfident in my role.'

Consequences: Jacqui is feeling stressed the week prior to giving the presentation as the forthcoming task is constantly on her mind. Feeling continually anxious is affecting her sleep patterns and distracting her from accomplishing tasks at work including preparations for the presentation.

Disputing: Using *Socratic questioning*, you can help Jacqui to see things from another perspective. If the Finance Director has asked her to present an analysis of strengths and weaknesses in the current audit procedure, a more helpful interpretation is that he values her opinion. Also, it is helpful to *normalise* her feelings of nervousness by pointing out that most of her colleagues would feel a little self-conscious performing in front of the team and they will probably empathise with her even if she does blush.

Effective Thinking: Using *Socratic questioning*, support Jacqui in formulating a more helpful outlook that will enable her to feel more confident about giving the presentation. Coach her in acknowledging her anxiety and then focusing on the task in hand as a strategy for dispelling anxiety. Encourage her to think of the presentation as an opportunity to showcase her talents and gain the recognition that she deserves.

In addition to the ABC model, all of the techniques outlined in Chapter 2 are extremely useful for helping clients to deal with stress in the workplace more effectively. If you want to use a very simple tool that will enable clients to reframe what they perceive to be stressful situations, you could try the 'SIT-SOT' model.

The 'SIT-SOT' model

SIT = Stress Increasing Thoughts: These are frequently distorted, inconsistent with reality and unhelpful in dealing with the challenge in question. Thoughts of this nature tend to magnify any problematic aspects of the challenge and consequently increase feelings of anxiety. They need to be countered with:

SOTs = Stress Overcoming Thoughts: These are consistent with reality, and focus the mind on constructive methods for dealing with the challenge.

To complete the SIT-SOT sheet with your client, follow these procedures:

1   Get your client to describe the stressful situation as they perceive it.
2   Ask your client to describe any negative thoughts they have about the situation that give rise to feelings of anxiety (or any other unhelpful negative emotions). Record these in the left-hand column.
3   For each SIT recorded in the left-hand column, work with your client to formulate an alternative SOT in the right-hand column. In this way, you act as facilitator by encouraging them to counter each negative thought with a practical solution.

Table 4.2   Jacqui's SIT-SOT analysis

Stressful situation: Giving a presentation to SMT

Stress increasing thoughts (SITs)	Stress overcoming thoughts (SOTs)
1 I'll blush and colleagues will see that I'm nervous.	1 Even if I blush, other people won't necessarily interpret it as a sign of nerves. I've seen people blush when giving presentations and not paid any attention to it.
2 My nerves will get the better of me and I won't be able to think clearly.	2 It's inevitable that I'll feel some nerves to start with. But if I memorise the first few minutes of the presentation, I won't have to worry about my mind going blank and I'll get into the flow.
3 Someone might throw me a curved ball and ask a question I won't know the answer to.	3 If I prepare thoroughly, I'll know more than most people in the room. Even if someone asks an awkward question, I'll field it as best as possible and promise to provide additional details to go out with the minutes.
4 I know Kalpana's presentation will be better than mine and she'll be a hard act to follow.	4 Kalpana's presentation style is different to mine. A number of people in the team are very analytical and will appreciate my discompassionate and considered approach.

Table 4.2 is an example of a completed SIT-SOT sheet constructed to help Jacqui deal with her stressful situation. You can see from this that the SIT-SOT model is a useful tool for encouraging clients to tackle what they initially perceive to be stressful situations with a problem-solving approach. It also *weakens* unhelpful thoughts and beliefs in a similar way to the zigzag model described in Chapter 1.

We now turn our attention to one of the most common causes of stress in the workplace: the challenge of time management.

Time management in the workplace

It is a well-known fact that British workers put in the longest hours in Europe. In her book *Willing Slaves: How the Overwork Culture is Ruling Our Lives* (2004), Madeline Bunting notes that British full-time employees work an average of 43.6 hours per week as opposed to their European counterparts who average 40.3 per week. She also points out that the number of employees toiling in excess of 48 hours each week has increased from 10 per cent of the working population in 1998 to 26 per cent in 2004. There is every expectation that this trend will rise in an increasingly competitive global economy. In addition to this, a Health & Safety Laboratory Report presents evidence on the relationship between increased working hours and poor psychological health symptoms (HSL, 2003: 16). And yet the UK has lower levels of productivity than many other European countries that adhere to the working-time directive limit of 48 hours.

You may encounter clients who persist in working long hours in spite of the fact that, by their own admission, this practice does nothing to increase their productivity and is actually having a negative effect on their mental and physical wellbeing. If you explore your client's *beliefs* about their work situation, you will usually find evidence of unhelpful thinking (e.g. 'I *must* be seen to work hard by my manager and colleagues'). This is a common attitude held by employees due to the rising trend of 'presenteeism', a term invented by Professor Cary Cooper, a psychologist at Manchester University and expert in organisational management. When employees feel insecure within the workplace, they often compensate by working longer hours – not just to cope with increased workloads, but to be seen to be working harder. In the long term this has the paradoxical effect of decreasing their productivity due to exhaustion and a deterioration in mental and physical health.

The first step to helping clients with this problem is to analyse their unhelpful beliefs using either an ABC or 5-area review formulation and explore the negative consequences this is having for them.

Example

Kirsty was promoted to head of the Maths department within her school 6 months ago. Conscientious by nature, Kirsty started to increase her work hours after taking the job to 'get up to speed'. This has now become a dysfunctional habit and Kirsty has developed two unhelpful beliefs: that she must be seen to put in extra hours by colleagues and her manager; and that she needs the extra time to accomplish tasks. In addition to getting in early and staying late, Kirsty works weekends and feels compelled to send colleagues emails on Saturdays or Sundays to provide evidence of her ongoing commitment. The findings of a 5-area review are shown in Figure 4.3.

Situation

Role as Head of Department

Thoughts

'If I don't put in long hours, people will think I'm slacking'
'I can't manage my workload without putting in long hours'

Physiology

Migraine headaches
Lower back pain

Feelings

Stressed
Irritable

Behaviour

Snaps at partner and colleagues
Unable to relax

Figure 4.3   Kirsty's 5-area review results

Once you have carried out a formulation with your client, they may gain a new perspective on the dysfunctional nature of their work habits. However, this new understanding may just be an *intellectual* insight and your client may remain sceptical about changing their unhelpful thoughts and behaviours. The next step in the process could involve a cost and benefit analysis (CBA) as outlined in Chapter 3 to deal with any ambivalence your client may feel about changing their dysfunctional behaviour.

Kirsty's CBA is shown in Table 4.3; completing it gave Kirsty an *emotional* insight. Weighing up the advantages and disadvantages of working long hours in this way gave Kirsty a visceral feeling that she needed to change her attitudes and behaviours in relation to her job.

Table 4.3   Kirsty's cost and benefit analysis

Costs and benefits of: Working long hours

Costs (disadvantages)	Benefits (advantages)
Short-term	**Short-term**
I'm having problems getting a decent night's sleep	My manager and colleagues will think I'm diligent
I'm suffering with back pain and migraine headaches	I'm better able to keep on top of my work load
I've started drinking wine last thing every night to help me unwind	
I don't spend much quality time with Jack and the kids	
I'm often irritable at home and in work	
Long-term	**Long-term**
I think my relationship with Jack could run into problems	If I show commitment, I could go for a
My health will probably suffer as I'm not looking after myself	deputy head post in a couple of years
I'll alienate people at work with my bad moods	
I'll become dependant on alcohol to relax	

Having elicited your client's commitment to change their dysfunctional beliefs and habits, you can support them in developing appropriate strategies at both a cognitive and behavioural level. You can use *disputing* and *Socratic questioning* to help your client change their unhelpful attitudes and beliefs about working long hours. Like Kirsty, they may insist that it is not possible to get the job done without putting in long hours but this belief is often the result of a distorted perception. You could point out that individuals like the prime minister of the UK and the president of the USA have 24 hours in each day, exactly the same as your client, and probably with far greater workloads. The answer to the problem could lie in more effective time management.

There are a variety of methods for managing time in the workplace and a particularly useful model is the time management matrix featured in Steven Covey's *The 7 Habits of Highly Effective People* (1999).

The time management matrix

The time management matrix (see Table 4.4) is divided into four quadrants that enable activities to be identified in terms of urgency and importance. You can use it with your client to analyse the way in which they manage their time.

Table 4.4   The time management matrix (Covey, 1999)

	Urgent	Not Urgent
I M P O R T A N T	**I** ACTIVITIES: • Crises • Pressing problems • Deadlines	**II** ACTIVITIES: • Prevention of problems • Personal development (training, education) • Building work relationships • Forward planning • Creating new opportunities
N O T I M P O R T A N T	**III** ACTIVITIES: • Interruptions • A high percentage of emails • Many phone calls • Some meetings • Other people's priorities	**IV** ACTIVITIES: • 'Busy' work • Irrelevant emails • 'Gossipy' phone calls • Chatting • Surfing the Internet • Too many tea or coffee breaks

Quadrant I: Urgent and important

The types of activities that fall within this section require immediate attention and cannot be postponed. They are often problems that need resolving as soon as possible or emergency situations. Typical examples include looming deadlines, complaints that need dealing with or sudden opportunities that would be lost if not acted upon. Everyone has to deal with these activities at some stage but some people spend most of their working life 'fire fighting' in quadrant I. If your client identifies a number of activities in this quadrant, it is worth exploring the antecedents leading up to them. A common reason certain activities become urgent is because of procrastination: the task may be challenging or unpleasant, leading to postponement. A related reason is that some individuals experience difficulty in finding the motivation to take action until the deadline looms and the sense of urgency triggers an adrenaline rush. The workplace is full of people who become addicted to the feeling of 'living on the edge'. While this may seem energising, the problem with spending too much time on these activities is that they are extremely draining leading to symptoms of stress and burnout in the long term.

Quadrant III: Urgent but not important

If your client identifies activities within this quadrant, it is likely that they initially thought themselves to be carrying out urgent and important work. If you examine each activity, you may find that they are in fact urgent for other people rather than your client. Examples of this include interruptions from colleagues asking for support because they have a deadline looming in addition to emails and telephone calls requesting an urgent response. Obviously there are exceptional circumstances in which your client will need to prioritise supporting other colleagues in an emergency, but it is worth exploring how many of these diversions could have been deflected. We have already emphasised the importance of maintaining focus on specific tasks in the workplace and every interruption will cause your client to lose their momentum as well as giving away valuable time to others. Exploration of activities in this quadrant may reveal that your client requires support in developing the assertiveness skills outlined in the earlier part of this chapter.

Quadrant IV: Not important and not urgent

This is the least productive quadrant of all and time spent here will be invariably wasted. Activities typically include gossiping with colleagues and indulging in frequent tea or coffee breaks in addition to excessive trips to the water cooler. A huge time waster that many people are unaware of is the tendency to tinker excessively with emails that are not important and could be dealt with briefly after priority tasks have been completed. If you analyse the way in which your client is spending their time, you may discover that they often spend the whole day at work being 'busy' without achieving anything significant. If spending time in quadrant IV is so unproductive, why do many people expend a great deal of energy here? We have already noted that the mind has a tendency to avoid uncomfortable states if left unchecked: postponing writing an important but demanding report, for example. We have also described the way in which the mind is constantly seeking a more 'pleasurable' experience even when there is an initial focus on an important task. Quadrant IV activities provide ample opportunities for procrastination and other forms of mental distraction. Another reason why people spend time in quadrant IV is to obtain some respite from mentally and physically exhausting activities that are urgent and important. Perhaps your client has delivered a major presentation the previous day that has been emotionally and mentally draining and feels entitled to 'coast' the following day. This behaviour is perfectly understandable but runs the risk of establishing a vicious cycle of recovering in quadrant IV by engaging in undemanding but unproductive tasks while neglecting activities that will eventually become full-blown emergencies.

Quadrant II: Important but not urgent

According to Steven Covey, this quadrant is at the heart of what he describes as 'effective personal management' and is the area where successful people focus most of their energy – hence our reason for presenting it last. In some respects this notion resembles the Pareto principle, often quoted as a rule of thumb in the world of business, whereby 80 per cent of fruitful outcomes derive from 20 per cent of productive activities (e.g. 80 per cent of sales come about as the result of 20 per cent of clients targeted). Examples of these activities include:

Forward planning: taking time out to develop long-term strategies that propel the individual, team or organisation in a chosen direction. At an individual level this might involve reviewing career objectives and developing a time-bound action plan in order to achieve these, similar to the one outlined in Chapter 3. At an organisational level this will routinely involve constructing a 1 to 5 year strategic plan including targets for growth and new areas of business development.

Developing relationships: team building within the organisation and developing networks of support that can be called upon when there are emergencies to deal with or unexpected opportunities that require an immediate response. Unless your client is working in isolation, it is highly likely that their success in the workplace will depend on cultivating these supportive relationships and this process requires the investment of time. There is, however, a subtle balance to be struck between socialising at work (chatting about non-work related matters) and engaging in mutually beneficial activities (gaining a better understanding of one another's roles and potential areas of collaboration).

Increasing skills and knowledge: formal and informal learning within and outside of the workplace. A passive approach to this area of development might involve participating in mandatory training events provided by the organisation. A more proactive approach to personal development involves not only participating in formal education and training but also encouraging your client to remain up to date with the latest in the chosen occupation (e.g. reading professional journals reporting on new technologies). Other self-development activities such as meditation and maintaining a physical fitness regime can be included within this category as they also lead to increased productivity.

As we have seen, a common feature that all of the above activities share is that they do not *have* to be done in the short to medium term. In the absence of any sense of urgency, it requires a certain amount of self-discipline and a proactive approach to engaging with these activities and maintaining focus until they have been achieved – there will always be something more interesting, easier and *seemingly* urgent to distract your client. The first step to enabling your client to become more effective in their time management is to help them see how they are currently spending their time. You can use the time management matrix combined with a weekly activity log to do this.

First, get your client to detail what they have been doing for each hour on the weekly activity log for five days. This will require some discipline as it represents yet another task in your client's already busy schedule, so you need to use your powers of persuasion to convince them that their effort will be repaid

Table 4.5 Raj's weekly work activity log

Time	Monday	Tuesday	Wednesday	Thursday	Friday
7–8 am	Commute and read novel	Commute and read novel	Commute and read novel	Commute and read novel	Commute and read novel
8–9 am	Coffee with Alan	Research on youth offending	emails	emails	emails
10–11 am	emails	Travel to Compton Youth Service	Travel to Compton YOT	Prepare team meeting presentation	emails
11–12 pm	emails	Meeting with Compton Youth Service	Meeting with Compton YOT	Prepare team meeting presentation	2 phone calls – unscheduled
12–1 pm	Lunch with Alan	Meeting with Compton Youth Service	Meeting with Compton YOT	Lunch with team	Lunch with Jane
1–2 pm	Meeting with supervisor	Working lunch with Youth Service Manager	Working lunch with YOT Manager	Chair team meeting	Clive dropped in for help – unscheduled
2–3 pm	Meeting with supervisor	Client case work	Client case work	Chair team meeting	Writing monthly report
3–4 pm	Jane dropped in for help – unscheduled	Client case work	Client case work	Organise team rota	Writing monthly report
4–5 pm	1/2 year budget forecast	Client case work	Client case work	Organise team rota	Writing monthly report
5–6 pm	1/2 year budget forecast	Admin.	Admin.	Admin.	Writing monthly report
6–7 pm	Commute and read novel	Commute and read novel	Commute and read novel	Commute and read novel	Commute and read novel

by saving time and increasing productivity in the long run. It is also advisable that your client logs each activity shortly after it has taken place in order to gain an accurate representation of how they are spending time: hastily completing the log last thing at night (or just before they see you) will not provide you both with quality information to work on. Table 4.5 gives an example of a weekly activity log completed by Raj, a project manager working for a charity that supports young offenders.

Next, examine the recorded activities with your client and allocate these to the appropriate quadrants within the time management matrix. Table 4.6 shows Raj's completed matrix.

Using the time management matrix enabled Raj to see a number of behavioural patterns that were not previously apparent. For example, Raj noticed that he had a tendency to put some tasks off until the end of the day, in the case of administration and budget forecasting, and the end of the week when it came to his least favourite task – the monthly management report. He also left preparing his presentation for the team meeting until the last moment and should have tabled the team rota at the meeting. Raj admitted that he needed the sense of urgency from an impending deadline as a prompt but found working in this way stressful. He also recognised his tendency to start the week at a leisurely pace (when possible) to get into the rhythm of work by having a

Table 4.6 Raj's time management matrix

		Urgent	**Not Urgent**
I M P O R T A N T		**I** ACTIVITIES: • Writing monthly report • ½ year budget forecast • Preparing team meeting presentation • Organising team rota • Administration	**II** ACTIVITIES: • Research on youth offending • Working lunch with Youth Service Manager • Working lunch with YOT Manager
N O T I M P O R T A N T		**III** ACTIVITIES: • 60% of emails • Jane's unscheduled visit • Clive's unscheduled visit	**IV** ACTIVITIES: • Coffee with Alan • Reading novel whilst commuting • 40% of emails • Lunch with Alan • Lunch with Jane

long coffee and lunch break with Alan. Raj also noticed a similar tendency to use emails as a way of easing himself into the chores of the day but often with the consequence of spending an unjustifiable amount of time on this activity.

On the positive side, Raj recognised that he didn't *have* to spend his lunch hour with the Youth Service and YOT managers, but doing so helped strengthen these working relationships by building on mutual trust and shared understanding of professional objectives. Additionally, time spent reading the latest research on youth offending was not urgent but vitally important for Raj's role as project manager. Raj gained further insight into his behaviour in that he is able to engage in quadrant II activities if they play to his personal strengths – dealing with people and academic study. Raj now realises that he must *consciously* prioritise quadrant II activities that he is less keen on (e.g. report writing, budgeting) instead of *unconsciously* allowing them to drift into quadrant I, causing stress and damage to professional reputation.

It is apparent from this analysis that Raj can steal time from quadrant's III and IV, invest it in quadrant II and thus gradually shrink quadrant I, creating a virtuous rather than a vicious circle.

Reflect and discuss

1   Which problems in terms of clients' motivation and lack of focus do you most commonly experience in your work? What strategies have you learned and how would you use these with clients?
2   Think of a time when you felt anxious in a social situation and/or found it difficult to assert yourself. What were the factors that caused you to feel this way and how would you handle the situation differently with what you have learned in this chapter?
3   Think of as many quadrant II activities as you can that apply to your professional and personal life. What factors prevent you from completing these activities and what strategies could you use to overcome these blockages?

5

Supporting Unemployed Clients

This chapter is designed to help you to:

- gain an understanding of the effects of unemployment on physical and mental health
- consider gender differences and the impact of unemployment on mental health
- obtain an overview of strategies for supporting unemployed clients combining CBT with career counselling and coaching
- construct detailed formulations to gain an understanding of clients' problems within the context of being unemployed
- use behavioural activation strategies to motivate unemployed clients in job seeking
- teach unemployed clients a range of problem-solving skills

Unemployment and its effect on physical and mental health

Early studies within industrial psychology provide evidence that unemployment leads to poorer mental health and negative self-esteem. Warr used cross-sectional and longitudinal comparisons to demonstrate the negative impact of unemployment on aspects of psychological wellbeing including reduced self-esteem (1987: 197). Tyrell and Shanks (1982) noted that long-term unemployment produces secondary effects to poverty including the loss of self-esteem. Buss, Redburn and Waldron (1983) carried out research into the psychological effects of mass unemployment in Youngstown, Ohio where a steel-mill town experienced large-scale redundancies in the wake of recession. They observed that the individual's self-esteem is likely to decline if they believe that failure to find work is an indication that their skills are 'no longer needed or valued' (p. 16). The very term 'redundant' has connotations of uselessness, and to be made redundant increases the likelihood that the individual will engage in negative thinking and endorse unhelpful self-critical beliefs.

Unemployment has also been seen to impact on behaviour patterns in a negative way leading to inactivity and depression: a vicious lethargy cycle.

Many unemployed individuals fall into a pattern of going to bed late and sleeping until the early afternoon because they do not have the structure of work to provide daily routines and develop increasing levels of despondency, mental avoidance and depression as a result. As Haworth and Evans (1987) note, if individuals are in employment they have to 'get up, get organised and participate in society in order to earn a living. Employment thus provides traction' (p. 245). Alternatively, unemployment *removes* traction.

More recent research commissioned by the UK Department for Work and Pensions (Waddell & Burton, 2006; Department for Work and Pensions, 2009) suggests that there is a positive link between employment and mental health and that conversely being unemployed can lead to deterioration in physical and mental health which inevitably makes it harder for the individuals concerned to find employment. Being unemployed can seriously damage your health as there is a strong correlation between unemployment and mortality and also the need for increased healthcare (Yuen & Balarajan, 1989). This situation is exacerbated by the fact that one in four people are challenged by mental health issues at any time in England (Freud, 2007) and may become unemployed as a result. These two factors combine to form a vicious circle that keeps many people trapped in long-term unemployment. Once individuals challenged by mental health issues become unemployed they find it increasingly difficult to obtain work, and the cycle of worklessness reinforcing mental health problems continues to perpetuate itself. Research by the British Society of Rehabilitation Medicine (2001) indicates that if someone is out of work for over six months, there is only a 50 per cent likelihood of them returning to work. This drops to 25 per cent after being out of work for more than 12 months, and after 2 years chances of returning to work are almost non-existent. This bleak outlook is confirmed by evidence that the number of unemployed people requiring help with mental health problems is over 50 per cent higher than those in employment (Paul & Moser, 2009). Further evidence of the negative impact of unemployment on mental health was obtained through the UK's Pathways programme targeted at unemployed incapacity benefit claimants.

In October 2003 the UK government launched the Pathways to Work initiative ('Pathways' for short) with the aim of encouraging individuals

Table 5.1   The Pathways research findings into mental health problems in the UK

Type of mental health problem	%
Alcoholism	4.3
Depressive episode	53.5
Dissociative disorders	0.0
Drug abuse	6.8
Eating disorder	0.1
Manic episode	0.1
Mental and behavioural disorders associated with puerperium, not elsewhere classified	0.8
Mental disorder not otherwise specified	1.5
Other anxiety disorders	13.6
Other neurotic disorders	5.6
Persistent delusional disorder	0.2
Persistent mood disorder	0.0
Pervasive development disorders	0.1
Phobic anxiety disorders	0.4
Reaction to severe stress	9.0
Recurrent depressive disorder	0.1
Schizophrenia	1.3
Specific development disorders of scholastic skills	1.1
Specific personality disorders	0.2
Unspecified dementia	0.1
Unspecified mental retardation	0.1
Unspecified mood disorder	0.5
Unspecified non-organic psychosis	0.7
Sample size	8,741

Source: Bewley, Dorsett & Haile (2006: 25)

claiming incapacity benefits to find employment. The initiative was launched as a response to the large increase in the number of incapacity benefit claimants (approximately 2.7 million in 2002), many of whom had officially recorded mental health problems. In 2006 an evaluation of the impact of the Pathways programme was carried out by a consortium of research organisations (The Policy Studies Institute) on behalf of the Department of Work and Pensions using qualitative and quantitative techniques. At the time of the evaluation the Pathways programme covered 40 per cent of England. The evaluation findings were summarised in a detailed report (Bewley, Dorsett & Haile, 2006). One of the most striking findings was that 39 per cent of the 8,741 sample were officially recorded as having a 'mental or behavioural disorder'. The information was obtained from GPs' medical certificates sent to Jobcentre Plus (the UK government agency supporting jobseekers) as part of the individual's incapacity benefits claim. The breadth of mental health problems can be seen in Table 5.1.

Type of mental health problem among the pilot population recorded as having a 'mental or behavioural' disorder

It is quite apparent from this detailed survey that a high percentage of unemployed people in the UK suffer from psychological problems, and a high percentage of benefits claimants may have suffered from these problems *prior* to becoming unemployed and their condition has prevented them from working (e.g. 53.5 per cent depressive episode; 13.6 per cent anxiety disorders; 5.6 per cent neurotic disorders; 9.0 per cent reaction to severe stress diagnosed by GPs). Interestingly, one of the key aspects of the Pathways strategy was to offer a condition management programme (CMP) to all claimants to offer support with physical and/or mental conditions to enable entry into sustainable employment. One of the most commonly used CMP methods of support for unemployed claimants with mental health issues is cognitive behavioural therapy (CBT) varying from one-to-one sessions, telephone support and access to clinically approved CBT computer-based programmes (FearFighter and Beating the Blues).

Gender differences and the impact of unemployment on mental health

Much of the recent evidence that has been gathered to demonstrate the negative effects of unemployment on mental health relates only to the male sex. In the Royal College of Psychiatrists study *Men Behaving Sadly* (1998) it is stated that approximately one in seven men who lose their jobs develop mental health problems with depression within six months. Lewis and Sloggett (1998) found that being unemployed may increase the chances of men committing suicide by twice as much.

A recent study published in the *Journal of Epidemiology and Community Health* (Tiffin, Pearce & Parker, 2005) suggested that women are less affected by the change in social and economic status associated with unemployment and thus less likely to suffer from poor mental health as a result. The reason given for the difference in response between genders is that many men suffer from low self-esteem if they are unable to maintain their role as the main provider. Dr Paul Tiffin and a team of academics from Newcastle University surveyed 503 men and women aged 50 about their psychological wellbeing. Their analysis of the results involved identifying socioeconomic status throughout the lifetime of the men and women based on the head of the household's occupation. Their findings indicated that women did not exhibit any marked differences in mental health if they moved up or down in social status. The results were dramatically different for men as those who had experienced a decline in social status were four times more likely to suffer from depression than those who had moved up the social ladder. Dr Tiffin, who also works as an NHS psychiatrist, offered a number of possible reasons as to the study's findings. The first suggestion is that women are simply more psychologically resilient than men when it comes to coping with loss of social status. But the study authors also present a more complex view, namely that the men suffering from depression in the survey shared a typical 'post-war' mentality: that the man is expected to be the main breadwinner and that unemployment frequently leads to loss of self-esteem. Women, it is suggested, may view having a successful family life as more important than career achievement.

However, the interpretations within Tiffin et al.'s study need to be regarded with some caution as they are confined to a particular age group and geographical location. With the increase in divorce rates and the rising number of single-parent families, women are often the 'main breadwinners' and unemployment may lead to a deterioration of mental health for a variety of reasons associated with joblessness. Also, other studies have provided evidence that women, as well as men, attach psychological importance to having a job. Warr (1982) found that single women were more likely to exhibit commitment to employment than married women, and that this tendency was stronger among younger women of higher occupational status. Henwood and Miles (1987) carried out an experiment by getting 117 men and 107 women to complete a questionnaire with single-item measures against Marie Jahoda's access to certain categories of experience (ACE) in the workplace. These experiences were deemed crucial to psychological wellbeing (e.g. social contacts, status, time structure, activity and being part of a collective purpose). Their findings led them to the conclusion that unemployment had similar negative psychological consequences for both men and women.

Another aspect that needs to be taken into consideration when comparing the negative psychological effects of unemployment between men and women is that official statistics are mostly based on paid work and do not take account of other forms of unpaid employment (e.g. caring). The difficulties in providing clear evidence are outlined by Allen, Waton, Purcell & Wood (1986) when they describe an investigation into the relationship between parasuicide and unemployment among women. The difficulties occur because women (especially those who are married) may not register as unemployed because they are not eligible for benefit. They describe this as 'yet another example of how methods of determining who is employed and who is unemployed render women invisible in studies which seek to explain the consequences of unemployment' (p. 6).

There are further complexities that need to be considered when the effects of ethnicity combined with gender are taken into account. A study of the impact of unemployment on demand for personal social services carried out in 1985 (Balloch, Hume, Jones & Westland, 1985) found that attempted suicides had increased among Asian women in the Bradford area and that unemployment among their husbands was seen as a major cause. The reason given is that because Asian people are often expected to contribute to the wider community, unemployment and loss of income leads to a sense of failure within the whole family. This can be further exacerbated by the notion that any resulting mental illness is regarded as a punishment from God and difficult to acknowledge publicly.

Although previous research suggests that there may be *differences* in the way in which men and women suffer from mental health problems in response to becoming unemployed, there is sufficient evidence to suggest that both genders suffer negative psychological consequences and are equally in need of support.

Strategies for supporting unemployed clients combining CBT with career counselling and coaching

If unemployment can be regarded as a major causal factor leading to deterioration in mental health, its consequences can also be measured in economic terms. The London School of Economics' *Depression Report* (Layard, 2006) highlighted the loss of output as a result of depression and chronic anxiety to be worth approximately £12 billion per year (or 1 per cent of national income), and more recent research (Centre for Mental Health, 2010) estimated the cost of mental health problems in England to be £105.2 billion in 2009/10.

Given the huge costs in terms of both economic impact and human suffering, the UK Government commissioned extensive research into potential strategies for enabling unemployed people to return to work with a focus on providing support for mental health issues (Freud, 2007; Layard, 2006; Waddell & Burton, 2006). This has led to the recent development of government-funded programmes that utilise cognitive behaviour therapy (CBT) with the aim of supporting unemployed individuals in their return to work.

The UK Government launched the Improving Access to Psychological Therapies (IAPT) programme in 2005 to provide increased access to tested psychological therapies (predominantly CBT) for individuals suffering from depression and anxiety disorders. The early IAPT pilots proved successful and the UK Government committed £400 million in 2008/09 to expand the programme under the new name of 'Talking Therapies' throughout the whole of

England by 2015 (Department of Health, 2011). Employment support is seen to be an integral part of the strategy and since 2009 employment advisers have been recruited to work alongside CBT practitioners to provide clients with a combination of CBT and career counselling and coaching to meet their needs under the 'Working for Wellness' strand of the strategy. Until recently the two professions have worked largely in isolation from one another. This recent development suggests that there is growing recognition for the efficacy of combining CBT with career counselling and coaching as a means of empowering clients to overcome both practical and psychological barriers while pursuing their vocational goals.

There is also evidence to suggest that career counselling and coaching has a *therapeutic* value as an intervention with clients. A recent report by the UK National Institute of Adult Continuing Education (NIACE) noted that effective information advice and guidance (e.g. career counselling and coaching) can contribute to the benefits of education for people experiencing mental health problems:

> *Support to access the most appropriate learning opportunities maximises the chances of success and is crucial in building an individual's confidence in their ability to be an independent and successful learner under the Disability Discrimination Act. (James, 2005: 6)*

In addition, the recent Freud report on the future of the UK's welfare to work strategy (Freud, 2007) draws attention to Waddell and Burton's (2006) assertion that 'Work can be therapeutic and can reverse the adverse (mental) health effects of unemployment'. Using cognitive behavioural approaches to career counselling and coaching can facilitate this therapeutic intervention.

Using formulations with unemployed clients

As you have seen from the research in the previous section, the experience of unemployment can have a devastating effect on clients' beliefs about themselves and the way they perceive their life circumstances. Many clients' self-concept is closely linked to their occupation: they regard themselves as 'a carpenter', 'an accountant', 'an executive'. If they have invested in their identity within the workplace to the detriment of other domains within their lives (e.g. family, social interaction, hobbies) they will be more vulnerable to experiencing unemployment as a loss of their sense of self with all the debilitating consequences that this negative view implies. Other considerations that may cause distress include the client's age, particularly if their previous occupation is representative of a younger demographic, and financial uncertainty. All of these aspects may increase the likelihood that clients will endorse negative, self-defeating beliefs which may chronically undermine their ability to obtain subsequent employment.

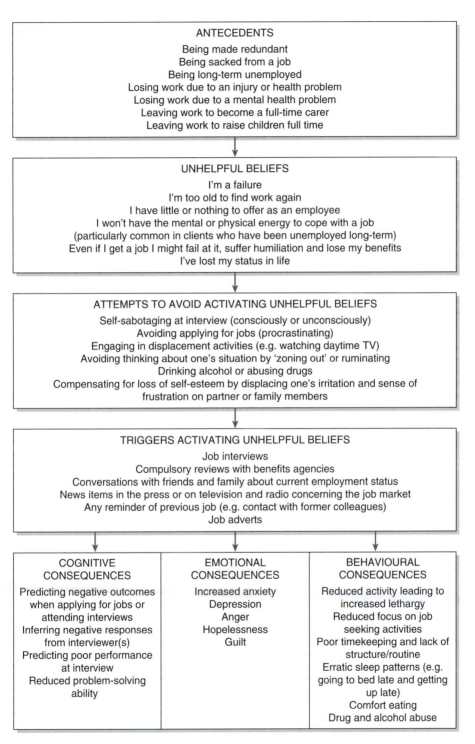

ANTECEDENTS

Being made redundant
Being sacked from a job
Being long-term unemployed
Losing work due to an injury or health problem
Losing work due to a mental health problem
Leaving work to become a full-time carer
Leaving work to raise children full time

UNHELPFUL BELIEFS

I'm a failure
I'm too old to find work again
I have little or nothing to offer as an employee
I won't have the mental or physical energy to cope with a job
(particularly common in clients who have been unemployed long-term)
Even if I get a job I might fail at it, suffer humiliation and lose my benefits
I've lost my status in life

ATTEMPTS TO AVOID ACTIVATING UNHELPFUL BELIEFS

Self-sabotaging at interview (consciously or unconsciously)
Avoiding applying for jobs (procrastinating)
Engaging in displacement activities (e.g. watching daytime TV)
Avoiding thinking about one's situation by 'zoning out' or ruminating
Drinking alcohol or abusing drugs
Compensating for loss of self-esteem by displacing one's irritation and sense of
frustration on partner or family members

TRIGGERS ACTIVATING UNHELPFUL BELIEFS

Job interviews
Compulsory reviews with benefits agencies
Conversations with friends and family about current employment status
News items in the press or on television and radio concerning the job market
Any reminder of previous job (e.g. contact with former colleagues)
Job adverts

COGNITIVE CONSEQUENCES	EMOTIONAL CONSEQUENCES	BEHAVIOURAL CONSEQUENCES
Predicting negative outcomes when applying for jobs or attending interviews Inferring negative responses from interviewer(s) Predicting poor performance at interview Reduced problem-solving ability	Increased anxiety Depression Anger Hopelessness Guilt	Reduced activity leading to increased lethargy Reduced focus on job seeking activities Poor timekeeping and lack of structure/routine Erratic sleep patterns (e.g. going to bed late and getting up late) Comfort eating Drug and alcohol abuse

Figure 5.1   Longitudinal formulation of experiences and responses of being unemployed

Given the potential complexity of unemployed clients' challenges, it may be helpful to construct a detailed *longitudinal formulation* of their current circumstances and in the following section, we explain this method in detail. This type of formulation details the antecedent events leading up to their current situation, unhelpful beliefs that they have developed and the impact these have on their thoughts, feelings and behaviour. The example in Figure 5.1 describes a typical range of experiences and responses following on from the experience of becoming unemployed. (A longitudinal formulation worksheet for use with clients can be downloaded from www.sagepub.co.uk/sheward.)

Once you have constructed a comprehensive, detailed formulation of your client's situation within the context of being unemployed, you will both be in a better position to understand potential cognitive, emotional and behavioural blocks to progression and devise appropriate strategies to address these. You have already learned how to use the ABCDE model to help clients challenge unhelpful beliefs and devise constructive cognitive, emotional and behavioural goals. You can now draw on the more detailed longitudinal formulation to isolate specific unhelpful thoughts, beliefs and behaviours for action within the ABCDE model. The longitudinal formulation will also help you to identify any ambivalent attitudes your client may hold about the prospect of applying for or obtaining employment following a close study of the 'Attempts to avoid activating unhelpful beliefs' section. You can raise the issue of ambivalence with your client by normalising this response to unemployment and sharing with them the fact that it is perfectly understandable to have mixed feelings about resuming work after one's confidence has been temporarily reduced. You can assist your client to work through their conflicting thoughts by helping them construct a detailed CBA exploring the advantages and disadvantages of maintaining a particular outlook or behaviour for themselves and others in both the short and long term.

In the following example Steve is working with Michael, aged 55, who has recently been made redundant from his job as personnel manager within a medium-sized marketing company. This is their first session together and Steve wants to gain an understanding of Michael's current situation, how he is coping with unemployment and if he is experiencing any problems in motivating himself to find suitable work. Michael has referred himself to Steve because he feels 'stuck' and has become increasingly despondent.

Example

Steve: OK Michael, this is our first session together and I thought it might be helpful if we could get an overview of your current situation, how you're feeling and if there are any blocks to moving forwards – you mentioned feeling 'stuck' and experiencing difficulty in motivating yourself to seek work.

Michael: That's right. It's been four months since I was made redundant and I'm finding it a lot harder to remain optimistic and keep applying for jobs. My mood has deteriorated lately and I find myself feeling either down or anxious about the future.

Steve: Why don't we try to unpack that – do you mind if I jot things down on the whiteboard?

Michael: No, go ahead.

Steve: Perhaps you can tell me something about events leading up to your being made redundant. What was happening within your organisation?

Michael: Basically the company had lost a couple of major contracts and had to make savings on back-office costs – the Personnel Department was the first place to be hit and I was placed on a list of staff at risk of redundancy.

Steve: Did the Personnel Department restructure?

Michael: Yes. They went from two personnel managers to just one within the new structure and I had to compete with my younger colleague – he won.

[Steve notes on the whiteboard:]

ANTECEDENTS
Placed at risk of redundancy
Competed for job unsuccessfully with younger colleague

Steve: Is that a fair summary of what happened?

Michael: Pretty much.

Steve: You mentioned that you are feeling stuck in terms of motivation. I was wondering if what happened had an effect on the way you view yourself and whether any negative thinking has crept in?

Michael: I guess it did come as a bit of a blow. I worked my way up within the company since leaving university and my job was a big part of my life.

Steve: A lot of people feel that their job is a major part of their identity – is that true for you?

Michael: I suppose so. I feel that I've lost my status, you know: the company car, the job title and all of that. And what was particularly galling was the fact that I was sidelined by a junior colleague.

Steve: What did that mean to you?

Michael: That I'm past it – over the hill.

[Steve notes on the whiteboard:]

UNHELPFUL BELIEFS
I've lost my status
I'm past it and over the hill

Steve: It sounds pretty painful to think that way.

Michael: It is, now you come to mention it.

Steve: Do you do anything to avoid situations that might make you think and feel this way?

Michael: I've avoided seeing friends and relatives because I'm a bit embarrassed about my situation. I've also avoided applying for jobs with companies that have a youthful image because I don't want to risk rejection and a further reminder that I'm past it.

[Steve notes on the whiteboard:]

> ATTEMPTS TO AVOID ACTIVATING UNHELPFUL BELIEFS
> Avoids seeing friends and family
> Avoids applying for jobs with 'youthful' companies

Steve: But in spite of avoiding situations that prompt you to think negatively about yourself, some things still trigger off these thoughts?

Michael: It's surprised me how many items there are in the media about having a mid-life crisis. Every time I read things like that I think, 'What's my life all about?' Also, all these gloomy news items about the job market make me feel I'm on the scrapheap.

[Steve notes on the whiteboard:]

> TRIGGERS ACTIVATING UNHELPFUL BELIEFS
> Media articles about mid-life crisis
> News items about contractions in the job market

Steve: So when you think these things about yourself like, 'I've lost my status' and 'I'm over the hill', does it lead to other negative thoughts?

Michael: Usually I start thinking that I'll never work again and if I get a job interview, I'm pretty sure I won't be successful.

[Steve notes on the whiteboard:]

> COGNITIVE CONSEQUENCES
> Predicting failure at interview
> Predicting long-term or permanent unemployment

Steve: And how would you describe your feelings when you think about yourself and your situation in these negative ways?

Michael: Well, I feel pretty depressed, hopeless and anxious about the future.

[Steve notes on the whiteboard:]

> EMOTIONAL CONSEQUENCES
> Depression
> Hopelessness
> Anxiety

Steve: Now, a really important question is, what do you do or avoid doing when you think and feel this way?

Michael: As I mentioned earlier, I'm applying for fewer jobs because my confidence has declined and I find myself watching daytime television to take my mind off things and fill the time. I find also that I'm having problems sleeping so that I'm getting up later in the morning.

[Steve notes on the whiteboard:]

BEHAVIOURAL CONSEQUENCES
Reduced job seeking
Increased television watching
Going to bed late, getting up late

Steve: Can you see how this all fits together Michael?
Michael: Yes, looks like my life right there on your whiteboard!

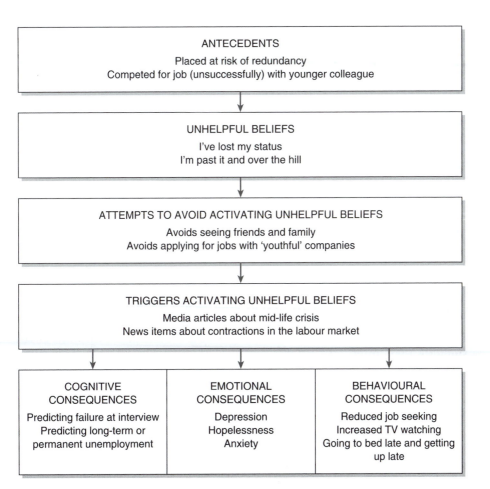

Figure 5.2   Michael's longitudinal formulation of experiencing unemployment

As you can see from the above example, constructing a detailed formulation of your client's situation on the whiteboard provides a sense of you both working collaboratively on a problem. This Socratic process offers a number of advantages over a verbal discussion of the client's situation in that it:

- validates the client's experience
- compartmentalises different aspects of the problem thus preventing the client from feeling overwhelmed
- enables the client to see the *interaction* between different aspects of their problem
- makes the client an active participant in the process and prepares the way for collaborative problem solving

Having gained an understanding of your client's situation within the context of being unemployed, an important next step is to assess how they are currently spending their time and what impact the activities they engage in have on their mood and energy levels.

Using behavioural activation with unemployed clients

The research set out at the beginning of this chapter provides evidence that being unemployed renders people vulnerable to becoming depressed, less active and, as a result, less able to find subsequent employment. There are a number of important reasons for this tendency. First, being unemployed is an unpleasant experience for most people and dwelling on this situation will inevitably lower mood. Second, unemployment removes daily structures and routines so that there is a danger of drifting into a state of mental and physical entropy if insufficient attention is paid to maintaining a daily routine. Third, unemployment provides large amounts of time for rumination: worrying about the future and dwelling on negative events in the past or present.

One of the most effective recent approaches for helping people overcome depression (and low mood in general) is behavioural activation. Empirical evidence (Martell, Dimidjian, Herman-Dunn & Lewinsohn, 2010) suggests that unlike other CBT approaches that recommend challenging negative thoughts and beliefs, behavioural activation is more successful in helping people overcome depression because it places the emphasis on *action* rather than *thought* and its techniques are equally helpful for unemployed clients.

Having carried out detailed formulation of your client's situation, you will have both gained an insight into their thoughts and feelings, how both of these aspects have impacted on their behaviour and whether this has led to a decline in activity. If this proves to be the case, it will be helpful to share with your

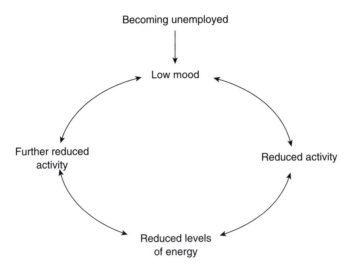

Figure 5.3   The lethargy cycle

client the way in which being unemployed can contribute to the development of a *lethargy cycle* (see Figure 5.3) and how this can lead to ever declining levels of activity if left unchecked, resulting in low mood and reduced energy.

The first step to recognising the extent to which this cycle has become an obstacle for clients in their job-seeking activities is to ask them to complete a detailed *activity and mood diary* between sessions (a diary form for use with clients can be downloaded from www.sagepub.co.uk/sheward).Instruct your client to detail their activities hour by hour and indicate their mood on a scale of 0 to 10 where 0 = least and 10 = most intense. We recommend that you elicit your client's own terms to describe the moods they experience as suggesting that they are suffering from 'depression' and 'anxiety' may alarm them (even if this is the case). If it becomes apparent that your client is suffering from high levels of depression and/or anxiety and you both agree that this has become their primary problem, it is advisable that they seek suitable treatment from their medical practitioner.

In the example in Table 5.2, Michael has partially completed an activity and mood diary as a homework assignment and has suggested the term 'down' to describe the feeling of low mood that he often experiences and which has a negative effect on his motivation: consequently D = 'down' in the example below.

Completing the log has provided both Steve and Michael with a great deal of valuable information to work on. You will notice that Michael has got into the habit of going to bed near or after midnight and is getting up late in the morning. This has a negative effect on his mood and energy levels as he often lies in bed not sleeping but ruminating about his situation. This tendency is also apparent when Michael engages in passive activities such as sitting for

Table 5.2   Michael's activity and mood diary

Time	Monday	Tuesday	Wednesday	Thursday	Friday
7–8 am	Asleep	Asleep	Asleep	Asleep	Asleep
8–9 am	Asleep	Asleep	Breakfast and shower D=6	Asleep	Breakfast and shower D=6
9–10 am	Asleep	Asleep	Travel to job centre D=5	Asleep	Travel to careers centre D=4
10–11 am	In bed awake D=8	In bed awake D=8	Visit job centre D=4	Asleep	Visit career counsellor D=2
11–12 pm	Breakfast and shower D=6	Breakfast and shower D=6	Walk to town centre D=3	In bed awake D=9	Use careers library D=1
12–1 pm	Computer: job search D=6	Computer: job search D=6	Visit local college D=2	Breakfast and shower D=8	Do weekly shopping D=2
1–2 pm	Computer: job search D=6	Computer: job search D=7	Lunch in park D=1	Walk to buy newspaper D=6	Lunch with friend D=1
2–3 pm	Watch TV D=6	Walk to buy newspaper D=4	Sign up with temp job agency D=2	Computer: job search D=6	
3–4 pm	Watch TV D=6	Prepare job application D=4	Computer: job search D=4	Computer: job search D=7	
4–5 pm	Watch TV D=6				
5–6 pm	Prepare dinner D=2				
6–7 pm	Meal with partner D=2			Meal with partner D=2	Visit friends D=1
7–8 pm	Do washing up D=2				Visit friends D=1
8–9 pm	Watch TV D=4				Visit friends D=1
9–10 pm	Watch TV D=5				Visit friends D=1

Time	Monday	Tuesday	Wednesday	Thursday	Friday
10–11 pm	Watch TV D=7				Visit friends D=1
11–12 am	In bed 12 am D=8	Watch TV D=7	Watch TV D=7	Watch TV D=7	In bed 11.30 pm
12 am onwards	Couldn't sleep D=9	In bed 1 am D=8	Watched TV until 2 am	Couldn't sleep D=9	Sleep

hours at his computer or watching television. When asked about his concentration levels during these activities, Michael admits that his mind often wanders and he finds himself dwelling on negative thoughts. Conversely, when Michael has a compelling reason to get up in the morning and do something (e.g. visit the job centre or career counsellor for scheduled appointments), his mood is lifted, creating momentum for further activities. This mood lift is also evident when he engages in modest activities that give him respite from dwelling on his problems such as talking to his partner, spending time with friends or simply walking to the shop for a paper.

Having identified the specific patterns of behaviour that contribute to your client's low mood and reduced motivation, your next priority is to schedule activities that will reverse the lethargy cycle. As previously mentioned, one of the major problems with unemployment is lack of structure leading to reduced activity, increased rumination and consequently, unhelpful negative emotions. Drawing your client's attention to the negative effects of their dysfunctional routines will prepare the way for negotiating and scheduling a range of constructive activities aimed at improving mood and increasing motivation towards active job seeking. As a starting point you could select activities from your client's diary that have made a demonstrable improvement to their mood and schedule these for the following week. The purpose of the activity and mood diary now becomes one of scheduling activities calculated to improve mood as well as recording patterns of behaviour and their effects on mood.

It is vitally important that you help your client to understand that they need to carry out scheduled activities even (and especially) if they do not feel motivated to do so. To encourage them in this endeavour, share with clients the fact that research shows that when individuals act in accordance with plans rather than mood, the feeling of motivation will follow (Martell et al., 2010). This is what Martell and colleagues refer to as the 'Just do it!' principle, similar to Nike's advertising slogan. You could provide a concrete example of this by asking your client to recall a situation in which they were required to get up early and go to work even if they did not feel like it (e.g. on a rainy Monday morning following a holiday). Further questioning will probably reveal that once they got to work and became focused on necessary

Table 5.3   The agreed range of activities to help Michael improve his day

Time	Monday	Tuesday	Wednesday	Thursday	Friday
7–8 am					
8–9 am	Breakfast and shower	Breakfast and shower	Breakfast and shower	Breakfast and shower	Breakfast and shower
9–10 am	Travel to temp agency	Travel to local library	Travel to job centre	Travel to offender mentoring charity	Travel to career counsellor
10–11 am	Sign up with temp job agency	Internet search for job vacancies	Visit Job Centre	Enquire about voluntary work	Visit career counsellor
11–12 pm					Use careers library
12–1 pm					
1–2 pm	Swimming	½ hour walk	½ hour walk	Swimming	½ hour walk
2–3 pm					
3–4 pm					
4–5 pm					
5–6 pm	Prepare dinner	Light gardening			
6–7 pm	Meal with partner		Visit friend		Visit friends with partner
7–8 pm					
8–9 pm					
9–10 pm					
10–11 pm					
11–12 am					
12 am onwards					

tasks and engaged socially with colleagues, their mood and energy levels improved. Table 5.3 shows a range of activities agreed between Michael and Steve aimed at providing daily structure, a sense of purpose and increased motivation.

Michael has learned from his initial diary record that if he schedules activities early in the morning, he is more likely to galvanise himself into action and overcome inertia and low mood. Michael has also agreed to fill the time available with less passive activities (like sitting at the computer for hours) and more constructive routines like volunteering to mentor teenage offenders. He has noticed that even modest amounts of physical exercise provide a mood lift and increased energy and has scheduled at least one daily activity around lunchtime aimed at maintaining positive momentum throughout the day. Michael is now aware of the fact that too much television watching invariably leads to rumination whereas time spent with his partner or friends prevents him from becoming withdrawn and dwelling on problems.

When scheduling activities with clients, it is important to foster a sense of *experimentation*. You are not offering a magical solution but rather encouraging clients to try different approaches in order to evaluate what effect they will have on their mood and energy levels. It is also very important that clients continue to record all other activities they have engaged in during the week and their effect on mood in addition to the ones you have scheduled. This will provide ongoing additional information and enable you both to further refine the behavioural activity schedule based on your evaluation of what works best.

In addition to monitoring low mood (e.g. Michael's scoring of 0 to 10 for feeling 'down'), it is also helpful for clients to record positive feelings that they experience when carrying out scheduled activities and, in particular, aim at obtaining a balance between *pleasure* and *mastery*. For example, Michael may record carrying out 'light gardening' as 4 for pleasure and 8 for mastery. Conversely he may record 1 for mastery and 8 for pleasure when having a meal with his partner. Similar to instructing clients to record examples of low mood, it is helpful for them to come up with their own terms to describe mastery and pleasure.

Teaching unemployed clients problem-solving skills

In addition to experiencing low mood or depression, unemployed clients are more likely to suffer from increased levels of anxiety and both of these emotions are likely to contribute to what Dugas and Robichaud (2007: 38) describe as 'negative problem orientation': the sense that problems are threatening, difficult or impossible to solve and will have a negative outcome whatever action is taken. This perspective frequently leads to avoidant behaviour (e.g. avoiding dealing with the problem until it becomes an emergency) or continuing to worry about the problem without seeking to resolve it. Both of these dysfunctional strategies inevitably increase anxiety and a sense of helplessness and hopelessness. Given the nature of unemployment, it is highly likely that your client will be confronted with an increased number of challenges in their life and learning effective problem-solving skills to deal with these is vitally important. Teaching the following steps are recommended and you may also wish to refer to D'Zurilla and Nezu (1999) who provide a detailed outline of problem-solving therapy. It will be helpful if you complete this exercise using a whiteboard or at least on paper so that your client can be actively engaged in solving their problems while learning the sequence.

Step 1: Define the problem

Encourage your client to be as specific as possible in describing the problem they are facing. This is important because you may both find that your client's worries are hypothetical and outside of their control. If this is the case you are advised to teach them the worry tree exercise outlined in Chapter 2. Also, engaging in behavioural activation and job-seeking related activities will prevent your client ruminating on hypothetical worries.

Step 2: Consider as many strategies as possible for solving the problem

Having defined the problem clearly, encourage your client to be as creative as possible in considering potential strategies to resolve it. It is important to caution your client against censoring their thoughts by dismissing potential solutions as they occur as this may stifle their mental flow. Suggest that they note down everything that comes to mind no matter how ridiculous or unrealistic it may seem. If your client gets stuck at this point, it may be helpful for them to use the 'best friend's argument' technique: asking, if they had a best friend facing the same problem, what advice would they give? In our experience of running groups with clients, it is often much easier for them to come up with solutions for others than think of strategies for resolving their own problems. This is invariably because it is difficult to remain objective about one's own problems and the above technique helps clients to see their problem from a different perspective.

Step 3: Consider the advantages and disadvantages of each strategy and rate them according to difficulty and usefulness

This is a similar process to the costs and benefits analysis (CBA) we have used with clients in other situations but is less focused on resolving ambivalence and more designed to give a clear ranking of the various solutions in terms of their individual utility. The advantages and disadvantages of each strategy are considered and a rating on a scale of 0 to 5 given for difficulty and usefulness respectively.

Step 4: Select the 'best fit' strategy

Having gone through the above evaluation, your client will be in a better position to select a potential strategy from the range available. They may at this point express the view that the strategy in question is not perfect and this is seldom the case. However, the important thing for them to do is choose a serviceable strategy and take action as inactivity will usually cause even greater problems and lead to increased anxiety.

Step 5: Describe the individual steps needed to carry out the best fit strategy

Your client needs to break down their strategy into a series of detailed steps describing what they intend to do and when they will carry out each action. It may be worth revisiting the SMART objectives in Chapter 3 to help ensure that the steps are specific, measurable, attainable, realistic and time-bound. It is also important for your client to identify any potential obstacles they may encounter when attempting to carry out their strategy and consider contingency plans for dealing with these. This offers two advantages: anticipating potential problems increases motivation to carry out the strategy; and it is easier to counter problems with a pre-planned solution (if they occur) rather than deal with them in the heat of the moment.

Step 6: Evaluate the outcome

Your client needs to develop objective measures to determine whether or not their chosen strategy has been successful (or partially successful). Questions they may ask themselves include:

- Has the problem been solved?
- Are there any remaining aspects of the problem that need to be dealt with?
- What has been learned from carrying out the strategy?
- What changes need to be made to the strategy for the next attempt to solve the problem?

In the following example Steve is working with Barry, who has recently been made redundant from his job over the last two decades as an assembly worker for a large car manufacturer in the local area. The company was the biggest provider of employment opportunities within the region and has gone bankrupt following the loss of a major overseas contract. This is their third session together and Steve has been coaching Barry in job-search skills and interview techniques as it is the first time he as had to apply for work in 20 years. Barry appears to be very dejected and lacking in enthusiasm during the session.

Example

Steve: You seem pretty down today Barry– is there anything I can help you with during our session today?

Barry: I suppose since we last met I've been wondering if there's any point to all of this. It's OK putting together a CV but there's hardly any work in the area and I'm worried about falling behind with the mortgage. It doesn't help that the kids are getting older and we're paying out more for school trips and clothing.

Steve: I can understand that you've got a lot on your mind right now. Would it help if we tried to get more of a focus on one of your problems and came up with ways of tackling it?

Barry: Well I don't know what you're going to do about the local job situation but I suppose we could give it a try.

Steve: OK. We need to be as specific as possible about your problem so that we can pin it down – can you describe it in a nutshell?

Barry: I just don't think I'm going to find suitable work in the area. All that's available are call-centre jobs – they're low paid and I'm not cut out for that sort of work.

[Steve notes on the whiteboard:]

PROBLEM: Lack of suitable job opportunities

Steve: If you had to come up with different ways of solving this problem, what could you think of?

Barry: That's just the problem – I can't think of any solutions.

Steve: What if one of your friends who've just been made redundant from the car plant came to you and said, 'I need work, I'm struggling financially but I don't know what to do', what would you say?

Barry: Well, I suppose I might suggest moving to another part of the country to find a similar job, but that wouldn't work for me.

Steve: Let's just get the ideas written down no matter how crazy they sound. What else?

Barry: Call-centre work, but the money's lousy and you need IT skills.

Steve: Keep going!

Barry: A temporary fall-back in this area is to get work as a mini-cab driver but ...

Steve: Let's put that down anyway. Any other thoughts?

Barry: Bar work – bad hours, low wages.

Steve: Go on.

Barry: Actually, I've often thought about becoming a driving instructor, but you have to pay quite a lot for the course.

Steve: Any further ideas?

Barry: That's all I can come up with at the moment.

Steve: Well done. The next thing we need to do is look at each of your suggestions in terms of their potential advantages and disadvantages, how difficult they would be for you to carry out but also

how useful they would be in terms of solving your problem. Shall
we try that?

Barry: Might as well.

After some consideration Barry came up with the evaluation shown in
Table 5.4 of each potential strategy. (A strategy evaluation worksheet for
use with clients can be downloaded from www.sagepub.co.uk/sheward.)

Table 5.4   Barry's evaluation of potential job options as a first step
to problem solving

Strategy	Advantages	Disadvantages	Difficulty 0–5	Usefulness 0–5
Move elsewhere in the country to find similar work	Could do the same job Wouldn't need to re-train	Upheaval for family Children's education disrupted House prices higher elsewhere	5	4
Call-centre work	Employment opportunities available locally	Low salary Requirement to re-train	4	2
Mini-cab driver	Employment opportunities available locally Could use existing skills to maintain cab Well paid during evenings and weekends	Would see less of family working unsocial hours No long-term job security	2	3½
Bar work	Employment opportunities available locally	Would see less of family working unsocial hours No long-term job security Badly paid	2	2
Training to become a driving instructor	Local demand for driving instructors Reasonably well paid after training Freedom of running own business Could use existing skills to maintain vehicle	Some risk – earning potential might be affected by down-turn in local economy Initial investment on training course	4	5

After some consideration Barry decided that aiming at training to be a driving instructor offered the best-fit strategy for his circumstances. Although it would be relatively challenging in terms of financing the initial training while supporting his family, Barry thought that it offered a long-term means of making a living within the local community as well as drawing on existing mechanical skills that he possesses. When he began scoping out the individual steps needed to carry out this strategy, Barry realised that mini-cab work offered an interim solution for supporting his family and saving up money to pay for the driving instructor training course. The main obstacle that Barry anticipated was the additional childcare demands his wife would face while he works evenings and weekends. His contingency plan for dealing with this was to discuss the driving instructor option with his family and obtain their support. In terms of evaluating the outcome, Barry decided to measure the success of his strategy by calculating how long it would take him to save enough money for the driving instructor training course based on estimated earnings as a mini-cab driver and evaluate if he was on target after one month.

Reflect and discuss

1 What do you consider to be the key problems encountered by unemployed clients in your professional practice?
2 In what ways do differences in gender, ethnicity, disability and sexual orientation bring about additional challenges for unemployed clients?
3 Which other techniques previously described within this book would be particularly useful in working with unemployed clients?
4 How could you adapt the problem-solving skills described in this chapter for clients with literacy problems?

6

Supporting Clients in Education

This chapter is designed to help you to:

- gain an understanding of emotional intelligence and its role within education
- obtain an overview of recent developments within career counselling and coaching in educational settings
- help students to complete a barriers, thoughts, feelings, actions (BTFA) evaluation
- obtain commitment by completing a cost and benefit analysis (CBA) with students
- teach students problem-solving skills
- help students to complete a solutions, thoughts, feelings, actions (STFA) blueprint
- use metaphors to help students develop resilience

The role of emotional intelligence (EI) within education

As we have mentioned previously, Daniel Goleman has influenced the world of psychology with his seminal work *Emotional Intelligence* (1996) and the concept of EI has also influenced educational policy in both the US and the UK. This is because research suggests that enabling pupils to obtain better self-awareness, empathy and the ability to manage their mood (e.g. anger, frustration) leads to increased motivation and improvements in classroom behaviour and is an important factor in predicting academic success (e.g. Gumora and Arsenio, 2002; Lam and Kirby 2002; Catalano, Berglund, Ryan, Lonczak & Hawkins, 2004; Petrides, Frederickson and Furnham, 2004; Humphrey, Curran, Morris, Farrell & Woods, 2007). Implementing EI strategies within educational settings in conjunction with cognitive behavioural techniques provides a powerful combination for helping learners to succeed. Both approaches dovetail together as significant parts of Goleman's model are influenced by the same leading figures in the cognitive behavioural field presented within this book, namely Martin Seligman, Mihaly Csikszentmihalyi and Aaron Beck. There are five domains of EI and you will notice that each one is consistent with the aims of career counselling and coaching underpinned by cognitive behavioural approaches:

Self-awareness: understanding the way we respond emotionally to different situations and using this insight to manage our emotions optimally.

Emotional control: using different strategies to manage our emotions in order to cope with challenging situations and, as a consequence, manage our lives more effectively.

Self-motivation: managing our emotions to achieve a positive outcome. A typical example is managing short-term impulses and tolerating feelings of frustration in order to achieve a goal that will be of long-term benefit. This process can also lead to the state of 'flow' that we have described in Chapter 3, so that the task becomes a reward in itself by providing a sense of absorption and achievement.

Empathy: the ability to recognise emotional responses in others and imagine how they are feeling.

Handling relationships: Closely related to empathy, this skill is vitally important in managing any interpersonal relationships and helps to prevent or resolve any conflicts that may arise.

Goleman acknowledged the development of a curriculum within the USA specifically aimed at increasing emotional intelligence in learners and referred to *Self-Science: The Emotional Intelligence Curriculum* (Stone-McCown, Freedman, Rideout & Jensen, 1978) as a 'model for teaching emotional intelligence'. The curriculum is taught widely throughout the US and includes 54 lessons and 53 experiments aimed at providing learners with tools for resolving conflict, increasing self-motivation, improving communication and interpersonal skills.

At present a great many primary and secondary schools in the UK seek to develop pupils' emotional, social and behavioural skills through national curriculum subjects like Personal Social Education/Personal Social Health Education (PSE/PSHE) or Citizenship and use a range of curriculum materials designed specifically for this task (DfES, 2005). A key development within this academic area is the Social and Emotional Aspects of Learning programme (SEAL), a comprehensive approach to nurturing social and emotional skills to underpin effective learning, good behaviour, regular attendance and staff effectiveness (DfES, 2007). The programme aims to develop emotional health and wellbeing among both pupils and staff and enhance learning and academic achievement by cultivating motivation, empathy and social skills in learners. A substantial research study was carried out by the University of Cambridge Local Examinations Syndicate (Rodeiro, Bell & Emery, 2009) with the specific aim of investigating whether there is a causal relationship between attempts to develop EI in pupils and subsequent examination success. In order to test this hypothesis, 1,977 students from 31 schools in England completed the 'Trait Emotional Intelligence Questionnaire' prior to taking the 2007 secondary school GCSE science exams. The questionnaire is a 153-item self-report instrument that measures the individual's perception of their own abilities and trait EI. The results showed that certain aspects of trait EI significantly predicted academic attainment and supported the hypothesis that emotional factors play a role in students' performance and progress. This was supported by a number of the key findings outlined within the final report:

- Self-motivation and low impulsivity were significant predictors of attainment in almost all subjects.
- Academic ability is not the only predictor of educational achievement and EI has a very important effect on learning.

Interestingly, the study found that trait EI does not seem to have a huge influence on the academic performance of high-ability students but may help low-ability students to cope with stress or anxiety. The authors conjecture that vulnerable or disadvantaged students are more likely to experience stress and emotional difficulties than higher ability students and are more likely to benefit from being taught EI strategies.

Given the growing emphasis on helping students to acquire EI as both a life skill and a method for improving academic achievement, the role of career counselling and coaching will become increasingly important in facilitating this process. Using cognitive behavioural approaches as part of the practitioner's repertoire will undoubtedly strengthen this approach.

The role of career counsellors and coaches in education

Career counsellors and coaches perform an important role in helping clients to succeed within secondary, further and higher education and are employed by both the public and private sector. At the time of writing an estimated 7,500 personal advisers provide pupils and students with vocational advice and guidance within schools and colleges in the UK, although not all are formally trained as career counsellors (Children's Workforce Development Council, 2008). The UK Coalition Government has emphasised the importance it attaches to the role of careers guidance in empowering learners and, specifically, in increasing social mobility by ensuring that a greater number of disadvantaged young people gain access to further and higher education. Because of this importance, the UK Government has established a task force of leading experts to provide recommendations for strengthening the 'careers profession' and its work in the public, private, voluntary and community sectors. Among its many recommendations, the Careers Profession Task Force call for practitioners to achieve a minimum level-6 qualification (e.g. post-graduate) in career counselling and define the role in terms of a range of duties:

Careers advisers' duties

Careers advisers' duties typically include:

- interviewing clients on a one-to-one basis or in small groups
- carrying out a needs assessment
- providing information, advice and guidance about careers, education, employment and training
- helping students to apply for further and higher education, as well as work-based training and other employment opportunities
- assisting young people to draw up action plans for employment, education and training and supporting them to achieve these goals
- running small group sessions or larger presentations on all aspects of careers work
- keeping up to date with labour market information, legislation and professional and academic developments by visiting employers, training providers and training events run by educational and professional bodies
- using information and communications technology (ICT) to track labour market information and for administrative tasks such as recording interactions with and tracking clients
- using computer-aided guidance packages, skills assessment tools, psychometric tests and personality inventories
- supporting the transition of young people with learning difficulties and disabilities (LDD), and brokerage of specialist education and training opportunities for young people with LDD
- planning and organising careers fairs and conventions
- managing a caseload of clients
- assisting careers educators with the brokerage of work opportunities for students

(Careers Profession Task Force, 2010)

In addition to the careers advisers' duties, emphasis is placed on the motivational aspects of the careers professional's role in terms of helping learners to:

develop a strong sense of personal responsibility and the resilience to overcome barriers to achieve their goals

and:

broaden their horizons, raise aspirations and appreciate their potential to progress. (Careers Profession Task Force, 2010: 11)

Career counselling and coaching underpinned by cognitive behavioural techniques provides practitioners and trainees with effective tools for raising aspirations in students by helping them challenge negative beliefs about the self and replacing these with a more helpful evaluation of academic abilities and personal strengths. This approach is also ideally suited to helping students develop emotional and intellectual resilience by teaching a problem-solving approach to overcoming barriers to achieving goals, in particular by helping them identify any thinking errors leading to unhelpful emotional and behavioural consequences. This is consistent with a model of career counselling and coaching that places the emphasis on helping the individual to become self-sufficient in managing their career throughout life by increasing self-efficacy rather than relying on the practitioner as 'expert'.

Helping students to overcome barriers through problem solving

In Chapter 1 we introduced the 5-areas model in some detail and set out instructions for its use in helping clients to succeed at interviews in Chapter 2. We will now consider how an adapted version of the model can be taught to pupils and students as a motivational career counselling and coaching tool that will equip learners with a means of overcoming barriers to achieving their educational and vocational goals. The following procedure and supporting materials can be used effectively in one-to-one situations with clients or when working with small- to large-size groups.

Stage 1: Help the client to clearly define their educational/vocational goal(s)

It is highly likely that the client will have defined their educational or vocational goals if they have benefited from other career counselling or careers education support. For example, action planning is an important part of most career counselling practice and using the FIRST model set out in Chapter 3 will help clients to identify both goals and potential obstacles. If your client has not had the opportunity to identify their educational or vocational goal, we recommend using the FIRST model combined with setting SMART goals as a starting point. If the client identifies more than one goal, agree which one to work on as a priority. This decision will be dictated by how important the goal is to the client and also the degree of difficulty (e.g. the number of barriers) they are experiencing in achieving the goal.

Stage 2: Complete a barriers, thoughts, feelings, actions (BTFA) evaluation

Having agreed which goal to work on, use *Socratic questioning* and *guided discovery* (see Chapter 1) to elicit the client's barriers to achievement, typical thoughts they have when contemplating these barriers and the emotional and behavioural consequences of holding unhelpful thoughts in relation to their goal (see Figure 6.1). Your primary aim at this point is to help your client to see the way in which their thoughts, feelings and behaviours interact and that their *attitude* towards perceived barriers may initiate and maintain an unhelpful cycle. Your secondary aim will be to teach clients the BTFA evaluation model so that they can use it as part of a problem-solving approach to dealing with subsequent barriers that they will inevitably encounter while managing their

Figure 6.1   The BTFA evaluation model

career through life. (A BTFA evaluation worksheet for use with clients can be downloaded from www.sagepub.co.uk/sheward.)

There are two ways in which you can teach the model:

Method 1: Using a flip chart or whiteboard, ask the client to describe their goal, any barriers they perceive and make a note of these. Next, ask the client to describe any negative thoughts, feelings or actions they typically experience when contemplating their perceived barriers and note them down according to the layout in Figure 6.1. At this stage do not write down the headings (i.e. Thoughts, Feelings, Actions). After you have captured as many examples as possible, add the section headings and ask the client if they can see how these different aspects interact with one another. As they comment, link the individual sections of the diagram by drawing the connecting arrows and emphasise the negative cycle. Ask what conclusions they draw from this. The advantage of using this method is that you can use a very Socratic approach as the model 'emerges' on the flip chart or whiteboard as you and the client work collaboratively. In our experience this approach is far more powerful than simply teaching the model in a didactic fashion.

Method 2: Provide the client with a blank copy of the BTFA worksheet downloaded from www.sagepub.co.uk/sheward. Use the flip chart or whiteboard to teach the model by giving the client a hypothetical example of a goal, perceived barriers and resulting thoughts, feelings and actions. Ask them to complete the BTFA worksheet in the same way after selecting a goal they are experiencing difficulty in achieving. Review your client's evaluation and ask them to summarise the key learning points. The advantage with this method is that you can facilitate learning in a group situation more easily by issuing participants with copies of the worksheet and teaching the model in a Socratic fashion, drawing on the group to provide hypothetical examples for each section. You can also set homework assignments by asking clients to complete BTFA evaluations for further goals and barriers.

In the following example Rhena is working with Letitia who is currently experiencing difficulties in preparing adequately for her GCSE exams at the end of her secondary school education. Rhena has already carried out Step 1 and has identified Letitia's goal. She now uses Step 2 and Method 1 to help Letitia carry out a BTFA evaluation.

Example

Rhena: Now the goal you wanted to prioritise, Letitia, was revising for your GCSE exams, is that correct?

Letitia: Yes, I'm really struggling with doing the revision for the exams.

Rhena: Do you mind if I write this up on the whiteboard as we go along? It might help us to get a better overview of the problem.

Letitia: OK.

Rhena: When you say that you're struggling to do the work, how would you describe the barriers – what's getting in the way of doing the work?

Letitia: There are a couple of things. My friends are older than me and keep asking me to go out clubbing. Also, the exams are coming up soon and there's loads of work I'd need to do.

Rhena: So the barriers are ...

[Rhena writes:]

Pressure from friends to go clubbing
Huge amount of work and tight deadline

Letitia: That's right. I feel that if I let them down, they won't let me hang out with them. And when I think of all that work, I don't think I could cope.

Rhena: Do you have any other unhelpful thoughts?

Letitia: Yeah, I don't really know if it's worth all the effort.

[Rhena writes:]

My friends might reject me
I couldn't cope with the work
I don't know if it's worth it

Rhena: And when you think this way, how do you feel?

Letitia: Like it's too much and I can't go there.

Rhena: Can we call that feeling 'overwhelmed'?

[Letitia nods; Rhena writes:]

Feeling overwhelmed

Rhena: So when you feel this way, is there anything you find yourself doing as a result or that you avoid doing?

Letitia: Well, when it really gets on top of me I'll watch television, maybe play computer games or just go out with my friends because that way I don't have to think about it anymore.

[Rhena writes:]

Watch television
Play computer games
Go out with friends

Rhena: OK, let me show you something.

[Rhena adds:]

Thoughts, Feelings, Actions
[headings over each section; see Figure 6.2]

Rhena: Do you see what happens when you think about your barriers in this way?

[Rhena draws arrows connecting Barriers, Thoughts, Feelings sections.]

Letitia: Yeah, I feel really bad.
Rhena: And when you feel like that, does it help you to act in ways that'll enable you to overcome your barriers?

[Rhena draws an arrow connecting Feelings and Actions sections.]

Letitia: No, the exact opposite.
Rhena: And the next time you try to face up to your barriers, what's that like?

[Rhena draws an arrow connecting Actions and Barriers sections.]

Letitia: It makes it harder to deal with them and it looks as though it just goes round in one big circle.
Rhena: That's right!

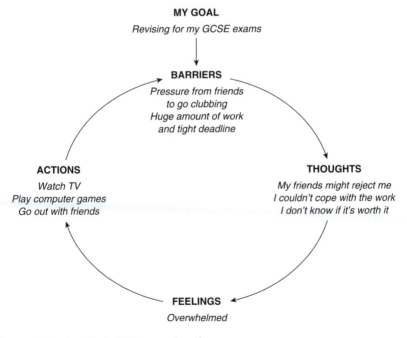

Figure 6.2   Letitia's BTFA evaluation

Stage 3: Obtain commitment by completing a cost and benefit analysis (CBA)

One of the barriers confronting your client may be a lack of sufficient commitment to achieving their goal or a sense of ambivalence about the outcome. If these issues remain unresolved, your client may be held back because they have not reconciled in their own mind the fact that it is worth making sacrifices and enduring a certain amount of discomfort in pursuit of their goal. The CBA will enable them to evaluate the short- and long-term advantages of achieving the goal for themselves and others as opposed to the short- and long-term disadvantages of ceasing to pursue the goal. In the following example Table 6.1 shows the CBA that Rhena has constructed with Letitia having identified some reservations about achieving her stated goal (e.g. Letitia's unhelpful thought 'I don't know if it's worth it').

Example

Table 6.1   Letitia's cost and benefit analysis

Costs and benefits of: *Revising for my GCSE exams*	
Costs (disadvantages)	**Benefits (advantages)**
Short-term	**Short-term**
For self:	*For self:*
Revising is hard work Sitting the exams will be scary	My parents will stop nagging me If I focus on revising, I might stop worrying so much
For others:	*For others:*
My friends see less of me	My parents will be relieved
Long-term	**Long-term**
For self:	*For self:*
I might lose my friends	If I pass my GCSE exams I can go to college and study Drama at A-level
For others:	If I pass my A-levels, I could go to drama school
My friends might think I've moved on and don't want to know them	I'll have more opportunities open to me if I pass my GCSE exams
	For others:
	If I pass my exams, mum and dad will be proud of me

Having gone through this detailed process, Letitia is surprised to find that she has identified more advantages than disadvantages associated with pursuing her goal and feels an increased sense of commitment as a result. This may seem like a rather mundane written exercise but the power of the CBA lies in helping the client to articulate any reservations they may have about pursuing their goal and off-set these against potential benefits rather than constantly ruminating about their conflicted thinking and remaining stuck. It also enables the practitioner to play the role of devil's advocate in challenging the client's assumptions about potential disadvantages. In this instance, Rhena has suggested that real friends would care about Letitia's best interests and want her to pass the exams, prompting Letitia to re-evaluate her unspoken fears about being ostracised from the group. This is similar to using a 'best friend's argument' to help clients resolve a problem (e.g. by asking the question 'What would your best friend advise you to do?'). Letitia can also see that even if the prospect of sitting the exams seems scary, taking action and revising will distract her from feelings of anxiety by providing a focus for attention and shifting her mind away from unhelpful rumination. This type of strategy can prove enormously helpful when dealing with *procrastination*, an exceedingly common problem for students facing exams (or course work in general) and who continually avoid the short-term discomfort of revising. (A copy of the CBA form for use with clients can be downloaded from www.sagepub.co.uk/sheward.)

Stage 4: Help the client overcome their barriers by teaching problem-solving skills

Having identified your client's barriers to achieving their goal, you now have an opportunity to teach them problem-solving skills for dealing with this situation and any subsequent challenges they may encounter. Teaching this approach and the various steps outlined in this chapter follow Gerard Egan's principle of 'seeing problem management as life-enhancing learning and treating all encounters with clients as opportunity-development sessions' (Egan, 2002). There are six steps involved in this process as previously described in Chapter 5.

Step 1: Define the problem
Encourage your client to be as specific as possible in describing the problem they are facing. This should flow naturally from the barriers identified within your BTFA evaluation and you should address each one in turn as part of the process. On this occasion, Letitia chose 'Huge amount of work and tight deadline' as her immediate priority.

Step 2: Consider as many strategies as possible for solving the problem

Encourage your client to be creative during this stage and come up with as many solutions as possible no matter how ridiculous they may seem. The important point of this exercise is for the client to get into the flow of creative thinking without self-censoring. If you can inject some fun into this step, so much the better. Letitia's potential strategies included:

- Leave the country and live with my grandparents in Jamaica.
- Get my sister to take my exams for me.
- Apply for jobs or apprenticeships and forget the exams.
- Take a year out and take my exams next year.
- Work out how much time I have left until the exams and plan my revision.

Step 3: Consider the advantages and disadvantages of each strategy and rate them according to difficulty and usefulness

In this step the client considers the advantages and disadvantages of each strategy and rates them according to difficulty and usefulness on a scale of 0 to 5. Rhena helped Letitia to evaluate and score her potential strategies as shown in Table 6.2.

Table 6.2   Letitia's evaluation and scoring of her problem-solving strategies

Strategy	Advantages	Disadvantages	Difficulty 0–5	Usefulness 0–5
Leave the country and live with my grandparents in Jamaica	I'd have a great time and avoid all the hard work	I'd miss my parents and friends and it would be hard to find work	1	1
Get my sister to take my exams for me	She'd probably do better at the exams	She'd never agree!	5	5
Apply for jobs or apprenticeships and forget the exams	I could earn money and train while I'm working	Most jobs and apprenticeships require qualifications	5	4
Take a year out and take my exams next year	I'd give myself more time to prepare for the exams	I'd still be faced with the same problems	1	1
Work out how much time I have left until the exams and plan my revision	I'd break a big problem into manageable steps	It would mean a lot of hard work	4	5

Step 4: Select the 'best-fit' strategy

It is unlikely that your client will identify a 'perfect solution' on this or future occasions when engaged in problem solving. The key teaching point to communicate is that it is far better to select a 'good enough' potential strategy and take action than to remain stuck and continually agonising about the problem. Two subsidiary questions the client may find helpful when selecting a potential strategy are:

- Have I enough information to help me make this decision?
- What's my deadline for making this decision?

Having carried out the evaluation in Table 6.2, Letitia decided that her 'best-fit' strategy was to *work out how much time she has left until the exams and plan her revision*. Letitia concluded that although this strategy would require a great deal of effort, it would offer a way forward after months of avoiding the problem while at the same time agonising about it.

Step 5: Describe the individual steps needed to carry out the best-fit strategy

This step leads into the action-planning stage that is common to most career counselling and coaching practice and requires the strategy to be broken down into a series of SMART objectives as described in Chapter 3. Letitia worked with Rhena to outline the following steps:

1 Obtain dates of subject exams.
2 Work out how many hours are available for revision in total.
3 Decide how much time to spend on each subject depending on predicted grades and importance of subject (e.g. English and Maths).
4 Develop a revision timetable plotting study time for each subject in evenings and weekends leading up to the exams.

Rhena also helped Letitia to identify a *potential obstacle* that might get in the way of carrying out the various steps in her strategy, namely that she may lack the motivation to commence working during the evening or weekend after studying at school all week (they both identified this as a recurrent negative pattern). After some discussion, Letitia was able to develop a *contingency plan* for overcoming the obstacle with Rhena's help. Letitia agreed that if she experienced difficulty in motivating herself to commence revision, she would sit down and work for at least 10 minutes *no matter what her mood was*. Rhena's hypothesis is that once Letitia gets started, motivation will follow.

Step 6: Evaluate the outcome

Any strategy needs to be reviewed in terms of its effectiveness so that it can be modified and subsequent action planned. Helping your client to develop *objective measures* to determine the success, or otherwise, of their chosen strategy is an important part of this process. Rhena and Letitia agree that a good measure of the strategy's effectiveness will be the number of actual hours spent revising against the number planned within the timetable. They agree also that if the amount of actual hours spent revising falls below 80 per cent of the planned hours, Letitia will need to revisit her strategy.

Having taught your client the six steps to problem solving on one barrier to progression, you can set them a homework assignment for carrying out exactly the same process with other barriers they have identified. This will have the effect of consolidating learning and increasing the client's ability to become their own 'career counsellor/coach'. Letitia agrees with Rhena that she will use the six steps to tackle her other barrier, 'Pressure from friends to go clubbing', and present her strategy at their next session.

Stage 5: Complete a solutions, thoughts, feelings, actions (STFA) blueprint

This is a similar process to carrying out the BTFA evaluation which helped your client to identify the vicious cycle of barriers to achieving their goal, resultant unhelpful thinking, behavioural responses and negative emotional

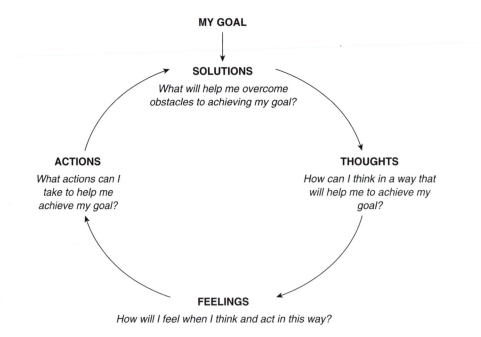

Figure 6.3   The STFA Blueprint Model

consequences. Having increased the client's motivation through a CBA and developed constructive strategies through problem solving, the STFA replaces the initial vicious cycle with a virtuous cycle (see Figure 6.3) and a blueprint for achieving success. (A STFA worksheet for use with clients can be downloaded from www.sagepub.co.uk/sheward.)

It is helpful to revisit the original BTFA evaluation with your client at this stage and the same Socratic approach can be used when formulating the STFA (e.g. Methods 1 and 2) as the following example illustrates.

Example

Rhena: Now that we've come up with some strategies for dealing with your barriers, I'd like to scope out a map that will help you keep travelling in the right direction. Are you interested in working on this with me?

Letitia: Sure.

Rhena: Now, we came up with a solution to the barriers you were facing at our last session and you came up with another solution since we met. Do you want to summarise the details and I'll write them on the whiteboard?

Letitia: We agreed that I'd work out how much time I have left until the exams and plan my revision. The other problem was pressure from my friends to go clubbing. I thought I could tell them that I had to put study first for the next couple of months but that I'd invite them to a party to celebrate right after the exams.

Rhena: That's a great idea – your way of paying them back for not seeing them for a while. Let's write down both those solutions.

[Rhena writes:]

> Work out how much time I have and plan my revision
> Postpone clubbing and celebrate with friends after exams

Rhena: Now when you carry out these plans, what kind of thoughts will help you to keep focused and positive, especially when the going gets tough?

Letitia: Well, when I look at what I was thinking last time [*points to BTFA*], I'm less worried about my friends rejecting me because I'm trying to be really reasonable. I think I can cope with the work in bite-sized chunks and I reckon it's worth the pain because I stand a chance of getting into drama school.

Rhena: OK, those are great thoughts, let's write them on the board. What I really like is the way you're acknowledging that it's going to be tough but the prize at the end makes it worth the struggle [*Rhena is reinforcing Letitia's effort to develop mental resilience and high frustration tolerance – see 'The use of metaphor' below*]

[Rhena writes:]

> I'm being reasonable with my friends
> I can cope with bite-sized work
> It's worth the pain for drama school

Rhena: So when you think in this way, how's it going to make you feel?
Letitia: Really determined, fired-up.
Rhena: That's great.

[Rhena writes:]

> Determined
> Fired-up

Rhena: Now, what are the main things you need to do to keep you heading in the right direction?
Letitia: As we said last time, I need to just sit down and start working even if I don't feel like it.
Rhena: So as NIKE says, 'Just do it!'
Letitia: Yeah, I like that – can we put that down? The other thing is, if I find myself worrying while I'm watching television or something, I can go and do some work instead of worrying.
Rhena: Great ideas – let's write them down.

[Rhena writes:]

> Just do it!
> Worry cues action

Rhena: Now let's see what kind of circle we have this time.

[Rhena adds:]

> Thoughts, Feelings, Actions
> [headings over each section]

Rhena: Do you see the difference when you think about solutions for achieving your goal instead of barriers?

[Rhena draws arrows connecting Solutions, Thoughts, Feelings sections.]

Letitia: When I think that way I get energy, I get motivated.
Rhena: That's right. And when you feel motivated like that, how does it help you to act in a positive way?

[Rhena draws an arrow connecting Feelings and Actions sections.]

Letitia: I'll be more able to just get on with the work rather than worrying about it all the time.
Rhena: And the next time you apply solutions to your barriers, what do you think will happen?

[Rhena draws an arrow connecting the Actions and Solutions sections; see Figure 6.4.]

Letitia: I'll have a better chance of knocking down the barriers.
Rhena: Because your thoughts, feelings and actions are all helping you to achieve your goal.

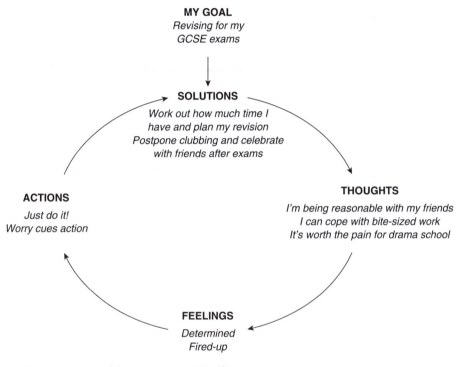

Figure 6.4   Letitia's STFA evaluation

A copy of the STFA worksheet for use with clients can be downloaded from www.sagepub.co.uk/sheward.

The use of metaphor to help clients develop resilience

We have mentioned the importance of using Socratic questioning as a way of teaching cognitive behavioural approaches to learners as part of career counselling and coaching practice in Chapter 1. This method can be enhanced through the creative use of metaphors to illustrate specific concepts. This is because metaphors utilise a combination of imagery and story-telling (in a concise way) and have far more *emotional* impact on the learner than simply presenting them with factual information. This is why working with imagery in therapy is receiving increasing emphasis as verbal cognitive processing is hypothesised to have less emotional effect (Dugas & Robichaud, 2007: 42). Whenever you describe an image or metaphor, you stimulate your client's imagination: they can see the image you have described from their unique perspective and invest it with personal meaning.

A detailed discussion on the use of metaphors is beyond the scope of this book. If you are interested in further reading on this subject we recommend *The Oxford Guide to Metaphors in CBT: Building Cognitive Bridges* (Stott et al., 2010). We will restrict ourselves to one specific use of metaphor which can be used to teach the value of learners acquiring *resilience* by means of the career counselling and coaching process.

As we have mentioned in Chapter 1, low frustration tolerance (LFT) is one of the main reasons why clients do not succeed in achieving their goals. This is because any meaningful endeavour will involve some form of physical, intellectual or emotional discomfort. You can help your client to strive for high frustration tolerance through the use of a 'psychological muscle' metaphor, as described below.

In the previous section we encountered Letitia who was struggling with applying herself to revision prior to her GCSE exams. This problem with *procrastination* is common among many learners and is a behavioural response to situations that trigger low frustration tolerance beliefs, namely:

A = Adversity: Revision prior to exams

B = Beliefs: 'I can't stand it'; 'It's too boring'; 'I should be having fun'

C = Consequences: Procrastination (behavioural); anxiety (emotional)

In the following example Rhena makes use of Socratic questioning and metaphor to teach Letitia the value of developing high frustration tolerance beliefs in order to help achieve her goals.

Example

Rhena: I was impressed by what you said about the chance of getting into drama school being worth putting up with the pain of revision. Have you thought like that before?

Letitia: Not really.

Rhena: It's a really important point. I mean how easy do you think it's going to be trying to achieve all your goals: GCSEs, A-levels, drama school?

Letitia: I guess it's going to be a struggle.

Rhena: But do you think it will be worth it?

Letitia: I think so.

Rhena: What do you think would help you with your struggle?

Letitia: I don't know.

Rhena: I guess you could say that aiming at your goals is a bit like running a race. If you were planning to run a marathon, what would you need to do?

Letitia: Get really fit.

Rhena: OK, so you'd need to start running and build up. If you wanted to develop your all-round physical fitness, where would you go?

Letitia: To a gym.

Rhena: That's right. You'd use weights to develop muscular strength and the running machine to develop stamina. Would this type of training be comfortable?

Letitia: No. You'd get sweaty and your muscles would ache.

Rhena: But if you wanted to run a marathon or get fit it would be worth the discomfort.

Letitia: I guess so.

Rhena: Can you see how this compares with your situation?

Letitia: It's similar. I've got to build up my mental stamina and learn to put up with the discomfort.

Rhena: And do you know what the great thing is? Every time you're faced with a challenging situation, like revising instead of watching television, it's a chance to develop your 'mental muscle'.

Letitia: Like a work-out in the gym?

Rhena: Exactly!

Reflect and discuss

1 What are the main advantages of teaching learners emotional intelligence and what criticisms could be levelled against this approach?

2 What are your views on the current developments within career counselling and coaching in education and what effect will they have on your professional role?

3 Consider five ways in which acquiring cognitive behavioural skills will increase your marketability within the education sector.

4 How could you adapt the written exercise described in this chapter for students with literacy problems?

5 Devise at least one additional metaphor for teaching the value of learning resilience to students.

7

Reflective Practice and Using Assessment and Self-help Tools

This chapter is designed to help you to:

- understand the relevance of reflective practice and evidence-based practice in relation to evaluating the effectiveness of cognitive behavioural approaches
- familiarise yourself with the revised cognitive therapy scale (CTS-R) and use it to evaluate your use of cognitive behavioural approaches
- understand Kolb's experiential learning cycle and apply and use it as part of your reflective practice
- use the wheel of life with clients to assess their current levels of success and satisfaction in various domains
- measure progress throughout the course of your work with clients by plotting increased success and satisfaction within each of the client's chosen domains
- help clients to identify personal values and signature strengths by using Professor Martin Seligman's on-line questionnaires
- become familiar with a selection of on-line CBT-based self-help tools that are particularly useful in supporting career counselling and coaching

Reflective practice

By comparison with counselling and psychotherapy, far less attention has been paid to process or outcome research in the field of career counselling and coaching, although slightly more in the US where career counselling is a branch of applied psychology (Kidd, 2006). Most career counselling and coaching practised within the UK is government funded and its effectiveness is measured largely by means of targets (e.g. the number of clients obtaining work, training or education following an intervention). While these impact measures provide a rationale for funding and performance management, they do little to evaluate the effectiveness of professional practice as many other variables may have contributed to the outcome (Keep, 2004); for example, a relative may have helped the client find work after the career counselling or coaching intervention. Also, no attention is paid to the quality of the experience for the client as Egan notes, 'If evaluation occurs at the end, it is too late' (2002).

The circumstances of your employment will largely determine the way in which you measure the effectiveness of your professional practice, whether you work for a government-funded agency or are self-employed. You may also follow guidelines from accrediting bodies or lead professional organisations such as the British Association of Counselling & Psychotherapy (BACP) or the Institute of Careers Guidance (ICG). However, there may be gaps in the processes or criteria that you are obliged to use and you may still find yourself asking the question 'What is the best way to evaluate my practice so that I can continually improve my professional skills?' If you are fortunate enough to have regular supervision of your work, you will be able to discuss this issue in detail and agree on criteria and methods for evaluating client sessions with your supervisor. Potential methods include recording sessions with clients, after obtaining written consent, and playing sections in supervision with specific questions. You may agree with your supervisor, for example, that you want feedback and advice on your practice of contracting with clients at the start of the session.

If no other means of regularly evaluating your professional practice are available to you, *reflective practice* is probably your best option. This process involves thinking about your work with clients before, during and after the session. Methods for facilitating this process include writing your observations in a diary or log and discussion with peers or mentors if formal supervision is unavailable. Reflective practice is often used in conjunction with *evidence-based practice*, a process which originated in medicine but is used widely within other fields including counselling. This approach aims to ensure that professional practice is based on evidence of 'what works best' and is informed by gathering empirical data (e.g. outcomes of random controlled trials evidencing effective practice). Even if your role is not informed by evidence-based practice in a formal way, it is still helpful to adopt its principle of trying to be as objective as possible in assessing the effectiveness of your practice rather than relying on methods that you prefer or are comfortable with (Baker & Kleijnen, 2000).

Although the most common method for engaging in reflective practice is keeping a written log of your observations, it is also helpful to have a set of criteria for evaluating the effectiveness of your work. Given that the aim of this book has been to equip you with a range of cognitive behavioural approaches to use as part of your career counselling or coaching practice, it seems appropriate to offer criteria for evaluating the effectiveness of this approach. At present the British Association for Behavioural & Cognitive Psychotherapies (BABCP) recommends that supervisors use the revised cognitive therapy scale, or CTS-R, to evaluate practitioner competency in delivering CBT interventions with clients. We offer a modified checklist of CTS-R criteria below as a means of strengthening your self-reflective practice and evaluating your competency in using cognitive behavioural approaches as part of your career counselling and coaching practice.

The revised cognitive therapy scale (CTS-R)

The scale was developed to measure therapist competency in using cognitive therapy by clinicians and researchers at the Newcastle Cognitive Behavioural Therapies Centre and the University of Newcastle upon Tyne (James, Blackburn, Reichelt, Garland & Armstrong, 2001). The CTS-R contains 12 items and is based on the original cognitive therapy scale (CTS) (Young & Beck, 1980, 1988). Each item is scored on a scale of 0 to 6 depending on the practitioner's competence level:

0 = Absence of feature, or highly inappropriate performance
1 = Inappropriate performance, with major problems evident
2 = Evidence of competence, but numerous problems and lack of consistency
3 = Competent, but some problems or inconsistencies
4 = Good features, but minor problems and/or inconsistencies
5 = Very good features, minimal problems and/or inconsistencies
6 = Excellent performance, or very good even in the face of patient (client) difficulties

You can use the above scores to evaluate your performance in utilising cognitive behavioural approaches as part of your practice against the following 12 items.

Item 1: Agenda-setting and adherence

In CBT it is good practice to set an agenda with clients at the start of each session. While this may seem formal, particularly when used in a therapeutic context, setting a brief agenda ensures that both you and the client pay sufficient attention to the most important issues and manage time effectively. It is also helpful if you bear in mind *learning objectives* for your client and give consideration to how these can be measured at the end of the session (e.g. getting the client to summarise key points – see item 2: Feedback). The agenda should be negotiated *jointly* and review items from the previous session (e.g. homework set) if appropriate. When assessing your ability in this item, ask yourself the following questions:

- Did you set the agenda with clear, discrete, realistic goals and stick to it?
- Can you identify at least two specific agenda items?
- Did you encourage the client to set the agenda in collaboration with you?
- Did the client understand what the session was going to cover?
- Did the agenda seem appropriate for the session?
- Were agenda items set in order of priority?

Item 2: Feedback

The practitioner should give and receive feedback throughout each session at regular intervals and particularly at the end (e.g. summarising key points and next steps). Feedback enables the client to focus on the main issues aimed at helping them to achieve their goal and splits the session into manageable components. It also enables the client and practitioner to obtain a shared understanding of the issues discussed. When assessing your ability in this item, ask yourself the following questions:

- Was the feedback appropriate and did you obtain it often enough during the session?
- Did you use feedback to split pieces of information into manageable chunks to help the client gain new insights?
- Did you encourage the client to provide feedback throughout the session?
- How effective was your use of feedback in helping the client to understand the main learning points of the session?

Item 3: Collaboration

It is helpful to think of yourself and the client as a team within this context and you should encourage them to participate fully throughout the session using skilful questioning, shared problem solving and decision making. You need to avoid being too directive, intellectual, controlling or passive while at the same time steering the client back to the agenda if they digress or ramble about irrelevant issues. You need to strike a balance between involving the client in working towards their goals while proving didactic input when appropriate. When assessing your ability in this item, ask yourself the following questions:

- Did you encourage the client to participate fully in the session as a team member?
- Did you establish a collaborative relationship with the client?
- Did you give the client enough time and space to think during the session?
- Were you too directive or controlling at any point during the session?

Item 4: Pacing and effective use of time

Having negotiated the agenda, the practitioner makes optimal use of the time available to ensure that each item is covered adequately, the client's needs are met and learning objectives are achieved. This will require a disciplined approach to pacing the session and limiting unproductive discussion on the part of both the practitioner and the client. The pace of the session and material covered should be adjusted to take account of the client's speed of learning and the agenda may need to be renegotiated accordingly. The practitioner should move swiftly to the next learning point after having checked that the client has grasped the essential detail, but avoid rushing through the agenda without giving the client sufficient opportunity to assimilate new learning. When assessing your ability in this item, ask yourself the following questions:

- Were you able to recognise the client's needs and adapt the session accordingly?
- Were there any instances when the session moved too slowly or too quickly when covering agenda items?
- Did you or the client engage in any unproductive digressions?
- Was sufficient time left to evaluate learning outcomes for the session and set homework assignments?
- Did you adapt the pace of the session to meet the client's learning needs?

Item 5: Interpersonal effectiveness

This is a vitally important skill for any career counselling, coaching or therapeutic approach and is essential for developing a good working relationship with the client. In order to evaluate interpersonal effectiveness it is helpful to call to mind Carl Roger's (1957) necessary qualities for practitioners of 'empathy, genuineness and warmth':

Empathy requires practitioners to enter the client's world momentarily and view the relevant situation from their perspective. It also requires the ability to communicate this imaginative insight to the client in order to facilitate a shared understanding of the issues that are important to them. Acting in a manner that may be perceived as negative, distant or aloof is the antithesis of empathic behaviour.

Genuineness is expressed through sincerity and openness – an egalitarian attitude where practitioner and client are equal in the helping relationship as human beings although there may be different levels of expertise. Hiding behind the mantle of 'expert', acting in a condescending or patronising manner is the antithesis of maintaining genuineness as part of professional practice.

Warmth should be communicated through both verbal and non-verbal behaviour and convey acceptance of the client as a person. Acting in a cold, judgmental or critical manner is the antithesis to showing warmth as a practitioner.

Actively demonstrating all of the above qualities is particularly important when dealing with clients who have had a series of negative life experiences (e.g. offenders, low-achievers) and who may be initially suspicious or reserved. In some instances, the practitioner may be the first person to have shown the client empathy, genuineness and warmth. When assessing your ability in this item, ask yourself the following questions:

- Was your working relationship with the client positive?
- Did you actively demonstrate empathy, genuineness and warmth?
- Did you show acceptance of the client while maintaining professional boundaries?
- Were you able to empathise with the client in terms of any difficulties they are experiencing and acknowledge them?
- Did the client's response indicate that they felt accepted and understood?

Item 6: Eliciting appropriate emotional expression

Clients may express a range of emotions during sessions in relation to challenges they are facing and seeking help with. The practitioner should be able to both acknowledge and work with the client's emotions within the context of helping them to achieve their goals. For example, if the client expresses frustration or anxiety, it will be necessary to ascertain the thinking and situational factors contributing to these emotions. It will also be necessary to elicit the client's emotions if they experience challenges to achieving their particular goal (e.g. anxiety prior to a job interview) as managing these feelings more effectively will be an important task to work on. When assessing your ability in this item, ask yourself the following questions:

- Did you pay sufficient attention to the client's emotions?
- Were you able to elicit the client's emotions in relation to any problems they were experiencing in achieving their goal?
- Did you deal with any emotional issues discussed with sufficient sensitivity?

- Did your activity during the session facilitate positive emotional change in the client (e.g. enthusiasm, confidence)?
- Were you able to set appropriate goals for reducing unhelpful emotions (e.g. strategies for decreasing anxiety prior to job interview)?

Item 7: Eliciting key cognitions

One of the key themes described in Chapter 1 was the way in which clients' cognitions can lead to unhelpful negative emotions and present additional barriers to achieving their goals. Therefore, it is important for the practitioner to be able to elicit these cognitions using the various techniques presented within this book (e.g. Socratic questioning, 5-area assessments etc). When assessing your ability in this item, ask yourself the following questions:

- Were you able to identify and elicit any unhelpful cognitions?
- How effectively did you use appropriate techniques (e.g. Socratic questioning, 5-area assessments) to elicit the client's cognitions?
- Did you adequately explain the effect of unhelpful cognitions to the client?
- Did you enable the client to identify subsequent negative cognitions?

Item 8: Eliciting behaviours

Clients often engage in a range of unhelpful behaviours that create additional obstacles to achieving their goal. For example, a student may engage in pro-crastination leading up to exams in order to avoid the discomfort of boredom or anxiety associated with the task. It is important that the practitioner elicits any unhelpful behaviours and the role they play in undermining the client's efforts to achieve their goal. When assessing your ability in this item, ask yourself the following questions:

- Were you able to identify and elicit any unhelpful behaviours?
- How effectively did you use appropriate techniques (e.g. Socratic questioning, 5-area assessments) to elicit the client's unhelpful behaviours?
- Did you adequately explain the effect of unhelpful behaviours to the client?
- Did you enable the client to identify subsequent unhelpful behaviours?

Item 9: Guided discovery

We have stressed the importance of Socratic questioning in Chapter 1 and elsewhere as a method for enabling clients to gain new insights for themselves rather than simply lecturing them. By using an open and inquisitive style throughout the session, the practitioner stimulates the client's thinking processes so that they are fully involved in examining their challenges from a different perspective and fully engaged in constructive problem solving. Using a sensitive and inquisitive questioning style strengthens collaborative working and encourages the client to become an active participant during the session. When assessing your ability in this item, ask yourself the following questions:

- Did you use appropriate questions to fully engage the client in the session?
- Have you made statements or didactic inputs that could have been turned into questions?
- Did your questioning style facilitate understanding and enable the client to gain new insights into their situation and challenges?
- Was your questioning style sufficiently sensitive and within range of the client's level of understanding?

Item 10: Conceptual integration

In Chapter 1 we presented in detail both the 5-areas model and the ABC model and described methods for developing a *formulation* of the client's situation in relation to their challenges, illustrating the links between thoughts, feelings, behaviours and physical sensations. We have provided a number of examples for using these models in different contexts by carrying out an idiosyncratic formulation of the client's situation and teaching them that the way they think, feel and act when attempting to achieve a goal significantly influences outcome. Developing formulations using these conceptual models provides a 'map' that guides both practitioner and client during the course of their working alliance. Enabling clients to understand these concepts can powerfully influence their ability to deal with present and future challenges and teaching them to use these models helps them to become self-sufficient. When assessing your ability in this item, ask yourself the following questions:

- Have you carried out a detailed formulation of your client's situation and challenges using either the 5-areas or ABC model?
- Have you enabled the client to understand the interaction between thoughts, feelings, behaviour and the way in which this cycle can be optimised in pursuing their goals?
- Have you integrated these concepts into your overall work in sessions?
- Have you taught the client to use these models to deal with future challenges?

Item 11: Application of change methods

We have presented a range of cognitive and behavioural methods within this book that are aimed at helping clients to make positive changes in their current strategies for overcoming obstacles and achieving goals. These include cognitive techniques such as the worry tree for developing a problem-solving approach to dealing with anxieties, and behavioural techniques such as activity scheduling to increase motivation and prevent deterioration of mood. The appropriate method(s) should be judiciously selected following a detailed formulation of the client's situation and challenges using either the 5-areas or ABC model. It is essential that the client understands the rationale for using the particular change method as failure to do so will compromise the effectiveness of the technique. It is also important that any change methods used are suited to the needs of the client and their ability to carry them out effectively. This will require discussion during the session and exploration of potential obstacles to the client employing the methods with contingency plans for dealing with these. When assessing your ability in this item, ask yourself the following questions:

- Did you check that the client understood the rationale for carrying out the change method?
- Did the method(s) flow naturally from your formulation of the client's situation and challenges?
- Were the techniques appropriate for the client in terms of their ability to carry them out successfully?
- Did you negotiate appropriate learning objectives for the client when deploying the change methods?

Item 12: Homework-setting

We have mentioned the importance of homework-setting in Chapter 8 in order to consolidate learning that has taken place during the session and build the client's independence and sense of self-efficacy. The tasks should be negotiated and agreed with the client in order to encourage compliance and be within their range of capability. It is important for clients to understand the rationale for carrying out assignments and, as mentioned above, potential problems in carrying out assignments need to be anticipated and dealt with. Sufficient time needs to be allocated for setting homework tasks towards the end of the session to avoid rushing through details with the client. When assessing your ability in this item, ask yourself the following questions:

- Did you check that the client understood the rationale for carrying out the homework assignment?
- Were the techniques appropriate for the client in terms of their ability to carry them out successfully?
- Did the homework assignment flow naturally from work carried out during the session?
- Was the homework assignment planned in adequate detail with sufficient time allocated during the session?

Asking for feedback

In addition to using the CTS-R to evaluate your use of cognitive behavioural approaches within career counselling and coaching, we recommend that you seek written or verbal feedback from clients. This can be obtained at the end of each session or at the last session if you have been working with the client over an extended period. Questions to ask include:

- Which ideas have you found most helpful during the session(s)?
- Which techniques did you find most useful?
- Is there any way in which the session(s) could have been improved?
- On a scale of 1 to 5, how would you rate the delivery of the session(s) in terms of warmth and openness?
- Are there any other comments you would like to make?

When requesting written feedback, you may wish to offer the client the option of returning it in a plain envelope in order to increase the chances of obtaining objective comments. If possible, it is good practice to schedule a brief follow-up contact time with the client (e.g. in 3 months) and ask the same questions to assess whether learning obtained during the sessions has been effective over a longer period.

Having evaluated your work with clients using the above methods, the next stage of reflective practice involves making sense of what you have learned and integrating this new knowledge into subsequent sessions. We recommend the use of *Kolb's experiential learning cycle* (Kolb, 1984) to facilitate this process.

Kolb's experiential learning cycle

David Kolb developed a theory of experiential learning set out within his groundbreaking 1984 book and presented a model (see Figure 7.1) that can be used as part of reflective practice.

As you can see from Figure 7.1, the cycle consists of four stages of learning and although each one can be entered at any point, Kolb and Fry (1975) maintain that all stages must follow sequentially in order for the individual to learn from experience. In the context of practising cognitive behavioural approaches as part of career counselling and coaching, it is not enough to simply carry out the techniques during a session with a client in order to learn how to use them effectively. It is also necessary to reflect on what you have done, make sense of the experience and plan how you will put this new learning into practice during the next session with the client. Although it is possible to begin at any stage of the cycle, it is helpful to follow the sequence set out below, starting with a particular action and learning from its consequences.

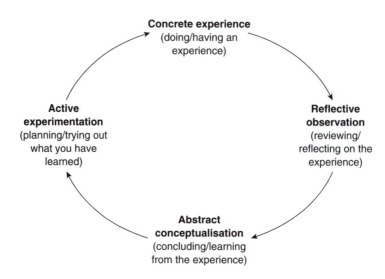

Figure 7.1   The experiential learning cycle (Kolb, 1984)

Concrete experience (doing/having an experience): Having obtained the theoretical knowledge set out within this book, you need to actually put it into practice in order to learn from the experience. This involves using the techniques and models you have learned with clients in groups or one-to-one sessions.

Reflective observation (reviewing/reflecting on the experience): After practising specific cognitive behavioural techniques or models during the session, you need to take time and evaluate how things went. You may experience an initial intuitive reaction or 'gut feeling', although it will be helpful to use more objective methods to evaluate what took place such as the CTS-R criteria or client feedback set out above. You may find it helpful to record your reflections in a log or journal as part of your ongoing professional development to avoid losing any valuable insights.

Abstract conceptualisation (concluding/learning from the experience): At this stage you need to consider the findings of your evaluation and draw conclusions from the experience. This might involve revisiting the theory set out within this book (abstract concepts) and considering what actually works in a live situation: how does practice compare with theory?

Active experimentation (planning/trying out what you have learned): Having gained a deeper understanding of specific cognitive behavioural techniques or models through implementation, reflecting on their effectiveness and relating the experience to relevant theory, you will now be in a position to plan your next session with a view to improving your practice. The key question to ask yourself at this point is 'What might I do differently to improve outcomes for the client?'

Although this is the final stage in the sequence it initiates a new cycle when you implement refinements in your practice, thus generating another concrete experience followed by reflective observation, further abstract conceptualisation and active experimentation.

Assessment tools

Conventional careers guidance approaches have traditionally involved the use of psychometric tests and inventories and the most widely used include:

- The strong interest inventory (Harmon, Hanson, Borgen & Hammer, 1994)
- The Minnesota importance questionnaire (Rounds, Henley, Dawis, Lofquist & Weiss, 1981)
- The 16-factor personality questionnaire (16PF) (Cattell, Eber & Tatsuoka, 1970)
- The career maturity inventory (CMI) (Crites, 1978)
- The career development inventory (CDI) (Super, Thompson, Lindeman, Jordaan & Myers 1981)

See Kidd (2006) for a fuller discussion on the use of these tools within a career counselling context. She correctly points out that problems practitioners and trainees often face are access to relevant journals and training in the use and interpretation of the various instruments. For example, in the UK it is a requirement to hold a British Psychological Society (BPS) Level A or Level B qualification to obtain and administer most tests and inventories. Faced with this dilemma, it is helpful if practitioners and trainees can turn to less formal, if non-validated, methods for assessing clients' occupational interests and life situations. In Chapter 3 we considered a number of ways to help the client make effective career decisions by identifying their personal values, and we presented the *value focus questionnaire* as a tool for assisting them in this endeavour. We now turn to a simple but effective method for assessing the client's life situation and measuring progress while they receive career counselling and coaching supported by cognitive behavioural approaches.

The wheel of life

The wheel of life (or life wheel) is a powerful model commonly used in coaching and particularly useful for helping clients to assess their current situation in various domains (e.g. work, education, social life). The wheel provides a holistic visual overview of the client's circumstances and can also be used to assess progress in specific areas of their life after you have supported them with the use of cognitive behavioural approaches. Figure 7.2 shows various dimensions of the client's life.

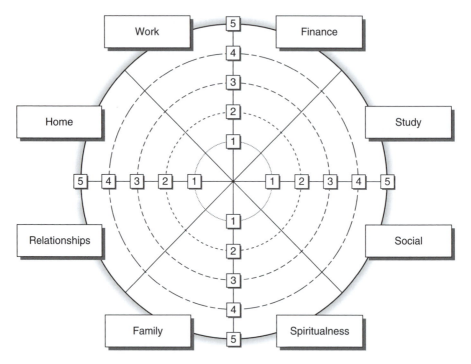

Figure 7.2   The wheel of life showing various dimensions of a client's life

As you can see from Figure 7.2, the client can assess their perceived level of success or satisfaction in each life domain on a scale of 0 to 5 (where 5 is the highest value) and plot the scores on the wheel. This visual representation of their current situation can be used as the starting point for negotiating various goals to be worked on collaboratively with their career counsellor or coach and progress within the different domains measured over time. In this way the effectiveness of the practitioner's interventions and the client's efforts can be measured empirically. A positive indication would be an expansion of the plotted pattern towards the outer rim of the wheel.

You can adapt the wheel to provide an idiosyncratic assessment of each client's life against a range of domains they wish to specify in order to measure progress between sessions. You can see from the example in Figure 7.3 that the client wished to focus on 'assertiveness', 'leadership', 'maintaining focus' among others.

One of the advantages in using this approach as a method for establishing a baseline and assessing progress is that you can create the wheel in a number of formats. Using a flip chart or whiteboard will enable you to sketch the wheel and engage the client in the process through Socratic questioning. If space is limited, you can draw the wheel on a blank sheet of paper (or use the blank template available to download from www.sagepub.co.uk/sheward). The following

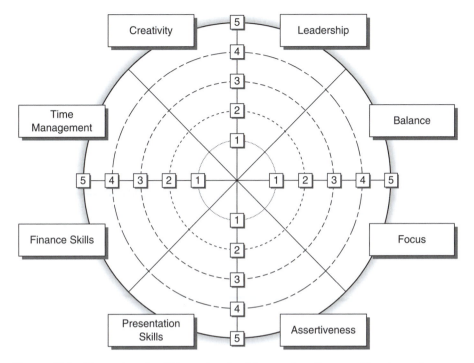

Figure 7.3   The wheel of life adapted to a client's specific domains

steps offer a guide to constructing a wheel of life with your client, although these can be adapted depending on your professional practice.

Step 1: Ask your client to describe aspects of their life they consider to be important and where they hope to see some improvement as a result of your work together. The more specific they can be, the better your chances of measuring the success of work undertaken during and between sessions.

Step 2: Write down a brief descriptor against each domain on the life wheel you have both decided to focus on in your work together.

Step 3: Ask the client to rate their current level of satisfaction and/or success by drawing a dot against each domain where 0 is the lowest and 5 the highest score.

Step 4: Draw lines connecting the dots until you have your initial baseline pattern. Ask the client for their reaction to the emerging pattern and its implications for the focus of your work together.

Step 5 (optional): Ask the client to plot their desired level of success/satisfaction against each domain that is *realistically achievable* in the course of your work together. This should result in two patterns set out within the wheel and offer a strong visual reminder of the gap that needs to be closed.

Step 6: Now turn your attentions to detailed *goal setting* with the client, assessing potential cognitive and behavioural barriers and using the approaches outlined in previous chapters to address these.

The wheel can be used during subsequent sessions as a visual check to assess progress towards the client's goals and as a motivational tool. Any positive results can be used as a means of encouraging your client to maintain any gains they have made in your work together by continuing to practise the approaches you have taught them

It is widely anticipated that the use of on-line career counselling approaches – or e-guidance – will become far more prevalent via the Internet as part of the digital revolution (Bimrose & Barnes, 2010). Significantly, a growing number of CBT-based resources are being made available on line as self-help tools, and the following methods can be used in conjunction with your practice of cognitive behavioural approaches as part of career counselling and coaching.

Identifying signature strengths and personal values

In Chapter 3 we considered Martin Seligman's signature strengths as a means of helping clients to identify their personal values. If your clients wish to measure their signature strengths, you can direct them to Professor Seligman's website at the University of Pennsylvania (www.authentichappiness.org) where they will be able to take the scientifically tested VIA survey of character strengths free of charge. The survey will take about 25 minutes to complete and will provide immediate detailed feedback on their personal profile. Clients who do not have internet access can complete the same survey set out in Seligman's book *Authentic Happiness* (2002). There are a number of other tests available at the site that may be of interest to clients including:

- the grit survey: measuring the character strength of perseverance
- the optimism test: measuring optimism about the future
- the work–life questionnaire: measuring work–life satisfaction
- the meaning of life questionnaire: measuring meaningfulness

In addition to helping clients identify their personal values, these tools can also be used to obtain a baseline measure of traits such as optimism and perseverance and satisfaction levels with regard to work and life in general. It may be interesting for your client to take these tests at the beginning and end of your work together and evaluate (a) whether there has been any improvement in scores and (b) to what extent the various approaches used contributed to this.

CBT self-help resources

A wide range of free resources can be found at www.getselfhelp.co.uk to supplement the approaches you have learned in this book or to provide additional support to your clients depending on the areas you are focusing on in your work together (e.g. managing stress). The following materials and tools available on the website are particularly useful in their application to career counselling and coaching:

- Positive steps to wellbeing
- Finding alternative thoughts
- Emotions: a summary of particular emotions and their associated thoughts, body reactions and behaviours
- Interpersonal effectiveness
- Communication styles: passive-assertive-aggressive
- Stress
- Sleep
- Relaxation
- Meditation
- Imagery (visualisation techniques)

Practising mindfulness

We explore the concept of *mindfulness* and explain its use in reducing stress in Chapter 9. The Mental Health Foundation is the UK's leading mental health research, policy and service improvement charity and has developed a website providing a detailed explanation of mindfulness at www.bemindful.co.uk. Visitors to the website can view the video clip of Mark Williams explaining the way in which stress has increased over the past few decades, its impact on the body and how mindfulness can combat the negative effects of stress. Mark is Professor of Clinical Psychology at the University of Oxford and founder of the Centre for Mindfulness Research and Practice at the University of Wales, Bangor.

The website provides a detailed explanation of mindfulness-based cognitive therapy (MBCT) and mindfulness-based stress reduction (MBSR) that is specifically relevant to the challenges clients face in the world of work. There is also a free stress test that can be completed on-line using the perceived stress scale (PSS). The test takes a few minutes to complete and provides an overall score. You can use this with clients to measure their stress level before and after completing selected exercises outlined in this book with your support. Alternatively they may wish to take the 4- week on-line mindfulness course available for a moderate fee, as participants report an average stress reduction of 35 per cent.

Reflect and discuss

1 How can you build reflective practice into your work structures to evaluate the effectiveness of your interventions with clients?
2 What other evaluative processes can you put in place to strengthen the quality of your practice (e.g. peer supervision, client feedback)?
3 Which elements of the modified CTS-R criteria are relevant to your practice and how can you integrate them into review processes?
4 Which other areas of your work can you apply Kolb's experiential learning cycle to?
5 How can you integrate the wheel of life into your current practice?
6 What caveats do you need to put in place when recommending on-line self-help resources?
7 What are the advantages and disadvantages of clients using CBT based self-help resources in conjunction with career counselling and coaching?
8 What other on-line resources can you use to strengthen your professional practice?

8

Ethical Issues

This chapter is designed to help you to:

- reflect on issues of diversity and the extent to which your cultural identity shapes your perception of others
- gain an understanding of the principles governing client confidentiality and their importance within the client–practitioner relationship
- learn essential steps for managing client risk
- integrate CBT methods within your professional practice to develop an effective working alliance with clients

Respecting and appreciating diversity and working towards impartiality

Pause for a moment and reflect on how your view of the world is influenced by your own specific cultural identity, gender, ethnicity, sexuality and religious or non-religious values. You may consider yourself to be open-minded and impartial, but your perspective will undoubtedly be influenced by these factors. The CBT model allows us to see that as human beings we only have partial knowledge of reality and that the lens through which we view the world can become distorted by our beliefs – particularly when we are unaware of their role in influencing our appraisals of interactions with other people. We have all developed an idiosyncratic paradigm, or map, of the world that influences our thoughts, feelings and actions. Approaching the issue of diversity within career counselling and coaching provides us with an exciting opportunity to test our perspective of reality by gaining a better understanding of how our clients view their particular situation within the context of their cultural values and individual circumstances.

It has been suggested that practitioners working within counselling and related fields should restrict themselves to working with clients from similar ethnic and cultural backgrounds as to do otherwise would risk providing a diminished service due to their limited awareness and potential prejudices (Simola, 1992; Sue & Sue, 1990). Providing a service with practitioners who share the same cultural attributes as clients is vitally important and many agencies strive to achieve this as far as possible through their recruitment practices. Examples include former drug abusers providing counselling to addicts; gay and lesbian advisers working with victims of homophobia; black or Asian social workers providing support to members of ethnic minority communities. However, in practical terms it would be difficult to provide an ideal ethnic and cultural match between practitioners and clients in every instance. The next best endeavour is to ensure that practitioners and trainees have a thorough understanding of cultural and diversity issues and that they engage in ongoing reflective practice to evaluate how their own cultural values influence work with clients. This can be achieved in a number of ways.

Reflect on your own cultural identity

This type of reflective practice is highly important if you are to avoid the pitfalls of making distorted inferences and developing unhelpful perspectives in your work with clients. As previously mentioned, we are all susceptible to forming core beliefs throughout the course of our lives that remain unconscious and may be strengthened by evidence that we constantly gather, often unknowingly. For example, an individual raised within a homophobic culture will be more inclined to notice negative examples of behaviour within the gay and lesbian community and automatically discount any positive evidence, thereby strengthening his or her unhelpful belief. Similarly, a man who holds the belief that women are worse drivers than men will be more biased to noticing poor examples of female motoring than taking into account positive data (e.g. that insurance statistics evidence the fact that women have fewer accidents than men). When considering your own cultural identity it is worth reflecting on how much your views are influenced by the following factors:

- Gender
- Age
- Sexuality
- Religion
- Class

- Political views
- Language
- Family

The above list is not exhaustive but gives some indication of the complexity of personal identity and challenges the notion that we are free from cultural bias. When working with clients it is helpful to bear these influences in mind and to continually monitor the way in which we form perceptions and develop opinions. This is consistent with CBT's empirical approach of gathering evidence and testing its validity, posing the question 'To what extent is our view of the client, their situation and our intervention based on an understanding that is free from bias and distortion?' Bearing this in mind will enable you to avoid what Gerard Egan refers to as 'diversity blind spots':

> *Helpers with diversity blind spots are handicapped. Helpers should, as a matter of course, become aware of the key ways in which they differ from their clients and take special care to be sensitive to those differences. (Egan 2002: 51)*

Gain a broad knowledge of cultural issues in general

It is essential for career counsellors and coaches to gain an understanding of issues related to ethnicity, race, culture, faith, class, gender, sexual orientation, disability and consider how these factors may need to be taken into account and influence professional practice (Tuckwell, 2002). It is also an opportunity for personal growth in terms of enriching your knowledge of the complexity and diversity of human society. This knowledge and understanding can be obtained through formal training, reading and, most importantly, maintaining a genuine curiosity in the lives of others.

Gain a detailed knowledge of client groups within your professional practice area

You need to develop a detailed understanding of specific client groups that you are likely to encounter in your practice on a regular basis. This could include members of ethnic communities represented within the local population, age ranges (e.g. young people or the elderly), long-term unemployed clients, members of the gay and lesbian community to name but a few categories. In addition to formal training and literature, utilising community resources can be invaluable for increasing your understanding as many of the above groups may be represented by different organisations. However, it is important to avoid cultural stereotyping by continually bearing in mind the fact that each of your clients is unique and that there may be huge differences within the specific groups.

Gain a thorough knowledge of your client within the context of their cultural identity

It is important to obtain as much relevant information as possible about your clients prior to or during your first session. However, this needs to be explained to the client within the context of providing the best possible support to meet their needs and that they are at liberty to decline providing certain items of information if they wish. In many cases it may not be appropriate to raise the issue of your client's cultural identity and they may find any attempt to do so intrusive. In these instances, the knowledge you have gained will sharpen your sensitivity to meeting the client's needs and enable you to monitor your thoughts and behaviour without addressing cultural issues in an overt way. On other occasions it may be necessary to raise these issues if they have a direct bearing on your client's support needs (e.g. using an interpreter) or if your client thinks they are relevant. The latter case provides an excellent opportunity for you to work collaboratively with the client to obtain a shared understanding of their unique situation and how you can tailor your support to meet their needs. Even if you do have some knowledge of your client's particular life circumstances, it is advisable to acknowledge their expertise and enlist their support in gaining a fuller understanding. This will also enable you to avoid any interpersonal cultural blocks and build a strong working alliance with your client.

Integrate principles of diversity and multiculturalism within your professional practice

As each client and their individual circumstances are unique, you will need to adapt to their needs accordingly as we have outlined. The following guidelines are offered as broad principles aimed at strengthening your work with clients while taking into account the richness and complexity of diversity and multiculturalism:

- Nurture a curiosity and genuine interest in your clients and regard difference as an opportunity to learn and broaden your perspective of human experience.
- Always remember that your perspective of clients and their situations is viewed through the perspective of your own cultural lens.
- Try to ensure that your own values do not have an impact on your ability to meet the client's needs.
- Seek to understand different cultures but beware of generalising and stereotyping. Remember first and foremost that you are dealing with an individual.
- Try to work collaboratively with your client to gain a shared understanding of their unique circumstances. Do not be afraid to seek clarification for fear of betraying ignorance. Clients will usually appreciate genuine interest and respond positively.

Client confidentiality

Gaining your client's trust and establishing good rapport is an essential requirement for building an effective working alliance. Clients often seek support from career counsellors and coaches when they are at their most vulnerable (e.g. unemployed or at a career crossroad) and asking them to use cognitive behavioural approaches frequently requires them to go outside of their comfort zones so that the issue of trusting your judgment as a practitioner becomes even more important. It is for these reasons that the issue of client confidentiality needs to be handled carefully and sensitively from the very outset.

The following suggestions concerning client confidentiality are general principles to guide you in your work. Your personal responsibilities with regard to client confidentiality will be determined to a large extent by the law of the country in which you practice, the professional body with whom you are accredited and your employer (unless you are in private practice), and it is advisable that you become acquainted with these specific requirements as failure to do so may result in legal or disciplinary action in the worst case scenario.

The optimum time to address issues of confidentiality is at the start of the first session as part of what Egan refers to as the 'client–helper contract' (Egan, 2002): what the client can expect from the process, mutual tasks and responsibilities as well as *values that will drive the process*. Depending on the organisational or legal parameters described above, you might introduce the subject of confidentiality by assuring the client that everything you discuss will remain completely confidential unless:

- the client gives permission to share written or verbal information with a third party
- they give you cause for concern that they may be a risk to themselves or others

Obtaining client consent and adhering to the principle of always acting in their best interests provides a sound ethical basis for dealing with any issues regarding confidentiality. However, in some exceptional circumstances where you believe there is a clear risk to the client or others, it may be necessary to take immediate action without seeking consent. Examples include disclosure of self-harming (e.g. cutting), the intention to commit suicide, sexual or physical abuse of or from another and the intention to harm others. In these (hopefully rare) circumstances it will be necessary to weigh the client's entitlement to confidentiality against the need to share information with a third party. A guiding principle that will help in making these difficult decisions is to consider how you will ethically justify any actions taken should you be called to do so.

If your client has agreed that you may share personal and/or sensitive information with others on a need-to-know basis, it is incumbent on you to disclose only that which is essential for third parties to carry out work on behalf of your client.

Example

A career counsellor working within an adult education college is supporting a female client who has disclosed that she dislikes the tutor and wishes
to change courses. The client is emphatic that she does not wish to report
the matter but enlists the career counsellor's help in brokering the transfer
to another course mid-term. Both have agreed that the justification for
changing courses is that the client feels she has made a mistake with her
chosen subject and will make every effort to catch up.

In the example above, it would be unethical for the career counsellor to disclose the fact that the student did not like the tutor.

Keeping detailed client records is normally an essential part of professional practice and sufficient care should be taken to ensure that this information is stored securely (e.g. paper copies locked in filing cabinets and
electronic records password protected). Legislation concerning clients' rights
to access information kept about them varies depending on where you practice
professionally (e.g. the UK Freedom of Information Act) and you are advised
to check this in detail. When recording notes of your session or other docu-
mentation relevant to your practice, the best principle to adhere to is that you
would be comfortable for your client to read anything that you have written
about them.

Having considered the above issues concerning client confidentiality you
will hopefully realise that there are no black-and-white answers on how to
proceed in certain situations. In such instances it is recommended that you
seek advice from a manager, supervisor or professional body in order to miti-
gate any risks to yourself of the working alliance with your client.

Managing client risk

Career counsellors and coaches do not routinely encounter clients who
report suicidal intent, but as you have seen from the statistics set out in
Chapter 5, unemployed clients are more likely to take their own lives than
those in work, and practitioners working with offenders and adolescents may
be more likely to encounter this type of risk. The role of career counsellors
and coaches has become increasingly complex and often involves working
with clients faced with extremely challenging circumstances. While it is
essential that you maintain appropriate professional boundaries and stay
within the parameters of your job specification, there is a possibility that you
may encounter situations in which your client discloses suicidal thoughts or
even plans. This can occur in situations where practitioners have developed
a positive working alliance with their client and may be the only person

sufficiently trusted with this disclosure. If your organisation has a clear policy on managing client risk, it is essential that you follow their procedures. If this is not the case or you work in private practice it will be helpful to keep the following guidance in mind in the unlikely event that you encounter suicidal risk in your work with clients.

The first point to make is that you may feel shocked and anxious if your client discloses that they have thoughts or plans about taking their life. This is a perfectly understandable response as even seasoned therapists who routinely deal with this type of situation find dealing with suicidal clients to be one of their greatest professional challenges (Reeves, Bowl, Wheeler & Guthrie, 2004). Try to remain calm by focusing on the content and manner of your client's communication and take brief notes if you are able. The important thing to stress is that your professional role does not enable you to provide support with emotional problems and that your client needs to see their medical practitioner to discuss this as a matter of urgency. Try to obtain your client's agreement to make an emergency same-day appointment with their medical practitioner immediately after their session with you. It is also helpful to include details of emergency services offering support to individuals at risk of suicide (Samaritans and Crisis lines in the UK) within your information resources in the unlikely event that you may need to provide them to your client.

If you have managed to get your client to agree to the above action, try to engage them in the work you had originally scheduled and develop a detailed action plan outlining tasks between sessions including a subsequent appointment with you as soon as practically possible. Hopelessness about the future is a key feature of suicidal thinking (Bennett-Levy et al., 2006: 221) so any positive focus on future goals will be helpful under these circumstances.

Finally, discuss the incident with your supervisor or manager immediately and seek their advice on next steps. It is essential that you make a detailed record of what your client disclosed and the action you took in case you are called upon to account for your actions. This is particularly important if you are in private practice and do not have any reporting mechanisms. You may also need to discuss your emotional responses to the situation in order to process your feelings adequately and to provide you with an opportunity to express any ongoing concerns you may have for your client.

The client–practitioner relationship

Throughout this book we have described a range of cognitive behavioural techniques aimed at helping clients to achieve their goals while working within a career counselling and coaching approach. The client–practitioner relationship can also be viewed as an important *method* for helping clients to achieve their aims and not merely a set of interactions during which clients are taught or coached in various skills. This requires a conscious decision on behalf of the practitioner to manage the relationship with their client in a certain way to optimise the chances of a successful outcome. This notion is not unique as many counselling theories stress the importance of the therapist–client relationship as a vehicle for facilitating change. Freudian psychodynamic theories emphasise the unconscious dynamics at work within the relationship as an essential part of the therapeutic process. Carl Rogers (1957) believed that offering 'unconditional positive regard, accurate empathy and genuineness' were both 'necessary and sufficient' for the client to make progress in therapy. The client–practitioner relationship within cognitive behavioural therapy places less emphasis on self-exploration and more focus on working collaboratively towards action that will result in positive change and is highly suited to the goal-orientated approach of career counselling and coaching. You may wish to incorporate some or all of the following principles into your approach to developing an effective working alliance with clients.

Maintaining appropriate professional boundaries

It is not uncommon for practitioners and trainees in helping roles such as counselling, coaching or therapy to experience sexual and/or emotional feelings towards their clients. However, acting on these feelings and forming relationships with clients outside the professional practice is explicitly precluded within most organisations' ethical frameworks. For example, the British Association for Behavioural & Cognitive Psychotherapies's (BABCP) *Standards of Conduct, Performance and Ethics in the Practice of Behavioural and Cognitive Psychotherapies* (2010) states that '[you] must not abuse the relationship you have with a service user, sexually, emotionally, financially or in other ways'.

If you find yourself experiencing sexual feelings towards your client, you need to be aware of the extent to which these feelings are affecting your professional practice. Examples may include spending longer than is necessary working with a particular client, both in terms of individual sessions and the overall course of your work together. Offering contact by telephone or email outside work hours and most forms of physical touch are further examples and breech most standards of conduct unless they form an essential part of your work and are explicit in your contract with the client (e.g. emergency contact or follow-up outside office hours).

If you receive supervision as part of your professional practice or as a trainee, you may wish to discuss this issue should it arise. Working with clients in a caring capacity can often trigger a wide range of responses in practitioners including sexual attraction, anger, irritation or pity and requires the ability to deal with these emotions without allowing them to adversely affect the support you are providing. One of the key precepts for maintaining appropriate professional boundaries is to listen to your emotions and pay attention to what they are telling you without being misled by them.

Showing appropriate warmth towards clients

The late Albert Ellis, founder of rational emotive behaviour therapy (REBT), advocated showing reasonable but not excessive warmth to clients in order to avoid the risk of them becoming overly dependent on the practitioner's approval and to foster a sense of self-efficacy in them (Dryden, 2004). You may find it helpful to maintain a friendly but businesslike approach with clients as much of your work will involve encouraging them to exert themselves in pursuit of their goals and this may require some firmness on your part.

Collaborative empiricism

The method of working described in this book typically involves carrying out a detailed assessment of the client's unique situation and devising strategies to help them achieve their goals. It also involves testing client's assumptions about future situations (e.g. that they will look stupid at an interview or dry up during a presentation). This is the style of collaborative problem solving and hypotheses testing advocated by Aaron T. Beck, founder of CBT (Beck, Rush, Shaw & Emery, 1979). The spirit of this approach is one of equality: as a practitioner you do not adopt the superior status of an 'expert' in which the client is subordinate to you. It is true, however, that you possess more knowledge than your client on strategies for helping them to achieve their goals whereas they are 'experts' about their life situation and the challenges they face. Adopting collaborative empiricism as an approach means that you combine your respective knowledge and test the effectiveness of various strategies and beliefs in pursuit of the client's goal.

Agenda-setting

We mentioned the importance of structuring sessions with clients in Chapter 3 and introduced you to Tol Bedford's FIRST model to help facilitate this. Agenda-setting is an explicit way of imposing structure on the session, helping achieve shared tasks within the time available and keeping both you and your client on track. This is a particularly helpful discipline if the client is verbose or prone to digression and it sets a businesslike tone within each session. You do, however, need to provide the client with a rationale for including an agenda – that you are trying to make best use of the time available for their benefit. It is also helpful at this point to ask clients for permission to interrupt them during sessions in order to keep you both on track. It is far better to socialise clients in your structured approach from the outset than risk offending them when it becomes apparent that you need to interrupt them at a later stage. Typical items that might be included on the agenda are:

- Review of work done on between session assignments (homework)
- Review of the client's goals
- Teaching further strategies aimed at achieving goals
- Review of main learning points
- Setting of further between session assignments

Always ask your client if they wish to add items to the agenda as this will strengthen your spirit of collaborative working. It is also helpful to add timings to each item (e.g. 'Review of work done on between session assignments': 15 minutes) in order that each topic receives sufficient attention. Agenda-setting and asking permission to interrupt are best dealt with during the initial contracting stage with clients.

Setting homework assignments

We have already stressed the importance of action planning and devising SMART goals for clients in Chapter 3. Using this approach will ensure that clients have an overall strategy for achieving their goals after you have carried out a detailed assessment of their situation. It will still be necessary for clients to carry out related tasks in between sessions unless you are working with them on just one occasion. If you anticipate working with clients for more than one session, it may be helpful to check with them during the first session that the term 'homework' does not have any negative connotations. If this proves to be the case, ask them to nominate an alternative description (e.g. 'between session assignments'). You also need to provide clients with a rationale for carrying out homework assignments: namely that you only have a limited amount of time together and you want them to consolidate what they have learned by practising their newly acquired skills and knowledge between sessions. When setting homework assignments with clients you need to ensure that three conditions are met:

- The client understands the nature of the tasks and how they relate to their overall goals.
- The client is committed to carrying out the homework assignment.
- The client is capable of carrying out the homework assignment.

It is also helpful if you both spend a few minutes anticipating any potential obstacles to carrying out the assignment and devise contingency plans for overcoming these.

As you have seen from 'Agenda-setting' earlier on in this chapter, it is important to review your client's homework assignment as a first priority during your next session together and devote sufficient time and attention to this task. Failure to do so will imply that you do not find the client's homework assignment particularly important, and this impression will create difficulties in motivating your client to carry out subsequent assignments. Reinforce achievement and review what the client has learned as this information can inform the content of your session. If the client has failed to complete any particular aspect of their assignment, check whether they have misunderstood what was required of them and renegotiate the assignment. If there are any other reasons for the client failing to complete their assignment, try to establish in specific detail what went wrong and work together on collaborative problem solving.

Helping the client become their own career counsellor and coach

Ideally the ultimate aim of your work with clients is to empower them to become self-sufficient in dealing with any future vocational or educational challenges that may arise. Teaching clients the strategies and techniques set out within this book will assist you in this endeavour but you also need to aim at getting them to achieve specific learning outcomes within each session, which is why we have included this subject on the agenda (above). If you are supporting your client over a period of time, it may be helpful to space out the final sessions (e.g. with a gap of two weeks followed by one month) in order to foster a sense of self-efficacy or getting the client to 'stand on their own two feet'.

Developing a blueprint for future success

If time permits, the final session should focus on reviewing and consolidating learning, setting medium- to long-term goals, anticipating any setbacks that may occur in future and agreeing contingency plans for dealing with these. Try to encourage your client to take detailed notes during this session as a written record will help them to recall the content of what they have leaned from you during your sessions together. Table 8.1 shows Tom's blueprint following his work with Rhena, described in Chapter 2.

A copy of the blueprint for future success worksheet for use with clients can be downloaded from www.sagepub.co.uk/sheward.

Table 8.1   Tom's blueprint for future success

Key learning points	Most useful techniques
1 Making a mistake in social situations does not make me an 'idiot'. 2 Thinking negatively about myself will have a detrimental effect on my thoughts, feelings and actions. 3 Just because I come from a working-class background does not mean that I am less capable socially – even posh people drop their food.	1 Using the ABC model to analyse how I think, feel and act in stressful situations. 2 Challenging negative automatic thoughts (NATs) as they occur. 3 Practising rational beliefs to counter negative thinking in stressful situations. 4 Acting 'as if' I am confident in order to begin feeling confident. 5 Practising diaphragmatic breathing for relaxation.
Potential setbacks	**Contingency plans**
I might find myself becoming anxious in other work/social situations if I am the focus of attention.	Carefully note any safety behaviours I might be engaging in and drop these. Deliberately focus my attention on my external environment and other people rather than monitoring my own performance.
Medium-term goals	**Long-term goals**
• Attend the buffet lunch at the law firm (1 month) • Attend Law Society conference and evening dinner (2 months) • Take part in Law Society Summer Ball (3 months)	• Complete course in public speaking (4 months) • Volunteer for slot as after-dinner speaker at Law Society function (5 months)

Reflect and discuss

1 How does cultural identity shape your view of clients (and others), and what action can you take to reduce biases and distortions from influencing your perceptions?
2 What potential ethical dilemmas might you encounter in your work with clients with regard to client confidentiality, and how could you resolve these?
3 If your employing organisation does not have a risk management policy, what do you think it should include? If you are self-employed, what should your risk management policy include?
4 Which principles outlined within this chapter would you adopt for use in improving the client–practitioner relationship? What impact do you think they will have on your work with clients?

9

Career Counselling and Coaching for Self-care

This chapter is designed to help you to:

- recognise the various symptoms of work-related stress and how they might impact on your professional practice
- use the ABC model and cost and benefit analysis to analyse situations in which you may be contributing to your own work-related stress and take steps to deal with this constructively
- utilise a range of methods that promote self-care and work–life balance
- learn the practice of mindfulness as a method for reducing stress and developing greater mental clarity

One of the greatest ironies within most caring professions is that practitioners and trainees are drawn to the work because they want to help others but frequently place insufficient emphasis on caring for themselves. This chapter seeks to redress that balance and draws on a number of the techniques we have already introduced you to with the aim of utilising them for self-help. Career counselling and coaching require highly developed interpersonal skills and, as a consequence, these occupations can be emotionally and intellectually draining. Add to this the pressure of targets imposed by employing agencies or the challenges of earning a sufficient income while self-employed and it is likely that professionals working within this sector will experience occasional, if not frequent, stress. The critical issue is to recognise when this becomes an ongoing problem rather than a temporary period that may be challenging but manageable. In order to prevent a slide from occasional to constant stress followed by burnout, it is essential to spot the early warning signs.

Danger signs of work-related stress

You may already be familiar with these indications through your work with clients and part of your role might include providing support with work-related stress. However, some of the following danger signals are quite subtle and more likely to occur in a counselling or advisory role. As such, they often go unnoticed until they become a real problem and so require vigilance on the part of the practitioner.

Deterioration in physical and mental wellbeing

Early indications might include minor ailments such as headaches, colds, muscular pains and gastric problems. All of these conditions can be eased by taking over-the-counter medication and the temptation is to carry on with the demands of work as normal. Most of the time this is an appropriate and necessary response, but if these symptoms persist it is sensible to consider what the underlying cause might be. Our body is a barometer of mental and physical health and may be trying to tell us something. The first sign of stress is its negative effect on the immune system and a reduced ability to fight-off minor ailments. If these warning signals are ignored and self-care neglected, the negative effects accumulate.

Emotional wellbeing is vitally important for those working in a caring profession as the emotions, as well as the intellect, are the most important tools that practitioners and trainees use with clients. Two of the most common indications of stress in terms of their impact on the emotions are symptoms of depression and anxiety. These include:

- **Low mood:** a lack of pleasure in activities that were previously enjoyed. A sense of hopelessness and pessimism (glass half empty rather than half full).
- **Irritability:** becoming easily annoyed with oneself, others or situations in general.
- **Difficulty concentrating:** drifting mental attention and 'zoning out'.
- **Ruminating:** constantly churning over worries in one's mind without engaging in problem solving.
- **Avoidance:** failure to deal with necessary situations and tasks that involve a certain amount of emotional discomfort (e.g. asserting oneself).

- **Nervousness:** feeling constantly keyed-up or on edge. Also having a low startle reflex.
- **Sleep problems:** difficulty falling asleep, or waking up in the middle of the night and unable to resume sleep.

It goes without saying that physical and mental wellbeing are interrelated and that a deterioration in one domain will usually have a negative impact in the other. Also, the emotional problems described above can become self-perpetuating. The experience of depression almost inevitably involves a reduction in energy which in turn leads to a decline in activity. This is know as the *lethargy cycle* and can lead to a downward spiral of increasingly low mood and reduced activity. This is why unemployment has such a negative impact on mental health. Similarly, heightened anxiety leads to increased avoidance of (perceived) stressful situations (e.g. going to meetings, giving presentations). Because this tendency to escape from challenging situations is immediately rewarded by a sense of relief, the behaviour is negatively reinforced, establishing within the individual concerned an even stronger urge to avoid challenging situations as their comfort zone shrinks in upon themselves.

The above danger signals of burnout may become apparent in or outside the workplace, but the following examples are particularly subtle and can occur within one's professional practice.

Over-empathy or lack of empathy

Empathy is a fundamental tool used by caring professionals but particularly by career counselling and coaching practitioners and trainees. We are constantly required to 'put ourselves in our clients' shoes' and consider situations from their perspectives. However, this can often involve over-identifying with the client's emotional state, with stressful consequences. Consider the following example:

Example

Melanie is employed as a career counsellor working with long-term unemployed clients in a deprived inner-city area. She has been helping Jill, a single parent who is desperate to find work because of mounting debts and the threat of eviction from her home. Jill has just disclosed that her young daughter has been diagnosed with autism and is particularly upset by the increasing number of challenges she has to contend with in addition to continued rejection from employers. That evening Melanie thinks of Jill and imagines how difficult it must be to live her life. Melanie finds Jill's situation particularly upsetting because she is a single mother and finds herself wondering how she would cope with unemployment and insecurity. She goes to bed feeling depressed, slightly anxious and finds it difficult to fall asleep as her mind keep going over Jill's situation.

While it is necessary to empathise with our clients in order that we are able to view situations from their perspective, it is important to establish appropriate psychological boundaries. This means paying particular attention when we find ourselves over-empathising to the point where it becomes emotionally disturbing and also constantly thinking about clients outside of the workplace. Many novice practitioners and trainees that we have supervised exhibit a tendency to become too emotionally involved in their clients' challenging situations and mistakenly believe that to do less (e.g. maintain an appropriate level of detachment) would be cold and unsympathetic. Upon closer examination, these beliefs are prompted by feelings of guilt because the practitioner or trainee is comparing their more comfortable existence with that of their client. If you find yourself engaging in this type of thinking, it is worth remembering that you have a duty to take care of yourself, emotionally, mentally and physically, so that you are better able to help your clients. Inability to maintain a healthy level of emotional detachment can lead to burnout and help neither you nor your clients.

The other sign of burnout is at the opposite end of the spectrum, when career counsellors and coaches become completely unable to empathise with their clients to the extent that this interferes with their professional practice. This is also described as *compassion fatigue* (Figley, 2002: 1434) and it occurs in other helping professions including counselling and psychotherapy. It is the culmination of over-investing oneself emotionally in clients and their challenging situations to the point where, often unknowingly, we develop psychological barriers to protect ourselves. Once again, maintaining appropriate professional boundaries prevents emotional burnout and the onset of compassion fatigue. Compartmentalising work with clients is a valuable part of this process. Mentally leaving the client and their problems in the workplace until their next designated session and regarding the home as a place of rest of recuperation is part of this professional discipline.

Lack of enthusiasm and energy

This state can develop gradually over a long period of time, but it usually becomes noticeable when motivation is low and the prospect of going to work prompts only negative feelings. The quality of individual sessions begins to suffer as practitioners become mechanistic in their approach, defaulting to a 'one size fits all' response rather than tailoring each intervention to best support the client. During sessions the practitioner may find their attention drifting and feel considerable relief when clients cancel. Preparation for client sessions becomes minimal and no time is invested in background reading, training or other professional development. This process is similar to the depression lethargy cycle described above as low motivation usually results in declining investment of energy which leads in turn to a growing sense of ennui.

Using ABC formulations for self-care

Hopefully you will have become familiar with using the ABC model to help clients challenge unhelpful thinking and behavioural strategies following the guidelines set out in previous chapters. The model can be equally effective for addressing your own work-related (or personal) challenges. Next time you experience an unhelpful negative emotion, carry out an ABC analysis to determine the antecedents and the contribution your thoughts are making to the way you are feeling. The following is an example of how Melanie used the ABC model to address her own stressful situation at work.

Situation: *Working with long-term unemployed clients who have multiple social problems*

'A' = Client reveals that her daughter has autism

'B' = I should do more to help. How would I cope if it were me?

'C' = Depression; anxiety

Having established her beliefs about the situation and the way in which they contributed to feelings of depression and anxiety, Melanie detected some ambivalence in her thinking. On the one hand she recognised that maintaining this attitude made her feel low in mood and anxious, but on the other hand she regarded it as a sign of compassion that drove her on to do more in her role as helper. Melanie decided to examine her conflicting thoughts by means of a cost and benefit analysis (CBA), shown in Table 9.1.

Carrying out the CBA helped Melanie to see that there were a significant number of disadvantages associated with her unhelpful belief for herself and her daughter and these far outweighed the perceived motivational advantage of her thinking. One idea that had particular resonance for Melanie was the realisation that if she continued to maintain her current attitude to work she risked burnout, in which case she would be unable to help her clients. This insight enabled Melanie to construct a more effective outlook with regard to her work and an emotional goal of feeling empathic rather than depressed and anxious:

Situation: *Working with long-term unemployed clients who have multiple social problems*

'A' = Client reveals that her daughter has autism

'B' = I will do all I can within the context of my role but recognise the need for professional and emotional boundaries. I will help clients to find employment and signpost them to other agencies for support with social issues

'C' = Empathic

Table 9.1   Melanie's cost and benefit analysis

Costs and benefits of: Believing that I don't do enough for clients

Costs (disadvantages)	Benefits (advantages)
Short-term	**Short-term**
For self:	For self:
I feel constantly stressed and suffer from low mood	If I remain unsatisfied with my work, I won't become complacent
For others:	For others:
I don't fully attend to my daughter when spending time with her – my mind is often elsewhere	Holding this belief makes me try harder for my clients
My daughter has noticed how I have been feeling and has commented on it	
Long-term	**Long-term**
For self:	For self:
If I continue to experience this level of stress and low mood, my mental and physical health may suffer	I may get a promotion if I continue to work hard
If my health suffers, it will impact on my job and may affect my ability to earn a living	For others:
If I become ill, I won't be able to help my clients	
For others:	
My daughter's mood may become influenced by my anxiety and depression – she may become insecure	

Try using the above approach next time you are feeling stressed or despondent about your work. Applying techniques described in this book on yourself will also enable you to deploy them more effectively with clients, particularly as you gain confidence in their efficacy.

Other methods for self-care

Caring for your physical wellbeing

Most forms of physical recreation offer an excellent way of reducing stress, increasing serotonin and increasing energy levels. Physical exercise is also very important for cognitive functioning as it increases oxygen to the brain. Any physical pastime that you find enjoyable will serve this purpose, but a combination of aerobic activity and gentle stretching is particularly advantageous and a good counterbalance to working in a sedentary occupation. Reducing caffeine and drinking alcohol in moderation, eating nutritious meals and keeping hydrated by drinking sufficient amounts of water each day will also be greatly beneficial.

Maintain a work–life balance

Make sure you take regular vacations to recharge your energy levels. This does not necessarily require spending a great deal of money on travelling. The main aim is to engage in enjoyable activities that provide a respite from work. This approach should also apply on a day-to-day basis so that taking regular lunch breaks away from the desk or office become part of your routine. Try to resist the urge to 'get more done' during your lunch break (e.g. dealing with emails while snacking) as this will eventually lower your energy and have a negative impact on the quality of your work. Try practising the relaxation techniques outlined in this book as well as those on getting a good night's sleep, assertiveness and managing your time more effectively.

Invest time in relationships

It is essential to put sufficient time aside for your partner, family or friends as these relationships need to be constantly nurtured. The tendency to overwork is insidious and can gradually impact on relationships almost without knowing. A more subtle phenomenon is being present physically but mentally ruminating over problems at work. When you spend time with others, try to be fully present. It is also important to maintain positive relationships with work colleagues to prevent a sense of being isolated with the work. Although career counselling and coaching involves working with people on a frequent basis, ironically it can feel lonely due to the need to maintain a professional persona the whole time. This is particularly challenging for practitioners who are self-employed but can be addressed by joining professional networks or sharing a practice.

Invest in personal development

If you neglect continuous professional development (CPD), not only do you fail to keep up to date with the latest applications and developments, you also risk becoming stale in your practice and this will make the actual work seem less enjoyable and even stressful. Try to attend regular courses to update your knowledge and keep your practice fresh. It also provides an excellent opportunity to network and exchange ideas with other practitioners and trainees.

Protect your emotional wellbeing

As we have seen in the case of Melanie, it is essential to maintain appropriate emotional boundaries at work. Becoming too involved in your clients' problems runs the risk of increased stress and eventual burnout. An excellent way of dealing with this issue is to receive regular professional supervision. If this is not possible within your current role, you can still routinely review your professional practice and consider whether you are maintaining appropriate boundaries. Ask yourself what are the professional limits of your role and when does it become necessary to bring in support from other agencies or to signpost the client for help that you are unable to provide? Always endeavour to leave work *at* your place of work (mentally and physically). Of course it will be necessary to take work home occasionally, but maintaining a psychological separation between your professional practice and home life is essential. Our final piece of advice for maintaining emotional wellbeing is the regular practice of some form of meditation and we will now explore this topic in detail.

Mindfulness

As we have mentioned, career counselling and coaching involves working with the mind and the emotions on a daily basis and these resources can become depleted if they are not nurtured on a regular basis. It is helpful to think of your mind and emotions as the tools of your trade. If you were a gardener and neglected to carry out routine maintenance on your lawnmower, failed to sharpen your shears and protect them from rust, they would eventually let you down and prevent you from carrying out your work. Your mind and emotions also require 'routine maintenance' to enable you to function optimally at work and in your personal life. One of the best ways of caring for the mind is to practise some form of meditation as it provides much needed respite from thoughts and feelings and engenders calm. There are many different approaches depending on individual preference and you may wish to research these. It is worth emphasising that meditation does not have to take place within a spiritual context and can be practiced by adherents of different faiths without ethical conflict. It is for this reason that we offer the practice of mindfulness as a starting point for the practice of meditation as it is free from religious bias and is used as a relaxation technique by millions throughout the world. Mindfulness is also used within the British National Health Service (NHS) as a treatment for anxiety and depression because of its growing evidence base.

What is mindfulness?

Mindfulness was originally developed by Dr Jon Kabat-Zinn as a method for relieving chronic pain but has developed into a variety of different approaches since the publication of his seminal work *Full Catastrophe Living* in 1990. These approaches range from clinical applications to treat depression and anxiety to daily practice of the simple but effective techniques by people who use mindfulness as a way of maintaining equilibrium while coping with the challenges of modern life. Put simply, the practice of mindfulness is about focusing one's attention on what is happening here and now – right this instant – without letting the mind drift to thoughts about the future or past. Although it may sound easy, maintaining this focus on the here-and-now is subtly challenging and requires practice. You can try this right now by stopping reading for a moment and focusing on your surroundings. Take a couple of minutes to look around you and pay attention to what you can see and hear. Now consider how difficult it was to maintain your focus of attention without some thoughts intruding and getting between you and your experience of the present moment. Try to be aware of this tendency that your mind has to wander away from the present moment for the rest of the day. You may, for example, be enjoying the most beautiful sunset and feeling a deep sense of calm when a thought occurs to you about work the next day. Without realising, your focus shifts from the present moment and you imagine the client you have to deal with who was quite challenging on a previous occasion. Almost imperceptibly your mood changes from a state of serenity to slight concern. Ironically, you remain watching the sunset with your eyes but you no longer see it in your mind because your imagination is presenting you with a picture of your awkward client. Kabat-Zinn describes this all too common experience:

> When you begin paying attention to what your mind is doing, you will probably find that there is a great deal of mental and emotional activity going on beneath the surface. These incessant thoughts and feelings can drain you of a lot of energy. They can be obstacles to experiencing even brief moments of stillness and contentment. (1990: 25)

There are two important points worth emphasising: (a) when our attention wanders from the here-and-now we do not fully appreciate the present – we drift through life partially experiencing what is happening to us; and (b) we waste huge amounts of mental and emotional energy. Consider your work with clients. If your mind is trying to attend to what the client is presenting while at the same time thinking of the next client or what you have to do that evening, you are placing a number of burdens on your mental processes simultaneously. But how can you become more adept at being fully present in the moment and thereby conserving mental and emotional energy? This question brings us to the practice of basic mindfulness.

Calming your mind and focusing on the present

We have already introduced you to a simple relaxation technique for use with clients experiencing anxiety at the prospect of attending an interview in Chapter 2. The principles that we outlined for focusing on the breath are equally important for the practice of mindfulness and you may wish to revisit them. The next exercise goes a stage further as it aims to both calm your mind and enable you to focus more adequately on the present moment.

Exercise

Step 1: Find a quiet place where you are unlikely to be disturbed. Try to allocate 15 minutes for the whole session, although you may wish to begin with 5 minutes and increase the time gradually as you become more proficient. It is preferable to carry out this exercise first thing in the morning in order to start the day in a calm frame of mind. As you will see, the exercise also helps focus the mind on the present so that you will be better able to stay in the moment throughout the day. In the same way that you eat breakfast to provide nutrition and energy for your body, engaging in meditation first thing nourishes your mind.

Step 2: Sit comfortably with your back straight and your shoulders relaxed. It is helpful if you move forward slightly and adopt an upright position so that you do not rely on the chair's backrest for support. This is because you are aiming to focus on your breathing while remaining calm and alert but not to fall asleep and slump in the chair. Obviously if health problems prevent you from adopting this posture, adapt the exercise to suit your personal needs.

Step 3: Close your eyes if you feel comfortable as this will minimise visual distractions. Alternatively, focus your eyes on a spot approximately 60 cm (2 ft) in front of you with a relaxed gaze. Try to focus on feeling completely safe within your chosen environment and that you are free from disturbance or capable of dealing with any unlikely intrusions. Next, cultivate an attitude of intentionality at the start of each session and commit yourself to carrying out the exercise within the timeframe you have allocated.

Step 4: Breathe naturally and focus your attention on your stomach, feeling it gently rise on the in-breath and fall on the out-breath. As we described in Chapter 2, you are now practising diaphragmatic breathing rather than shallow chest breathing. Just focus on the sensation of each breath entering and leaving your body, paying attention to the gentle, soothing feeling that this engenders. You may notice subtle aspects of the sensation, that the air you breathe in is slightly cool and warmer when you breathe out. Don't try to control you breathing; just let it follow its own natural rhythm.

Step 5: Keep the focus of your attention on each breath for the duration of each inhalation and exhalation. You will find your mind wandering and this is quite natural. When you notice this happening, gently bring your attention back to your breathing. You may find it helpful to count each breath from one to ten to assist your focus. Again, when you notice yourself counting beyond ten or thinking of something else, gently bring your attention back to the count and the breath.

Step 6: Notice the 'pull' of your mind and the way in which different thoughts and feelings come quite spontaneously. If you haven't practised any form of meditation before, you may be surprised to find how active your mind is during quiet moments. Don't get carried away with your thoughts, but at the same time resist the urge to block them out. Instead, let each thought pass through your consciousness like floating clouds while you gently bring your attention back to the breath.

Step 7: If you find yourself becoming frustrated or impatient with your practice of meditation, just notice this response and return your focus on breathing. This is quite a common reaction as we are conditioned to constantly strive for some outcome. Meditation, however, consists of letting go and simply being in the moment without judging it as good or bad. If you *try* to empty your mind or feel more relaxed you will defeat yourself because you are engaging in *thinking* rather than simply being.

Step 8: Gradually bring your meditation to an end by gently focusing your attention on your surroundings. Notice how you are feeling and reflect on any positive aspects of your meditation. Don't be despondent if your mind was particularly active and you did not achieve a deep sense of calm. Each meditation is different and the benefits of practising accrue gradually over time. This form of 'non-striving' may seem counter-intuitive but becomes easier to understand through regular practice. After your meditation, try to resist the urge to get up immediately and rush to do the next thing. Seek instead to carry any feeling of calm you have obtained with you to the next activity so that you set a positive tone for the rest of the day.

If you practise this gentle form of meditation regularly you may begin to notice subtle changes in your thoughts, feelings and actions. For example, you may become aware of any negative or stressful automatic thoughts that occur to you and the way in which your attention is constantly drawn away from the present moment. Simply being more aware of this tendency will enable you to gently bring your focus back to the present and attend to what you are doing more fully. In fact, everything you do throughout the day offers an opportunity to practise mindfulness. When you are working with clients, focus completely on what they are saying and observe their body language. When you eat lunch, put time aside to fully engage in the experience instead of doing it with partial awareness (e.g. eating while reading or working at your computer). Really concentrate on the taste and texture of your food, eat slowly and savour each mouthful. Consider the many ways in which you can practise mindfulness by becoming fully engaged in the moment.

> **Reflect and discuss**
>
> 1 Have you ever experienced any symptoms of work-related stress? What were they and how did they impact on your life?
> 2 Which current challenging situations could you apply the ABC model to? Can you use the cost and benefit analysis to help you make a decision you are struggling with?
> 3 Which self-care methods do you currently practice? Which additional self-care methods do you need to adopt and what steps can you take to put these into practice?
> 4 Which everyday situations can you think of that will give you an opportunity to practise mindfulness?

References

Allen, S., Waton, A., Purcell, K., & Wood, S. (1986). *The experience of unemployment*. London: Macmillan.

Baker, M. & Kleijnen, J. (2000). The drive towards evidence-based health care. In N. Rowland & S. Gross (Eds), *Evidence-based counselling and psychological therapies: research and applications*. London: Routledge.

Balloch, S., Hume, C., Jones, B., & Westland, P., (1985). *Caring for unemployed people: research into the impact of unemployment on demand for social services*. London: Bedford Square Press.

Beck, A. T., Rush, A. J., Shaw, B. F., & Emery, G. (1979). *Cognitive therapy of depression*. New York: Guilford Press.

Bedford, T. (1982). *Vocational guidance interviews: a study by the Careers Service Inspectorate*. London: Careers Service Branch, Department of Employment.

Bennett-Levy, J., Butler, G., Fennall, M., Hackmann, A., Mueller, M., & Westbrook, D. (2006). *Oxford guide to behavioural experiments in cognitive therapy*. Oxford University Press.

Ben-Shahar, T. (2008). *Happier*. New York: McGraw Hill.

Bewley, H., Dorsett, R., & Haile, G. (2006). *The impact of pathways to work: a report of research carried out by the Policy Studies Institute on behalf of The Department for Work and Pensions*. Leeds: Corporate Document Services.

Bimrose, J., & Barnes, S.A.. (2010). *Careers information, advice & guidance: the digital revolution and repositioning of labour market information*. Coventry: Warwick Institute for Employment Research.

British Association for Behavioural & Cognitive Psychotherapies (2010). *Standards of conduct, performance and ethics in the practice of behavioural and cognitive psychotherapies*. Bury: BABCP. Available at www.babcp.com/Files/About/BABCP-Standards-of-Conduct-Performance-and-Ethics.pdf.

British Society of Rehabilitation Medicine (2001). *Vocational rehabilitation: the way forward*. London: BSRM.

Bunting, M. (2004). *Willing slaves: how the overwork culture is ruling our lives*. London: Harper Collins.

Buss, T. F., Stevens Redburn, F., & Waldron, J. (1983). *Mass unemployment: plant closing and community mental health*. London: Sage.

Butler, G., & Hope, T. (2007). *Managing your mind: the mental fitness guide*. Oxford: Oxford University Press.

Careers Profession Task Force (2010). *Towards a strong careers profession: an independent report to the Department for Education*. London: Department for Education.

Catalano, R. F., Berglund, M. L., Ryan, J. A. M., Lonczak, H. S., & Hawkins, J.D. (2004). Positive youth development in the United States: research findings on evaluations of positive youth development programs. *American Academy of Political and Social Science*, *591*: 98–124.

Cattell, R. B., Eber, H. W., & Tatsuoka, M. M. (1970). *The 16-factor personality questionnaire*. Champaign, IL: IPAT.

Centre for Mental Health (2010). *The economic and social costs of mental health problems in 2009/10*. London: Centre for Mental Health.

Children's Workforce Development Council (CWDC) (2008). *Occupational summary sheet: Connexions Personal Advisers*. Nottingham: Department for Education and Skills.

Clark, D. M., & Wells, A. (1995). A cognitive model of social phobia. In R. Heimberg, M. Liebowitz, D. A. Hope, & F. R. Schneier (Eds), *Social phobia: diagnosis, assessment and treatment*. New York: Guilford Press.

Covey, S. (1999). *The 7 habits of highly effective people*. London: Simon Schuster.

Crites, J. O. (1978). *The career maturity inventory*. Monterey, CA: California Test Bureau.

Csikszentmihalyi, M. (1991). *Flow: the psychology of optimal experience*. London: Harper Perennial.

Csikszentmihalyi, M., & LeFevre, J. (1987). *The experience of work and leisure*. Paper presented at the Third Canadian Leisure Research Conference, Halifax, May 22–25.

Csikszentmihalyi, M., & LeFevre, J. (1989). Optimal experience in work and leisure. *Journal of Personality and Social Psychology*, *56*(5): 815–822.

D'Zurilla, T. J., & Nezu, A. M. (1999). *Problem-solving therapy: a social competence approach to clinical intervention*. New York: Springer.

de Botton, A. (2009). *The pleasures and sorrows of work*. London: Penguin.

Department for Education and Skills (2005). *Social and emotional aspects of learning: guidance*. DfES report 1378–2005. London: Department for Education and Skills.

Department for Education and Skills (2007). *Social and emotional aspects of learning for secondary schools (SEAL). Guidance Book*. London: Department for Education and Skills.

Department for Work and Pensions (2009). *Health, work and wellbeing: working our way to better health*. Norwich: Department for Work and Pensions.

Department of Health (2007). *Commissioning for a brighter future: improving access to psychological therapies*. London: Department of Health.

Department of Health (2011). *Talking therapies: a four-year plan*. London: Department of Health.

Dryden, W. (2004). *Reason and therapeutic change*. London: Whurr.

Dryden, W., & Branch, R. (2008). *The fundamentals of rational emotive behaviour therapy*. Chichester: Wiley.

Dugas, M. J., & Robichaud, M. (2007). *Cognitive-behavioural treatment for generalized anxiety disorder*. London: Routledge.

Egan, G. (2002). *The skilled helper*. Pacific Grove, CA: Brooks/Cole.

Ellis, A. (1963). Toward a more precise definition of 'emotional' and 'intellectual' insight. *Psychological Reports*, *23*: 538–540.

Figley, C. R. (2002). Compassion fatigue: psychotherapists' chronic lack of self-care. *Journal of Clinical Psychology*, *58*: 1433–1441.

Frankl, V. E. (1984). *Man's search for meaning*. New York: Washington Square Press.

Freud, D. (2007). *Reducing dependency, increasing opportunity: options for the future of welfare to work*. London: Department for Work and Pensions.

Goleman, D. (1996). *Emotional intelligence*. London: Bloomsbury.

Gumora, G., & Arsenio, W. F. (2002). Emotionality, emotional, regulation and school performance in middle school children. *Journal of School Psychology*, *40*(5): 395–413.

Harmon, L. W., Hansen, J. C., Borgen, F. H., & Hammer, A. L. (1994). *Strong interest inventory: applications and technical guide*. Palo Alto, CA: Consulting Psychologists Press.

Hartmann, L. M. (1983). A meta-cognitive model of social anxiety: implications for treatment. *Clinical Psychology Review*, *3*: 435–456.

Haworth, J. T., & Evans, S. T. (1987). Meaningful activity and unemployment. In D. Fryer & P. Ullah (Eds), *Unemployed People – Social and Psychological Perspectives*. Milton Keynes: Open University Press.

Henwood, F., & Miles, I. (1987). Unemployment and the sexual division of labour. In D. Fryer & P. Ullah (Eds), *Unemployed People – Social and Psychological Perspectives*. Milton Keynes: Open University Press.

HSE (Health and Safety Executive) (2008). *Working together to reduce stress in the workplace: a guide for employees*. Health and Safety Executive.

HSL (Health & Safety Laboratory) (2003). *Working long hours*. Crown Copyright.

Humphrey, N., Curran, A., Morris, E., Farrell, P., & Woods, K. (2007). Emotional intelligence and education: a critical review. *Educational Psychology*, *27*(2), 235–254.

Irvine, W. B. (2009) *A guide to the good life (the ancient art of stoic joy)*. Oxford: Oxford University Press.

James, A., Blackburn, I. M., & Reichelt, F. K.; Collaborators: Garland, A., & Armstrong, P. (2001). *The manual of the revised cognitive therapy scale (CTS-R)*. Newcastle: Newcastle Cognitive Behavioural Therapies Centre and the University of Newcastle upon Tyne.

James, K. (2005). *Learning and skills for people experiencing mental health difficulties*. Leicester: National Institute of Adult Continuing Education (NIACE).

Kabat-Zinn, J. (1990). *Full catastrophe living*. London: Piatkus.

Keep, E. (2004). *The multiple dimensions of performance: performance as defined by who, measured in what ways, to what ends?* Nuffield Review of 14–19 Education and Training Working Paper 23. London: Nuffield Foundation.

Kidd, J. M. (2006). *Understanding career counselling*. London: Sage.

Kolb, D. A. (1984). *Experiential learning: experience as the source of learning and development*. Englewood Cliffs, CA: Prentice-Hall.

Kolb, D. A., & Fry, R. (1975). Toward an applied theory of experiential learning. In C. Cooper (Ed.), *Theories of group process*. Chichester: Wiley.

Lam, L. T., & Kirby, S. L. (2002). Is emotional intelligence an advantage? an exploration of the impact of emotional intelligence on individual performance. *Journal of Social Psychology, 142*(1): 133–143.

Layard, R. (2010). *A campaign for psychological therapies: the case*. London: London School of Economics.

Layard, R. (2006). *The depression report: a new deal for anxiety and depression disorders*. London: Centre for Economic Performance's Mental Health Policy Group, London School of Economics.

Lewis, G., & Sloggett, A. (1998). Suicide, deprivation and unemployment. *British Medical Journal, 7168*: 1283–1287.

Magee, B. (1987). *The great philosophers*. London: BBC Books.

Martell, C. R., Dimidjian, S., Herman-Dunn, R., & Lewinsohn, P. M. (2010). *Behavioral Activation for Depression: a clinicians guide*. New York: Guilford Press.

McEwan, I. (2005). *Saturday*. London: Vintage.

Miller, W. R., & Rollnick, S. (2002). *Motivational interviewing: preparing people for change*. New York: Guilford Press.

Mitchell, L.K., & Krumboltz, J.D. (1996). Social learning approach to career decision making: Krumboltz's theory. In D. Brown, L. Brooks, & Associates (Eds), *Career choice and development: applying contemporary theories to practice* (3rd ed.) San Francisco, CA: Jossey-Bass.

Neenan, M. (2009). *Developing resilience: a cognitive-behavioural approach*. London: Routledge.

Neenan, M., & Dryden, W. (2011). *Rational emotive behaviour therapy in a nutshell*. London: Sage.

Paul, K., & Moser, K. (2009). Unemployment impairs mental health: meta-analysis. *Journal of Vocational Behaviour, 7*(3): 264–282.

Petrides, K. V., Frederickson, N., & Furnham, A. (2004). The role of trait emotional intelligence in academic performance and deviant behaviour at school. *Personality and Individual Differences, 36*: 277–293.

Ree, M., & Harvey, A. (2006). Insomnia. In Bennett-Levy, J., Butler, G., Fennell, M., Hackman, A., Mueller, M., Westbrook, D. & Rouf, K. (Eds.), *Oxford Guide to Behavioural Experiments in Cognitive Therapy*. Oxford: Oxford University Press.

Reeves, A., Bowl, R., Wheeler, S., & Guthrie, E. (2004). The hardest word: exploring the dialogue of suicide in the counselling process – a discourse analysis. *Counselling and Psychotherapy Research Journal, 4*(1): 62–71.

Rodeiro, C. V. L., Bell, J. F., & Emery, J. L. (2009). *Can trait emotional intelligence predict differences in attainment and progress in secondary school?* Cambridge: University of Cambridge Local Examinations Syndicate.

Rogers, C. R. (1957). The necessary and sufficient conditions of therapeutic personality change. *Journal of Consulting Psychology, 21*: 95–103.

Rounds, J. B., Henley, G. A., Dawis, R. V., Lofquist, L. H., & Weiss, D. J. (1981). *Manual for the Minnesota importance questionnaire*. Minneapolis, MN:

Vocational Psychology Research, Department of Psychology, University of Minnesota.

Royal College of Psychiatrists (1998). *Men behaving sadly*. London: Royal College of Psychiatrists.

Seligman, M. E. P. (2002). *Authentic happiness*. New York: Free Press.

Seligman, M. E. P. (2006). *Learned optimism: how to change your mind and your life*. New York: Vintage.

Seligman, M. E. P. (2007). *The optimistic child: a proven program to safeguard children against depression and build lifelong resilience*. New York: Houghton Mifflin.

Simola, S. (1992). Differences among sexist, nonsexist and feminist family therapies. *Professional Psychology: Research and Practice*, *23*(5): 376–381.

Soho, Takuan (1986). *The unfettered mind: writings from a Zen master to a sword master*. Translated by William Scott Wilson. New York: Kodansha International Ltd.

Stone-McCown, K., Freedman, J. M., Rideout, M. C., & Jensen, A. L. (1978) *Self-science: the emotional intelligence curriculum*. San Francisco, CA: Six Seconds.

Stott, R., Mansell, W., Salkovskis, P., & Lavender, A. (2010). *Oxford guide to metaphors in CBT: building cognitive bridges*. Oxford: Oxford University Press.

Sue, D. W., & Sue, D. (1990). *Counseling the culturally different: theory and practice* (2nd ed.). New York: Wiley.

Super, D. E., Thompson, A. S., Lindeman, R. E., Jordaan, J. P., & Myers, R. A. (1981). *Career development inventory*. Palo Alto, CA: Consulting Psychologists Press.

Tiffin, P. A., Pearce, M. S., Parker, L. (2005). Social mobility over the lifecourse and self-reported mental health at age 50: prospective cohort study. *Journal of Epidemiology and Community Health*, *59*: 870–872.

Tuckwell, G. (2002). *Racial identity, white counsellors and therapists*. Buckingham: Open University Press.

Tyrell, R., & Shanks, M. (1982). *Long-term unemployment: why it is a problem and what we can do to solve it*. London: National Westminster Bank, Work and Society.

Waddell, G., & Burton, A. K. (2006). Is work good for your health and well-being? Commissioned by the Department for Work and Pensions. London: The Stationery Office.

Warr, P. B. (1982). A national study of non-financial employment commitment. *Journal of Occupational Psychology*, *55*: 297–312.

Warr, P. B. (1987). *Work, unemployment and mental health*. Oxford. Clarendon Press.

Young, J., & Beck, A. T. (1980). *Cognitive Therapy Rating Scale Manual*. Philadelphia, PA: University of Pennsylvania.

Young, J., & Beck, A. T. (1988). *Cognitive Therapy Rating Scale Manual* (rev. ed.). Philadelphia, PA: University of Pennsylvania.

Yuen, P., & Balarajan, R. (1989). Unemployment and patterns of consultation with the general practitioner. *British Medical Journal*, *298*(6682): 1212–1214.

Index